THE FOUR FOUNDATIONS OF GOLF

HOW TO BUILD A GAME THAT LASTS A LIFETIME

JON SHERMAN

For Melissa, Jordan, Hayden, Ellen, David and Mark

If you want to continue your education after finishing the book, you can take The Four Foundations of Golf Video Masterclass.

To credit you for your book purchase, you can use coupon code **READER** at checkout to receive a $25 discount. Please visit the following URL to learn more:

https://fourfoundationsofgolf.com/masterclass

The video course gives the information from the book in a more visual, conversational format. Additionally, there are more examples and bonus materials from other coaches.

CONTENTS

INTRODUCTION

MY STORY

When I was eleven years old, I spent a lot of time at my grandmother's house. She was one of my best friends. One afternoon, I went through her garage and found an old set of clubs. I was obsessed with just about every sport but had never tried golf before.

So I took the antique clubs with their wooden shafts across the street to a schoolyard. For a while, I struggled to get the ball airborne. Then I stacked a pile of dead grass and placed the ball on top of it as a makeshift tee. I struck the ball perfectly, watched it sail through the air down the field, and I was hooked. Until that point in my life, nothing had given me the same satisfaction. I have been chasing that feeling ever since.

Like any love affair, my relationship with golf since then has taken a lot of twists and turns. I devoted most of my teenage years to improving at the game and competing. My mother used to bring me to the driving range and sit patiently as I hit 250 balls until my hands bled. While I was never a standout player, I became the captain of a mediocre varsity golf team. I then walked on to a Division III team at

New York University and abruptly quit when I realized I had no interest in the game anymore.

Though I became a decent player, probably a four-handicap at best during those years, I genuinely struggled to enjoy the game at times. My obsession with scores made it difficult for me to have fun on days when I didn't play all that well.

For the next decade, I would have an unfortunate relationship with golf. Living in New York City, which is not conducive to being a golfer, I would only get the chance to play sparingly. Instead of using those experiences to enjoy time with friends, I still held myself to a high standard of play. When I didn't reach it, I would lose my temper. Eventually, I knew that I could no longer play the game I loved unless I hit the refresh button.

When I turned 30 and became a father, naturally, my perspective changed on many things in life. My wife and I decided to leave the city for the suburbs. In a minor coincidence (well, not really), we moved within a two-minute drive of a golf course. For the first time in years, I could find time to practice and play more. With a renewed mindset, my game started to flourish.

My thousands of hours of work as a junior player instilled a strong set of skills. Combined with my new "dad perspective," I started to unwind from many mistakes I made as a teenager. Within a year, I got my handicap close to scratch and was having more fun than ever on the course.

My approach to golf, and many other sports, was always a bit unorthodox. While I never had textbook techniques, I found ways to execute well through practice methods that were a little "out of the box." In the latter part of 2014, I started to think I had something to offer other players. Like every other golfer, I had read tons of books and magazine articles about getting better at the game but never really found something that made a meaningful difference. So I started to look at the game-improvement advice available online and felt that I could offer a different perspective.

I believed that most golf advice was focused too much on the swing. On top of that, much of that advice was conflicting. Golfers would digest swing tips, pass them along to their buddies, and get stuck in a vicious cycle of constant change (with no results).

As a player who was able to reach a high level, I knew that there were so many other topics that were being ignored. So I started a website called Practical Golf in early 2015. I wrote about topics that I felt were just as important as the swing - managing expectations, practice habits, strategy, and the mental game. My ideas were very unrefined, and upon reflection years later, I got a few things wrong. But people started reading the articles and enjoying my perspective as a "player-coach."

Throughout the past seven years, I have refined my approach to the game. I have learned a lot from my personal experiences, closely watching golfers of all levels and interacting with some of the top coaches in the game. I have written close to 400 articles on my website, which millions of golfers worldwide have read. My first book, *101 Mistakes All Golfers Make (and how to fix them)*, was one of the bestselling golf books on Amazon in 2016. Additionally, the podcast I co-host with Adam Young, The Sweet Spot, has become the top game-improvement show.

In addition, I have continued to take my game to another level. When this book was released, my handicap index was a +2. I have tested my game in more than 100 tournament rounds over the past five years against elite amateurs and professionals and have built a promising mid-amateur career. I have been able to qualify for some of the top amateur and professional events in the New York Metropolitan area, such as the Long Island Open, Ike Championship, and Met Amateur. Every time I put my game to the test, I learn something new that can benefit players of all levels. While I am not perfect, I try to practice what I preach when I play.

I have wanted to write a more comprehensive guide to golf for a long time. But I tried to remain patient as my philosophy crystallized. I have interacted with thousands of golfers through my email inbox and social media. I've listened very carefully to their problems and tried to develop solutions. I have also been fortunate to form relationships with some of the top minds in the game.

Writing content on the internet can be a gut-wrenching experience, similar to a stand-up comedian. When your material falls flat, the silence can be deafening. In a sense, for the past seven years, I have been working on my "60-minute special." I have continually released content and paid attention to what was helping golfers the most and what fell flat. This book is the culmination of that long, arduous journey.

Nothing I discuss is revelatory. You have likely seen some of this advice elsewhere. Mark Immelman, a broadcaster, and coach, once described my advice as "hiding in plain sight." But like any book, I have tried to organize everything and communicate it to lead you to a much higher level of understanding of what it takes to lower your scores and have more fun.

If I had to state what you stand to gain from this book succinctly, it would go back to a conversation I had when I first met my dear friend Woody Lashen, a prominent clubfitter, shortly after I started Practical Golf. He asked me about the site and what I was trying to do. I muttered a few statements about how I wanted to help golfers from a player's perspective and help them organize their games outside of the swing. He simply responded, "oh, you're offering coaching, not swing instruction."

So you can think of me as your coach to guide you on your journey through this game. I will point you in the right direction, but the rest will be up to you!

HOW TO READ THIS BOOK

My father always taught me that providing value to everyone you meet is the key to success. I am flattered that you used your money to purchase this book, and I feel an immense obligation to provide you with as much value as possible.

When I first started writing *The Four Foundations of Golf,* I had no clue how long it would be. I intended to fill these pages with everything I have learned about the game in my 25-year journey. To be honest, it was one of the hardest things I've ever done in my life.

As a reader, I always was irked when authors would promise to teach you about a topic but leave out the most tangible lessons. I have tried my best to fill the forthcoming pages with as much detail as possible. I will spell things out as clearly as possible for you and leave little up to interpretation. More importantly, you will find that everything is communicated in as simple and straightforward a way as possible.

However, I want you to avoid a common pitfall. Absorbing information and putting it into practice in golf are two entirely different things. You might get to the end of this book, and feel you have the game figured out. But this is only the first step for many of you.

You cannot possibly execute all of the lessons at once. And I don't want you to. You have to do your best to pick and choose certain concepts to focus on, especially the most relevant ones to your game. You will get hundreds of ideas, but all it takes is two to three to make a meaningful impact. I hope this book stays on your bookshelf (or eReader) for years and that you refer back to it. Almost everything I discuss will remain pertinent for as long as you play the game. But please resist the temptation to confuse knowledge with skill. The former will give you a better chance of improving the latter.

CAVEATS, CAVEATS, AND MORE CAVEATS

To be fully honest, I cannot account for all of the variables in your games. While I try to make my advice relevant to every player level, you are all unique snowflakes in golf.

Whether you are an absolute beginner or even an aspiring playing professional, I believe there is something for you to learn. But at the same time, I want you to be mindful of your circumstances. Certain concepts I talk about might not be appropriate to you because of your time limitations, current skill level, or even what you want out of the game.

However, I want you to resist the urge to assume that just because you disagree with something I say doesn't mean it can't help you. I can't tell you how many times I have received messages from players who say, "that all sounds great, but my game is different." In most cases, that's not true. I was resistant to many of these concepts at first, and I'm glad I changed my mind!

Do your best to keep an open mind and a discerning eye to what feels genuinely relevant.

This Is Not a Book About the Golf Swing

In case I have not made this abundantly clear, this is not a book about the golf swing. I am not a swing instructor, and if you are looking for technical advice, you have come to the wrong place!

My coaching is focused on everything *but* the golf swing. These topics get glossed over in the instructional world, and I believe golfers are never really taught how to manage their games on and off the course. My goal is to give you the tools to be your own coach, improve efficiently, and, most importantly, have more fun.

Interestingly enough, many of the practice concepts I discuss will benefit your golf swing. But it won't be because I give you specific advice on what to do while you swing. I will challenge you to complete tasks and build your skill, which will get your swing to self-organize more functionally.

Don't Let Nostalgia Hold You Back

The challenging part about golf is that there is a lot of nostalgia. And there should be; it's a wonderful game with a rich history. However, when looking at information on improvement, many things said in the past are not true.

Whether it's the common swing tips like "keep your head down" or "swing smoothly," or phrases like "drive for show and putt for dough," golfers tend to distribute incomplete information that lacks nuance (or proof that they work). I will discuss topics like swing tempo, the value of distance, how scoring occurs, and give you more actionable advice.

There are timeless lessons in golf that will stay relevant forever, though. If anything, the guidance I give blends what the best players have always known in this game. But I also update certain concepts with modern analysis. However, at some point, you will confront something in these pages that goes against everything you have been taught. And I urge you to keep an open mind.

If you want to build a golf game that will bring you more satisfaction, this book will deliver a solid foundation. I genuinely believe the four sections will provide lifelong skills to help you excel at this game regardless of your experience level or goals.

I will give one final plea, and state this repeatedly in the coming chapters - be patient, and strive for incremental progress in your game!

PART ONE
MANAGING EXPECTATIONS

CHAPTER 1
WHY ARE YOU PLAYING THIS GAME?

GOLF CAN BE AN INTENSELY satisfying activity that brings a lot of joy into one's life. It is a way to spend time outdoors, get exercise, socialize with friends, travel, and fulfill your competitive side. Unfortunately, the game can also torture our souls in the worst way possible. Anyone who has fallen in love with golf and played it for years can attest to the highs and lows the game can bring.

Along the way, many of us can lose sight of why we are playing in the first place. Obsession with score and performance often can prevent enjoyment.

For years I was a miserable golfer. Looking back, it mostly had to do with expectations that were way out of line. The type of golf I wanted to play did not match my skill level and preparation. If I had to put my finger on it, this is one of the main issues that get in the way of most golfers enjoying their time on the course and even playing better.

I chose to start the book off with the topic of managing expectations because I strongly believe that if you cannot get this part of the game right, none of the other pieces will fit.

WHY ARE YOU PLAYING GOLF?

This question might sound silly, but I often ask players why they play this game.

For most of you, the answer will not be "to make a living." Playing golf as a profession is only reserved for an elite few, and even for them, it is probably not as fun as you think it is.

So if golf is not your profession, then you are choosing to spend time that could be used for other leisurely pursuits. As you know, golf is a very time-consuming activity. It is not uncommon for huge chunks of your day to be taken up by traveling to the course, practicing, warming up, and playing 9 or 18 holes.

How do you want to spend that time? Do you want to be endlessly frustrated by your mistakes, or even above average shots? Or have your day ruined because you didn't break 90?

Stepping back and looking at it from the outside, it should seem absurd that we choose to put ourselves through any kind of anguish for a non-professional pursuit. Yet every time we play, it is often an emotional rollercoaster. That's not to say that roller coasters can't be fun. You just want to make sure you have the right mindset going in.

FUN SHOULD BE IN THERE SOMEWHERE

I can't tell you how to play this game. You have to answer that for yourself. That's the beauty of golf - there are so many ways to enjoy it.

I play because I love golf and can't think of anything else I'd rather do with my free time (outside of spending time with my wife and kids). I also want to push myself to see how skilled I can become. I love to compete against myself and others in tournaments. At times, it can be stressful, but I thoroughly enjoy the pursuit. No matter how well or poorly I play, I am committed to remembering it comes from a place of passion and enjoyment.

For others, golf can be a way to exercise or spend time with your spouse. Your score can be a complete afterthought.

I hope that the phrase "have fun" is somewhere in your reasons for playing. I have seen way too many golfers who have lost sight of that simple notion, and it's a shame.

HELP IS HERE!

In the next few chapters, my goal is to help you reshape your expectations in golf. A lot of the information I will provide likely will come as a relief. Most of you reading this have probably been way too hard on yourselves.

Using statistics, anecdotal information, and plenty of other research I've done, you will have a much better understanding of how this game works.

But I want you to continually think about what kind of relationship you want to have with golf. If you want to improve, I have plenty of ideas for you. However, none of them may work if you don't enjoy the process. Many of the concepts I will explore will be revisited in different sections of the book. You can think of the expectation management section as a core fundamental - it's that important!

CHAPTER 2
THE FORMULA FOR GOLF HAPPINESS

When I first started my website, Practical Golf, one of my main missions was to help others avoid some of my past mistakes. Unfortunately, the game wasn't fun for me for years. I know many of you have fallen into similar funks, and it is why I like devoting so much time to helping others find their version of happiness out on the course. If you can't enjoy golf, you will have very little chance of improving. While I don't think there is a perfect recipe for each of you, I believe some fundamental conditions need to be met to have a rewarding experience.

I'm going to share with you a deeply embarrassing personal story to illustrate what I believe is the formula for golf happiness.

A HORRIBLE DAY IN FLORIDA

I'm on a beautiful golf course in the middle of winter, it's 80 degrees out, and I'm utterly miserable. What should be a fun day during a family vacation in South Florida with my father has turned into a complete disaster. I don't know it yet, but I'm about to reach the absolute low point of my "golf life" on the 13th hole.

The round was on a similar trajectory as most went during that time. Early mistakes led to anger and frustration, and my mood generally worsened as the day progressed. Golf wasn't enjoyable for me. It felt like something I should be doing, but I got very little joy out of playing. Despite not playing or practicing much, I felt entitled to shooting low scores, and at the first sign of trouble, I lost my composure.

After hitting a perfect drive on the 13th hole, I had a 140-yard approach shot with water guarding the right side of the green. I felt this was an opportunity to turn the day around with a nice approach shot.

SPLASH

Something in my brain exploded watching the ball sail 40 yards right of the green into the lake. Years of frustration all came out, and I launched my 9-iron at the golf cart. Everything seemed to go in slow motion as the club neatly severed my driver shaft just below the head. The driver's head launched in the air, flipping end over end and impaling itself into the ground. It was like a bad version of a trick shot video if anger and stupidity were the skills being shown off.

My father and I both stared at the decapitated driver and then at each other. Without saying a word, he walked off the course in disgust.

That was it, rock bottom. Golf had driven me to the worst outburst of anger I've ever had, and I quickly realized something had to change. Looking back, it's embarrassing. I'm ashamed to admit that it happened, but it was likely the most critical moment for me as a golfer.

My expectations and skill level were entirely at odds with one another, and the disparity between the two was making the game miserable for me. I know this is something every single golfer on the planet struggles with.

GOLFERS AREN'T TAUGHT THIS

When we take up the game, the focus is mainly on the swing and "the fundamentals" like stance, grip, and posture. Nobody sets us aside and tells us what we can reasonably expect from golf.

If golfers were given a master class on expectation management earlier, I believe the game would be far more enjoyable for most. On top of that, I think most players would be shooting lower scores. Instead, I continuously come across players in the same funk I used to be in.

Don't get me wrong; I'm not a monk - I still have plenty of flaws on display when I play. However, my enjoyment of the game is far better than ever. After 25 years of playing, going through probably too much heartache, I've settled on the following formula for golf happiness:

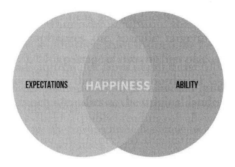

When you start to match up your expectations with your current skill level, that is where you can thrive in this game. The beauty of it is that there is no exact formula for all of us.

YOU HAVE TO ADJUST EACH SIDE OF THE EQUATION

When I realized I was not playing the golf I wanted to, and my driver incident made it clear that I couldn't continue on my current trajectory, I knew something needed to change.

I could either work harder to increase my skill level and ability, or adjust my expectations downward. At the time, I lived in New York City, which is not conducive to playing and practicing much - so I just decided that when I did get the chance to play, I wouldn't take things too seriously. Removing that burden made the game more enjoyable, and eliminating my obsession with score helped make golf a valuable part of my life again.

Years later, when my wife and I moved out of the city, I was able to play and practice more. As my skill level increased, it was not unreasonable to adjust my expectations accordingly because I was ready and willing to put the time in to become a better player.

WHAT IS YOUR VERSION OF THE EQUATION?

I think it is constructive to do a little self-examination from time to time. I know what golf means to you because it means that much to me. I want to help make sure that golf is a positive part of your life because why else would you spend a large chunk of your day doing something that doesn't bring you much happiness?

There is a golfer I met who is in his early nineties. He plays almost every day and even walks every hole. I've had the opportunity to play a few holes with him on several occasions, and he is probably one of the happiest players on the planet. He doesn't care about his score; he is just thrilled to be there. It's hard to bottle up his perspective because all of us hope to live that long and be able to play at that age. But it doesn't mean you have to wait that long to readjust your expectations in this game.

If you aren't happy with your current level of play, what will you do about it to meet your expectations? Are you going to take lessons to improve your technique? Will you adjust your practice, strategy, or mental game?

While it's clichéd, if you do the same old, you get the same old.

If you are not willing to increase your skills through better habits, and there's nothing wrong with that, then maybe it is time to reshape your expectations of the game? Not everyone needs to play to move their handicap lower. Golf can be a way to get outdoors, exercise, spend time with friends, and travel.

That's the beauty of the game; there is no right way to do it. If you've invested in this book, you're likely interested in the improvement route, and I'll give you plenty of ideas on changing your habits for the better.

No matter how you do it, shouldn't it be fun, though?

THE BIG IDEAS

- Golfers tend to struggle with happiness on the course when their expectations and skill level are far apart.
- Everyone's "happiness equation" looks different. To find the balance, you might need to make adjustments in how much time you can spend improving, or what you expect of yourself.

CHAPTER 3
INCREMENTAL PROGRESS

"Progress happens too slowly for people to notice; setbacks happen too fast for people to ignore."

- Morgan Housel

ONE OF THE hardest things in golf is to keep perspective of where your game stands. You can have weeks or months of great play, and all it takes is one shaky round to have you staring into the abyss. I struggle with it; I know you struggle with it, and even the best players in the world are not immune to this kind of doubt.

Progress in golf is not always about significant breakthroughs; it's more about small incremental changes that build over time. If more golfers can start to understand this concept, I believe they will enjoy the game more and allow themselves to actually improve rather than continually make changes without giving them proper time to work.

The concept of incremental progress is fundamental to this entire book. So whether I'm discussing how to improve your strategy off the tee or work on your wedge play, please remember that you will not conquer these things immediately. My role is to point you in the right direction, and then you can start doing more efficient work on your game. Over time, you will build a golf game that you can be proud of.

THERE IS NO SUCH THING AS A FIX

I don't like the word fix when speaking about golf. It implies that something is permanent or done forever. I believe you are setting yourself up for disappointment whenever you think something is "fixed." How often have you been at the range and declared victory on a swing problem only for it to show up again weeks later? I know I have.

Often, the notion of fixing is used to sell you a training aid or swing system.

"Fix your slice forever with this one tip!!!"

The truth of the matter is that you can't fix or eliminate a slice forever. Like I can't stop hooking the ball too much from time to time. We all have our swing flaws that show up.

Here's the good news, though - you can make these mistakes less often. So rather than thinking you are never going to lose a tee shot into the right trees, you can focus on having it happen maybe one or two times less per round in the beginning and build from there.

Getting better at golf is really about incremental progress. You want to build up a bunch of small wins that will mix in with some setbacks. Over time those will grow into something much bigger.

SMALL IDEAS, BIG CHANGES

Golfers are always on the search for answers. The game is complicated and frustrating, and we're all looking for help.

We tend to consume a lot of information throughout this process. I can remember reading plenty of magazines and books when I was a junior golfer, primarily focused on swing mechanics. Each time I put them down, I was filled with hope, optimism, and tons of great ideas. However, when I tried to put them into practice, I was discouraged because there weren't immediate results, and I had too many thoughts floating around in my head while I played.

It only takes one tiny kernel of an idea that can significantly impact your game. I am trying to disperse these kernels to all of you throughout this book. I hope you read the entire text, but more importantly, I hope you come away with a few major ideas that positively influence your game.

For example, years ago, I was frustrated that I wasn't making progress in tournament play. I sought the advice of a friend Scott Fawcett, the creator of a great strategy system called DECADE. All it took was one statement from him to make a meaningful impact on my game. He told me that if I wanted to succeed in competitive golf, I had to embrace my driver, which I had been avoiding at the time at all costs.

I took that information and focused on it for a long time. The driver is now my favorite club in my bag. This came through practice, equipment changes, and strategy alterations. It certainly didn't happen overnight, but that advice helped me self-organize.

STOP PUTTING SO MUCH PRESSURE ON YOURSELF

One of my challenges is that I don't want golfers to feel like they have to be perfect when they embark on any changes.

This book features an entire section on avoiding mistakes through optimal target selections that I know will save you strokes. The information is easy to understand, so you will likely think you'll have the game solved. However, the problem is execution and discipline.

Strategy is almost more about psychology, though. When you're in a recovery situation after you hit your tee shot into the trees, your instinct will be to play aggressively to make up for the mistake. But the smart play is to get your ball back to safety and take your medicine.

Even if you're committed to doing that during your next round, you will be lured into thinking you can thread your ball through the trees onto the green. Golf has a way of bringing out the inner gambler in all of us. If you choose the aggressive route, and it results in disaster, that's OK. You don't have to beat yourself up over it because mistakes will always happen.

But let's say you start making a more thoughtful decision a few more times during a round. You'll likely see some minor improvements in your score. Perhaps you avoid a couple of double bogeys and make bogeys instead. That's two strokes! If I told you before you teed off that you could eliminate two strokes, you'd probably take that deal in a heartbeat.

That's what incremental progress looks like.

THIS CAN BE APPLIED TO ANYTHING

Whether you are taking lessons and making swing changes, trying to alter how you practice, or only making a commitment to yourself that you won't lose your temper during a round - it's all about the small wins.

If you expect great results quickly, you are just setting yourself up for disappointment. It is precisely why so many golfers give up so fast. Also, if someone promises you too much too quickly, I'd caution you to take their words with a grain of salt.

Stay patient, and enjoy the ride.

THE BIG IDEAS

- Becoming a better golfer is more about incremental progress than significant breakthroughs. Small wins (combined with setbacks) add up over time, and it's essential to stay patient and maintain perspective.
- Beware of using the word "fix" or "eliminate." You'll be setting yourself up for disappointment. If you struggle with a slice, you're never going to make it disappear forever. A more appropriate goal is to have it occur less often.
- Small ideas can lead to significant changes over time. But you have to be patient, put in the right kind of work, and allow time for them to develop.

- Don't put too much pressure on yourself! The concept of incremental progress applies to everything in golf - swing changes, strategy, practice, etc.

CHAPTER 4
THE 2/3 RULE

As GOLFERS, we all have different interpretations of how our rounds went. Most players are way too hard on themselves and often have unrealistic expectations of their performance on the course. No matter how hard we try, we just can't accept that golf is primarily a game of mistakes.

I've played thousands of rounds over the past 25 years. Many of them were in competition with elite amateurs and some aspiring playing professionals. In all of this time, I have never seen anyone conquer every phase of the game.

I would like to dispel the myth that you need to fire on all cylinders in all facets of the game to become a better golfer. I'm going to introduce a concept called the ⅔ rule, which I think can help many of you.

THE THREE PHASES OF GOLF

I think about golf in three different areas for the sake of simplicity:

1) Tee Shots
2) Approach Shots
3) Finesse Shots (Anything inside 100 yards)

When I recall my better rounds, I have only succeeded in two of these areas. For example, I've had days where I shot par or better that featured great tee shots, outstanding iron play, but mediocre putting. I have shot those identical scores other times but had difficulties off the tee. I made up the difference through approach shots and getting up and down for par 5-6 times with my wedges and putter.

I shoot my average scores on most days when I'm only doing one phase of the game very well. When things go terribly, then it's a zero.

Interestingly, I still have never had a round where I succeeded at all three. I have never witnessed any other golfer accomplish this feat in person either.

I should also clarify that this scoring system is relative to every golfer. Whether you're looking to break 100, 90, or 80 – each golfer has their benchmarks for performance in each category.

THE GOOD NEWS

We put so much pressure on ourselves on the course to hit every shot well. The fear of messing up can paralyze us, resulting in more mistakes.

The good news is that you can shoot your target score while making some serious errors during your round.

(You should be breathing a sigh of relief right now)

Many golfers assume they need to be great at every part of the game when they step on the first tee. Consequently, they are on short mental leashes. The second their tee shot lands in the trees, they have already declared the hole over (and potentially the entire round). That's not how golf works if you want to become a better player.

ELIMINATING THE ZERO

We have all had rounds where things go our way, and the game might seem easier. Those are the rounds we remember, and they reveal our potential. However, if you want to lower your handicap and shoot better scores on average, you shouldn't be focusing on your best performances.

The rounds you want to concentrate on are where you score zero out of three. Those days can drag you down and rock your confidence.

I didn't become a better golfer until I started consistently posting rounds where I scored at least one out of three. Things began to change once I started moving away from the 0/3 days.

HOW DO YOU DO IT?

Consistency is a very misused term in golf. I believe most golfers are not as far from consistency as they might think. They are just looking at their games through the wrong lens.

Getting rid of the rounds where you score zero out of three isn't easy. You must make adjustments to how you approach the game at various levels. I'll focus more on the "how" in the coming sections. It will require changing your strategy, the way you practice, your mental approach, and several other categories.

Thankfully, I believe all of you reading this are capable of doing it (relative to your skill levels). Think of it as optimizing your golf game or a series of tweaks. I'm not here to tear things apart.

BEING PATIENT AND DIGGING IN

I'd like to put all of this together in one neat statement to summarize what I'm trying to say regarding the 2/3 rule.

Here goes:

You don't need to be perfect to have a great round of golf; you need to be patient. At least one part of your game is going to abandon you. If you can remind yourself that mistakes are OK and have the mental resolve to dig in, your scores will improve.

I will reinforce this statement through several different methods throughout the book. This is one of the core philosophies you need to adopt if you genuinely want to improve.

THE BIG IDEAS

- Most golfers are way too hard on themselves and expect much higher performance than necessary to achieve their scoring goals.
- The ⅔ rule breaks the game into three phases: tee shots, approach shots and finesse shots.
- You should never expect to score 3/3; at minimum, one part of your game will not perform above average.
- Shooting your lowest scores can come with a ⅔ score and average scoring can occur with only ⅓.
- The main goal is to start avoiding rounds where you score a 0/3, and everything in this book will help you do that!
- Keep reminding yourself that you don't need to be perfect to play your best golf; you need to be patient. At a minimum, one part of your game can feel like a struggle on any given day.

CHAPTER 5
THE PGA TOUR FALLACY

MOST GOLFERS ARE avid viewers of professional golf on TV. While watching the best players in the world can be very entertaining, it often does a great disservice to golfers to manage their expectations appropriately. In this chapter, I want to clarify a few things about the professional ranks and how it pertains to your game.

THERE ISN'T MUCH TO LEARN FROM THEM

The golf industry has done a great job marketing itself through PGA Tour players. Growing up, I voraciously read the top magazines to figure out how to improve my game. The same formula has been used for decades. All they do is pick the best players and write catchy head-lines like the following:

"Find out Dustin Johnson's 5 Keys to Power"

"Want to Putt Like Brandt Snedecker?"

For the most part, it's the same content over and over again. There isn't much substance in the articles, and week after week, you are being given new information without giving yourself the proper amount of time to work on the last swing tip. It's a vicious cycle that usually does not lead to success.

The best golfers in the world can do things with their bodies that recreational golfers cannot. You'd likely get hurt if you tried to make the same shoulder turn as Dustin Johnson! They have spent their whole lives preparing, have immense natural talent, and it's their job to practice and play almost every day. The rest of us are playing an entirely different game. So if someone tells you to recreate a move in Rory McIlroy's swing, I would suggest looking in the opposite direction.

The interesting part is that as good as the pros are, golf can be just as difficult and perplexing to them as it can be to the rest of us. Of course, it's on a different level, but they're not as good as you think!

WHAT YOU SEE IS MISLEADING

Television broadcasts are one of the main reasons golfers have unrealistic expectations. The network's primary goal is to keep you tuned in and to do that, they need to entertain you. Do you think that will happen by showing you shots of golfers you never heard of shooting a 76 and missing the cut? Probably not.

For the most part, golf on TV is a highlight reel. In the earlier rounds, they are cycling back and forth between massive drives, approach shots landing near the pin, and 25 footers dropping for birdie. There are usually close to 150 golfers playing, but you're being shown the most impressive performances from the biggest names. When it gets down to the weekend, they will focus on the players who are all playing the best that week.

So what happens when all of us watch these broadcasts repeatedly for years? We start to subconsciously view the game through a lens that is not realistic. I have seen golfers throw tantrums because they couldn't land the ball next to the pin from 100 yards out. Others will curse themselves for missing a 12-footer. Most of these outcomes are very reasonable for their skill level and even the pros, but it doesn't stop them from getting upset.

Don't get me wrong; the pros are genuinely incredible at golf. But I would like to share a few statistics that just might surprise you and hopefully get your mind in a better place on the course.

FOUR STATS THAT SHOULD PROVIDE RELIEF

My main goal in this section of the book is to remove a burden off your shoulders. I played the game for too long expecting way too much of myself, and I know it hindered my ability to enjoy myself and improve.

When it comes to PGA Tour stats, many of them are not relevant to ordinary golfers. The length of their drives, fairways hit, greens in regulation, and many of the other traditional stats are not helpful to your progress. However, there are a few numbers that I always like to remind people that can be very powerful. I'll revisit many of these later in the book in the strategy section and how you can use this information to make smarter decisions that will lower your scores.

The Green Light

One saying you've heard over and over again is that a golfer has the "green light" to go after the pin when they're in the fairway with a wedge in their hand. I am willing to wager a large amount of money that if I polled golfers and asked them how close, on average, a PGA Tour player can land the ball to the pin from 100-125 yards, they would get the answer wrong by a significant margin.

Over the past several years, the best player on tour from 100-125 yards was landing the ball just over 15 feet from the pin on average. The median was roughly 20 feet, and the worst performer was somewhere around 26-28 feet.

Think about that for a moment. The best golfers in the world cannot even come close to landing the ball within 10 feet of the hole on average. A lot of this has to do with strategy, but the fact of the matter is that landing the ball on the green from that distance should be a reasonable goal that most golfers should celebrate. If you give yourself a 20-foot look for birdies, then know you are keeping pace with the best of the best.

Additionally, this statistic has significance for all approach shots and what golfers should consider a "good shot."

Recovery Situations

PGA Tour players make bogey roughly 80% of the time in recovery situations, such as being in the trees. Of course, it seems like every time we see these shots on TV there is a miraculous outcome.

This is one of the most interesting statistics discussed in Mark Broadie's book *Every Shot Counts*. When most golfers hit an errant tee shot, their instinct is to get aggressive and try threading the ball through a small opening. Alas, it usually compounds the initial mistake and results in a double bogey or worse, which is one of the main reasons most players struggle to lower their scores.

If you make bogey from that situation, you'll be matching the performance of most PGA Tour players. I can't stress this statistic enough; please remember it when you're on the course.

Putting Is Hard for Everyone

I've always thought of putting as a different game within golf. Most golfers measure their success by a binary standard - the ball went in the cup or it didn't. Missing a putt of any length is usually met with disappointment. When you start to examine the statistics behind putting, and see what kind of odds golfers have at sinking putts from different distances, usually there is an element of surprise.

Distance	Tour Pro	Scratch Golfer	90-Golfer
3 Feet	96%	93%	84%
5 Feet	77%	66%	50%
8 Feet	50%	41%	27%
10 Feet	40%	33%	20%
15 Feet	23%	21%	11%
20 Feet	15%	14%	6%
30 Feet	7%	6%	2%

Source: Mark Broadie

The most eye-opening statistic for most is that from 8 feet, a tour pro only has a 50% chance of making the putt. Once they get outside that distance, their chances of holing out drop dramatically.

For now, try to internalize these numbers. I will discuss how you can use them to practice more effectively and how to improve your putting in later chapters.

Birdie Machines? Hardly Not!

If you didn't know, birdies are very hard to come by. Probably much harder than you think.

The best players on the PGA Tour typically average around 4.5 birdies per round, which is truly exceptional. The median on tour is about 3.5 birdies per round, and the last place can be anywhere from 2.5 to 3.

Additionally, most of those birdies are coming from Par 5s. Here is the PGA Tour scoring average for 2021 by hole:

Par 3: 3.08
Par 4: 4.05
Par 5: 4.63

It is very unrealistic for golfers looking to break 100, 90, or 80 to make many birdies. The real key to reaching those milestones is mostly avoiding big numbers. Choosing aggressive strategies to make more birdies will only push you further away from your scoring goals.

REMEMBER THESE STATS ON THE COURSE

Golf is a challenging game, whether you are a club player or trying to be the best in the world.

Time and time again, I have seen golfers beat themselves up on the course (myself included) for hitting shots that were quite good for their skill level. When your mood sours like this, it affects your mental ability to stay in the round. If you can adjust your expectations appropriately, it will save you strokes in the long run.

Keep these stats in mind and think about them during your rounds. Properly managing expectations is one of the greatest tools a golfer can have.

THE BIG IDEAS

- **Professional golfers are playing an entirely different game. Be careful assuming you have much to learn from them whenever you watch television broadcasts or read articles about their swing tips!**
- **TV is mostly a highlight reel of the best shots at any time. If they exclusively showed tour players at the bottom of the leaderboards missing cuts, you'd see a very different version of golf.**
- **A typical tour player will hit the ball about 20 feet from the hole with a full wedge shot in the fairway. This is an essential reference point for multiple reasons.**
- **A PGA Tour player will make bogey roughly 80% of the time in a recovery situation like being in the trees. Stop trying to be a hero!**
- **Putting is perhaps the most difficult and misunderstood part of golf. Golfers have their best chance of holing putts inside**

of 8 feet, and outside of those distances, it becomes more of a test of speed control and proximity.

- Birdies are very hard to come by, even for tour players. Lowering your scores is not about making more birdies; it's more about mistake avoidance.

CHAPTER 6
PRACTICE VS. PLAY

To become a better golfer, you'll need to devote some time to practice. However, there needs to be some balance between being on a golf course and working on your game. Many golfers who spend countless hours practicing, assume that alone will entitle them to lower their scores. Unfortunately, it doesn't work that way.

BECOMING A BETTER GOLFER REQUIRES EXPERIENCE

A lot can happen in 18 holes. You can go through periods of great play and then abruptly forget how to swing a club two holes later. The emotional swings that occur are part of what makes the game so unique and frustrating at the same time.

Golfers lose sight of the fact that you need to be on the course going through all of those trials and tribulations to gain experience. Advanced players will tell you the same thing; you need to be out on a course playing. All of the preparation in the world at the practice range cannot truly simulate what goes on during a round.

Simply put, you need to be comfortable on a golf course. There are so many little elements to this game that require a certain amount of experience, and if you can't play enough, it's hard to develop them. On top of that, gathering the proper feedback and analyzing your results on the course provides you with the template for your practice sessions.

WHAT IS A REASONABLE BALANCE?

I can't possibly quantify the number of hours or what kind of ratio you need to divide between practice and playing time. I can tell you that spending more time practicing at the expense of playing will likely yield diminishing returns at a certain point.

I know most of you have work, family, and other kinds of time commitments. That is why I talk about managing expectations so much. Many of us don't have unlimited time to work on our games and play as much as we would like. But if you use that time effectively, you can see improvement.

I'll discuss three hypothetical scenarios to illustrate my point:

Scenario #1 - Practice With Little Play: If you are a golfer who can get plenty of 30-60 minute practice sessions in but can only play one or two times a month - it usually makes sense to temper your expectations. Some players are more naturally talented than others. Still, if you cannot test your skills and learn from them during a round often enough, it's challenging to gain any meaningful return on your preparation. Overall, if you can't play enough, I wouldn't expect too much.

Scenario #2 - Practicing Instead of Playing: If you have more time to get on the course but choose to practice more instead of playing, I urge you to find more of a balance. Every time you tee it up, it's an opportunity to learn and challenge yourself. The things you've been working on at the practice facility, or your backyard, need a chance to be tested out in live-action.

Scenario #3 - All Play No Practice: Some golfers don't want to practice at all, and use all of their free time to play. I get it. While I think you still can learn and improve by playing plenty of golf, you are likely forgoing an opportunity to get better if you aren't working on your skills off the course. All of the clues about your game are hiding in your on-course performance. If you can take time to analyze what is happening during your rounds and use that information to work on some of the elements of your game that are lacking, there are usually some low-hanging fruit waiting to be picked.

IT'S ALL ABOUT COMFORT LEVEL

The best golf I have ever played is when I can play enough. I've also had the opportunity to learn from some highly-skilled players, and their feedback is quite similar. Better golf requires a certain amount of comfort level on the golf course. That is almost impossible to replace during practice.

If you can't play enough golf, that's OK - there is still an opportunity to get better at this game. However, I would caution you to be a little more patient with yourself. If you only get to play once a month, don't use that one round as a litmus test of your game. Playing once every 30 days is not enough to get any reasonable measure of where you stand. Please try to enjoy your time outside away from the world's distractions, and not put too much pressure on yourself.

Let's say you have an opportunity to play once a week. I think that's a much more reasonable opportunity to test what you've been working on in your practice sessions and strike a balance between playing and preparing. Indeed, there's no correct answer for every golfer. But the two main points I would like to get across are:

- You can only capitalize on your practice if you play enough.
- A large part of golf improvement is comfort level on a golf course.

I'll dive much deeper into how to practice more effectively later on in the book, but I think this chapter will give you an overall outlook on making sure you are striking the right balance between practice and play.

THE BIG IDEAS

- Striking a balance between practice and playing golf is crucial to improvement.
- There are so many elements of golf that you need to learn while playing. Additionally, establishing a comfort level of being on the course is often overlooked.
- Playing 9 or 18 holes is an opportunity to gather feedback, analyze, and use this information to make your practice sessions more efficient and productive.

CHAPTER 7
ACCEPTING THE RANGE OF SCORES

GOLFERS ARE CONTINUALLY MEASURING themselves by whatever score they shoot. Whenever a fellow golfer finds out that you played recently, the first question out of their mouth is not, "did you have fun?" It's usually, "so what did you shoot?" Then you'll likely tell the tale of your round and how it could have been a lower score had you not made the triple bogey on the 5th hole. It's part of the camaraderie of the game. We can't just say what we shot; it has to be put in the context of a story!

Because scoring is so important to most golfers, many use it to measure how their day went. While escaping this trap is hard, it is possible to have a good time despite not shooting the score you were hoping to. If most of you primarily focused on having fun, you'd likely see a drop in your scoring as a side effect.

One fundamental concept eludes most who play this game, though. Many golfers don't understand a reasonable range of scores for their ability level. When most tee it up, they are searching for that magical round where everything goes right. They want to tell their buddies how they broke 80 or whatever scoring milestone is important to them. The truth is that the majority of your rounds will not be your best stuff.

Rather than being disappointed by those rounds, I want you to start to learn how to accept them as typical outcomes.

IT'S ALL RELATIVE

Scoring is a very relative concept in golf. Shooting an 87 could be a complete disaster for one player, while the other would be jumping for joy and spreading the news far and wide that they finally broke 90. But no matter how good of a golfer you are, there will be a relatively wide range of scoring possibilities. Let's take a look at a PGA Tour Pro.

The name Richy Werenski probably won't ring a bell, but he made over a million dollars on the PGA Tour in 2021. At one point, he was the 101st ranked golfer in the world. Richy can play!

When most of us follow PGA Tour events, we pay attention to who is playing the best. The talent is immense these days, and we are used to seeing tour players shoot in the low to mid-60s at their best. However, touring pros who are not household names that miss cuts disappear into the background (along with their scores).

Let's take a closer look at Richy Werenski's range of scores. Richy averaged 71.1 strokes in all of the events he played, which is very respectable considering the difficulty of courses on the PGA Tour and the immense pressure. His best score was 61 in the second round of the ZOZO Championship. The next day he shot a 72 and then a 76 in the final round. So within 24 hours, he experienced an 11-shot swing and then a 15-shot swing one day after. Does that sound familiar to you?

You would think a player like him would never fail to break 80, but it happened. Werenski shot an 80 at The Player's Championship. He also recorded rounds of 78 and 79 twice. I'm sure he wasn't pleased, but those rounds represented his worst performances.

So even a PGA Tour player can have as much as a 20-shot swing from their best to worst. One day they can show up and shoot the best round of their life, and less than a day later, they can feel clueless.

NARROWING THE GAP

If you want to get better, there is something essential for you to under-stand about scoring. Generically speaking, the better a golfer is, the tighter window of scores they can shoot. For example, most of my rounds have scores between 70-76. Looking back a full year, my best score was a 68, and my worst was an 86. While it took me more than two decades to call myself a scratch golfer and tighten the range of those scores, one of the keys to getting better was limiting the damage on the days I was struggling.

When I look back at the kind of golfer I was compared to how I can play now, I would say one of the main differences is making my weaker performances not as bad. To give that context, I can take a day that usually would have ended up with an 83 and turn it into a 78. For you, that could be turning a 105 into a 98 - again, it is all relative.

So how do you do it? The first part is acceptance. Accept the fact that golf is an inherently volatile game. One day your swing can feel invin-cible, and all is well. In under 24 hours, things can feel like they completely fell apart, and your score balloons. It doesn't matter how skilled you are; it's what makes this game frustrating and addictive at the same time. We are chasing the unknown.

If you can accept that your score can change as much as 20, 30, or even 40 strokes between rounds, you're going to be in a much better place overall. Fortunately, I have a lot of tools to help you tighten those gaps a bit, but they will always exist.

Scott Fawcett, who you'll hear about several times in this book, gave me a helpful way to think about it in mathematical terms. Golfers' scoring trends typically follow the distribution of a bell curve.

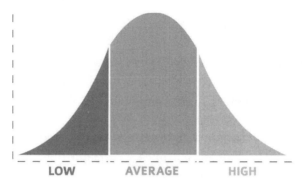

Sometimes it is helpful to visualize your scores as a series of outcomes.

The bulk of your scoring will usually settle itself within an average range. If you remember from your statistics class, 68% of a data set is generally within one standard deviation. As you move outside of that range, between two and three standard deviations, the probability of those events drops dramatically.

Golfers tend to get into trouble with the low-probability scores in both directions. They go out hoping for their best scores. Additionally, they have a tough time accepting their high scores.

These ranges are a fundamental truth about the game. You are in control of shifting your scoring ranges and making them tighter, but no matter how good you get, these rules will still apply.

So the next time someone asks you what you shot, even if it's not a score you are excited about, know that everyone who plays this game is in the same boat.

THE BIG IDEAS

- Golfers tend to use their scores to measure how their day went. Because of the game's inherent volatility, this can significantly alter enjoyment levels.
- Scoring ability is a relative concept in golf, but the scoring range is not. Whether you are a PGA Tour pro or a beginner,

your scoring can fluctuate tremendously from one day to the next. It's very normal!

- When most golfers improve, they typically can tighten their scoring windows and make their poor performances "not as bad." A lot of golf is about mistake avoidance.
- Thinking about scoring potential as a bell curve can be helpful. Don't expect low-probability events on the low side, and try to accept those that occur on the high side.

CHAPTER 8
WHAT IS A GOOD SHOT?

GOLFERS ARE INCREDIBLY DEMANDING of themselves, and it often hinders their ability to enjoy the game and play better. One area in particular where most of us struggle is how we evaluate the quality of the shot we just hit.

For most, if they don't land the ball within a small window of where they aim, the shot is a failure. The truth of the matter is many of those shots weren't that bad. Having a fundamental understanding of reasonable outcomes based on your skill level can be transformative for your game. Your mood can improve, you will make better strategic decisions, and your scores will drop.

We all know golf is hard, but I can assure you that whatever level you are looking to reach, you will not need complete control of your golf ball. You can make plenty of mistakes and achieve your goals. In a sense, you have to permit yourself to hit bad shots and at the same time understand what outcomes are reasonable. This chapter will give statistics that will paint a clearer picture of what constitutes a "good shot" by scoring ability.

TEE SHOTS

Where you hit the ball off the tee is extremely important in determining your eventual score on any given hole. Overall, your goal should be to advance the ball as far as possible while keeping it in play and giving yourself a chance to hit a green in regulation.

The measuring stick for success for most golfers is whether or not you hit the fairway. But as I will explore in the strategy section, it is not fairway or bust. In my opinion, fairways hit is one of the most misleading statistics in golf and doesn't take into account true success off the tee.

Most PGA Tour players average 50-65% of fairways off the tee. Looking at the recreational level, it moves to 50% or below, even for scratch golfers. You can't possibly tell if one golfer is more successful than another by evaluating their fairways hit percentage. It's more about how far they are hitting it and how often they avoid trouble (fairway bunkers, trees, penalty areas, out of bounds).

Here is the good news: you don't need prodigious length or laser accuracy to lower your scores with your driver.

Hitting the ball farther is an advantage, and I will give you plenty of ideas on doing it. There are clear trends between distance and scoring ability. But you don't need to hit 300-yard drives like the pros!

The USGA and R&A did a joint study on driving distance looking back as far as 1996. They found a typical male golfer hits their drives around 225 yards, and that number has not changed dramatically over the years. Cross-referencing shot-tracking systems like Arccos and Shot Scope, the numbers are similar.

AVERAGE DRIVING DISTANCE BY HANDICAP

	2017	2018	2019
0-5	244.4	244.5	242.6
6-10	231.4	231.5	229.7
11-15	220.5	220.1	219.0
16-20	209.9	209.8	209.0
21-25	201.3	201.6	200.9

Source: Arccos Golf

Even if you aspire to become a low-single-digit handicap, you can still get there while averaging less than 250 yards off the tee.

Shot distributions, also known as dispersion, are another critical concept for tee shot success. Typically, most fairways can range between 25 - 65 yards wide. You can consider 35-45 yards a medium width, and many PGA Tour setups are around 30-32 yards.

A fascinating exercise evaluates how wide a golfer's tee shot dispersion is from left to right after a series of shots. An elite amateur or professional player who hits it 300 yards can have distributions as wide as 65-70 yards, and still, play great golf! Typically, golfers who don't hit it as far will have a tighter distribution, but they still can be 45-50 yards wide.

Here is an example of a driver distribution pattern from one of the best amateur golfers in the world. This is a combination of multiple sessions on Trackman:

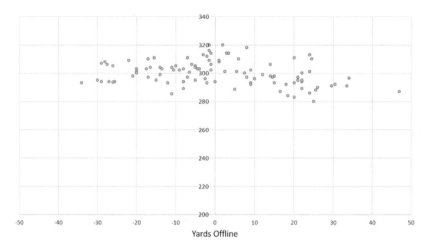

Source: Lou Stagner

So, no matter how accurate you think you are with your driver, it is reasonable to expect a fairly wide outcome. You are going to miss plenty of fairways!

The biggest limiter of scoring is trouble. Every time you land the ball in a fairway bunker, in the trees, a penalty area, or out of bounds, your scoring potential drops dramatically. Notice I didn't mention light rough. Rough is typically not nearly as big of a penalty. For many golfers, it usually is somewhere around .25 to .3 strokes. However, a fairway bunker can cost a player as much as 1.4 strokes and trees as much as 1.1 strokes.

Let's say you are a 15-handicap playing a 375-yard par 4 with fairway bunkers and trees. You hit your driver 225 yards into the light rough just left of the fairway. You have a good lie, a clear path to the green, and 150 yards left. Perhaps that tee shot discouraged you because you missed the fairway, but it's still a great shot!

I will use many of these concepts to help you pick smarter targets off the tee later in the book. Hopefully, seeing some of these numbers has given you a more realistic view of what constitutes a successful tee shot.

I also want to make one final point on tee shots. Playing the appropriate tee boxes for your skill level and distance ability is essential. Going too far back makes the game harder to enjoy. One simple formula you can use is multiplying how far you hit a 5-iron by 36 to give yourself a guide.

The PGA of America has also set forth these guidelines by driving distance:

Average Drive	Recommended Tees
300 yards	7,150 - 7,400 yards
275 yards	6,700 - 6,900 yards
250 yards	6,200 - 6,400 yards
225 yards	5,800 - 6,000 yards
200 yards	5,200 - 5,400 yards
175 yards	4,400 - 4,600 yards
150 yards	3,500 - 3,700 yards

APPROACH SHOTS

How well you hit your irons and other approach clubs has the most significant influence on scoring potential. Proximity to the hole plays a major factor in success, but most golfers have no idea what reasonable distances are.

You have to accept that landing the ball close to the pin is not a reasonable expectation no matter what kind of golfer you are.

In an earlier chapter, I shared that most PGA Tour players cannot land the ball within 20 feet of the pin on average from 100-125 yards in the fairway. This stat is always a great starting point because it removes the expectation of landing it close to the pin from just about any distance. Or at least, it should!

Evaluating whether or not you hit a good shot with an approach club is a mixture of whether or not you hit the green in regulation, or if you didn't, did you leave yourself a relatively easy wedge shot that you can get on the putting surface?

Hitting a green in regulation (GIR), no matter how far you are from the hole, should be celebrated, not expected. While fairways hit is not a great predictor of scoring success, a GIR is:

Handicap	Greens In Regulation %
0	52
5	38
10	35
15	26
20	21
25	15

Source: Shot Scope

Hitting greens are hard to come by. Even the top 1% of golfers barely hit more than half their greens each round.

The most significant separating factor in approach performance is proximity to the hole. Even when better golfers tend to miss greens, they are closer to the hole on average.

Let's look at proximity to the hole from all distances by handicap level:

75 - 125 Yards:

Handicap	0	5	10	15	20	25
Avg Prox	39 Feet	42 Feet	49 Feet	60 Feet	67 Feet	74 Feet

125 - 175 Yards:

Handicap	0	5	10	15	20	25
Avg Prox	45 Feet	61 Feet	70 Feet	88 Feet	107 Feet	114 Feet

175 - 225 Yards:

Handicap	0	5	10	15	20	25
Avg Prox	82 Feet	109 Feet	123 Feet	166 Feet	192 Feet	236 Feet

Source: Shot Scope

As you can see, even scratch golfers are quite far away from the hole on approach shots of all distances. So when you hit your 7-iron to 35 feet from the hole on the green, you might want to rethink whether or not you should be angry at yourself.

Similar to tee shots, mistake avoidance is critical as well. If you miss a green, avoiding bunkers, being short-sided, or penalty areas become important scoring influences.

Let's put it all together and think about what constitutes a good approach shot. For starters, pat yourself on the back whenever you hit a green in regulation. That is definitely a good shot!

The likelihood is that you will miss the majority of greens whenever you tee it up, though. I still believe you can consider certain outcomes successful. For starters, if you have avoided a bunker, and have a manageable lie in the rough or fairway, that's a positive. Additionally, if you have plenty of green to work with (not short-sided) between you and the pin, that is great too. Last but not least, the closer you are to the green, the better. You'll have a better chance of landing your wedge shot nearer to the hole for an easy bogey or a par save.

For example, if a 15-handicap had a 170-yard approach shot and landed it just off the green with an easy chip shot about 45-50 feet away from the hole, I would consider that a good shot. They've avoided the big trouble and outperformed golfers at a similar skill level in terms of proximity.

Great approach play is a mixture of mistake avoidance and proximity. Just remember that you don't have to be as close to the hole as you might think.

WEDGE PLAY

The recurring theme of proximity and mistake avoidance continues with wedge play. So many golfers feel pressure to land the ball within a 10-foot circle around the hole and often define success with an arbitrary distance that is likely way too difficult to achieve.

So what is a good wedge shot? Let's look at what the pros are doing for some initial guidance.

If you are a tour player, you are world-class with a wedge. Even the "worst" performers around the green are at a level that normal golfers find difficult to comprehend.

From 10-20 yards, which is a relatively close shot, a typical tour player will average about 7 feet from the hole. Hardly a gimmie. From 20-30 yards, the average moves further to about 9 feet. I can't stress how impressive these numbers are.

But when we look at recreational golfers and their proximity numbers, the picture changes dramatically. Here is a summary of performance by handicap level showing proximity to the hole and the likelihood of getting up and down.

10-20 Yards:

Handicap	0	5	10	15	20	25
Avg Prox	10.8 ft	11.6 ft	13.2 ft	16.2 ft	16.8 ft	18.6 ft
Up & Down %	57%	48%	41%	30%	30%	25%

20-30 Yards:

Handicap	0	5	10	15	20	25
Avg Prox	13.4 ft	14.6 ft	18.2 ft	22.6 ft	22.8 ft	26.1 ft
Up & Down %	42%	38%	26%	18%	16%	14%

30-40 Yards:

Handicap	0	5	10	15	20	25
Avg Prox	16.3 ft	22.5 ft	23.4 ft	27.6 ft	28.2 ft	30.1 ft
Up & Down %	27%	22%	22%	16%	15%	12%

Source: Shot Scope

No matter what level of golf you are playing, it's very unrealistic to expect to land the ball within the 10-foot circle on average with green-side wedge play. Of course, we'd love to have stress-free tap-ins for par, but golf doesn't work that way.

Our ambitions can be higher than approach shots since we are much closer to the hole. At a minimum, getting the ball on the putting surface inside around 20 feet is a good shot for most golfers. You've reduced your chances of making a double bogey quite dramatically at that point and also given yourself an opportunity to save par. That number can be adjusted a bit based on your skill level and how close you are to the hole, but I believe it's a good starting point.

So many golfers waste strokes around the greens because they fail to get the ball on the putting surface. This is a mixture of skill deficit and sometimes poor decision-making. Either way, if you were 25 yards away from the hole and landed the ball 12 feet from the pin, that's an opportunity to embrace a good shot rather than feel frustrated you didn't get that 5-footer for par.

PUTTING

Putting is perhaps the most misunderstood part of golf. There is a different set of rules and expectations to follow.

Performance usually gets judged from a binary perspective. You either make the putt, or you don't - and most interpret that as success or fail-ure. However, it is not that simple. I have been around golfers who I believe putted well during a round, but they interpreted their perfor-mance as a complete disaster. I've also fallen victim to this kind of behavior myself. It's tough to avoid.

Measuring putts per round is another statistic that can be incredibly misleading. Telling someone you had 30 putts might sound much better than if you had 34. But that doesn't take into account how many putts you holed from various distances, or how good your proximity to the hole was on longer lag putts.

I've got some good news and some bad news. Putting is very hard, actually much harder than you think. To make a putt, three things generally need to occur:

1. You need to read the slope of the green properly and pick the correct line to start your putt.
2. The putt must travel at the right speed to match your intended line.
3. Your stroke needs to start the ball on the correct line (not push it or pull it).

On top of that, you are rolling a ball on a living surface that is changing throughout the day. Golfers who tee off earlier in the morning are able to roll the ball on freshly mown and smoother grass. As the day progresses, more foot traffic and grass growth introduce imperfections. Lou Stagner, a skilled statistician, offered this analysis of putting make rates on the PGA Tour as the day progressed.

Distance to Hole	7:59 or earlier	8:00 to 8:59	9:00 to 9:59	10:00 to 10:59	11:00 to 11:59	12:00 to 12:59	1:00 to 1:59	2:00 to 2:59	3:00 to 3:59	4:00 to 4:59	5:00 or later
2'0" - 2'5"	99.0%	99.1%	99.1%	99.1%	99.1%	99.1%	99.0%	99.0%	99.0%	98.9%	98.8%
2'6" - 2'11"	98.0%	97.7%	98.0%	97.9%	97.7%	97.6%	97.5%	97.4%	97.2%	97.2%	97.1%
3'0" - 3'5"	94.4%	95.1%	95.2%	95.0%	94.8%	94.6%	94.3%	94.0%	94.0%	93.7%	93.7%
3'6" - 3'11"	91.7%	91.1%	91.1%	90.8%	91.0%	90.2%	90.1%	89.6%	89.3%	88.7%	88.0%
4'0" - 4'5"	85.6%	86.2%	86.1%	85.5%	85.0%	85.1%	84.7%	83.7%	83.8%	83.4%	83.1%
4'6" - 4'11"	80.8%	81.7%	80.7%	80.1%	80.0%	78.8%	79.0%	78.6%	77.9%	77.8%	77.9%
5'0" - 5'5"	76.2%	74.4%	75.5%	75.3%	75.0%	74.3%	73.1%	73.7%	72.2%	72.7%	72.6%
5'6" - 5'11"	70.6%	70.4%	70.5%	68.6%	70.1%	68.6%	68.5%	68.2%	66.4%	66.7%	67.1%
6'0" - 6'5"	66.7%	64.0%	65.2%	65.0%	64.5%	64.5%	63.5%	62.5%	62.4%	62.3%	61.4%
6'6" - 6'11"	60.5%	61.3%	60.8%	60.4%	61.0%	60.0%	58.8%	59.0%	59.2%	58.5%	57.6%
7'0" - 7'5"	58.9%	57.7%	56.0%	56.7%	56.0%	55.6%	55.2%	54.8%	54.4%	53.7%	53.6%
7'6" - 7'11"	54.7%	52.4%	52.8%	52.2%	52.0%	51.7%	51.3%	51.2%	50.7%	50.5%	50.7%
8'0" - 8'5"	50.6%	50.6%	50.2%	49.5%	48.9%	48.9%	48.8%	48.4%	48.4%	47.1%	47.4%

 @LouStagner   @LouStagnerGolf

On putts eight feet and in, where golfers have the best chance of making putts, their performance materially declined from the early morning to late afternoon.

Additionally, it is widely believed that on longer putts, irregularities on green surfaces are responsible for golfers missing many putts. Dave Pelz, a respected authority on short game performance, believes that even on a perfectly manicured putting surface, as much as 20% of putts will miss from 12 feet due to imperfections.

I'll discuss later in the book why I believe speed is the most critical factor of the three to get right, but long story short - it's a serious challenge to consistently hole putts.

The good news is that there are some actionable things you can do to lower your scores despite the inherent difficulty of putting. But first, let's set some realistic expectations.

How Hard Is It?

In the chapter on PGA Tour stats, I discussed how television broadcasts are partially responsible for golfers' unrealistic expectations. Putting performance is the most misrepresented part of golf whenever you watch the pros on TV. Usually, it's a highlight reel of players draining putts anywhere from 10-40 feet. You're not being shown how one golfer usually performs throughout 18 holes or even an entire tournament.

If I were to poll all of you reading this book, and ask how likely it is for professional golfers to make putts from various distances, I would wager that most of you would grossly overestimate their abilities. Mark Broadie compiled the following statistics, which shows the one-putt percentages from Tour Pros, scratch golfers, and a typical 90-shooter. Take a moment to allow these numbers to sink in:

Distance	Tour Pro	Scratch Golfer	90-Golfer
3 Feet	96%	93%	84%
5 Feet	77%	66%	50%
8 Feet	50%	41%	27%
10 Feet	40%	33%	20%
15 Feet	23%	21%	11%
20 Feet	15%	14%	6%
30 Feet	7%	6%	2%

The distances that usually surprise most golfers are from 5-8 feet. When players miss putts from those distances, they can become enraged. You can see that even for a professional golfer, they only have a 50% chance from eight feet. Once you get outside that range, their likelihood of making putts drops dramatically.

At 20 feet and beyond, the difference in skill level doesn't change the outcome as much. Whether they are on the PGA Tour or a weekend warrior, all golfers will likely miss from long range. But better putters will have far superior speed control. Take a look at the differences in three-putting probabilities from various distances:

Distance	Tour Pro	Scratch Golfer	90-Golfer
10 Feet	1%	1%	2%
20 Feet	2%	2%	8%
30 Feet	5%	9%	18%
40 Feet	10%	15%	30%
50 Feet	17%	23%	41%
60 Feet	23%	30%	51%

Source: Mark Broadie

That's not to say you should step up to all of your putts expecting to miss them. I'll discuss how routine is essential on the greens, and how you can practice more effectively later in the book. It is important to use these stats to help control your reaction to missed putts, and not let those negative emotions bleed into the rest of your game. Putting is largely a test of how many putts you can make inside of 10 feet, and how close you can leave it to the hole once you get further away from the hole.

In other words, be happy when you do hole a putt from just about any distance outside of three feet - that is a good shot! However, be more concerned about your speed control and proximity when you are outside the "make zone."

GIVE YOURSELF MORE CREDIT

The definition of a "good golf shot" eludes most players. Whether you have a driver, iron, wedge, or putter in your hand, you have to do your best not to let your expectations get the best of you. Remembering many of these statistics while you play can truly transform your enjoyment and performance.

THE BIG IDEAS

- Having a better understanding of what good shots are for your skill level can transform your golf game. You can improve your mood and make better strategic decisions. Who doesn't want to have more fun and lower their scores?
- Success off the tee is not all about hitting fairways. Some of the best golfers in the world have much wider dispersions off the tee than you would think. For most recreational golfers, it is about avoiding big trouble. You don't need prodigious length to lower your handicap, but you need to give yourself more opportunities to advance the ball to the green (or close to it).
- Approach play is not about how close you can land your ball

to the pin. Golfers at any level cannot expect to consistently be within 15 feet of the pin once they are outside of 100 yards. Hitting more greens is the most surefire way to lower scores. However, when you miss greens, proximity and mistake avoidance also dictate whether or not you have hit a good shot.

- Successful wedge play is not about leaving yourself tap-in pars. For many golfers, leaving yourself a 15-20 foot putt can be considered a good shot. Routinely getting the ball on the putting surface, and avoiding double bogeys is where many players lower their scores with wedges.

- Defining a good shot is often most difficult while putting. At any level, making a putt from 3-10 feet is a positive outcome. But you have to understand that the odds are stacked against you to make most of your putts. Three-putt avoidance and improved speed control are how most players lower their scores while modestly increasing their make rates inside of 10 feet.

CHAPTER 9
SCORING IN A NUTSHELL

For years, there were a lot of myths and misconceptions on where scoring primarily occurs amongst golfers and how players separated themselves from one another.

As a junior golfer, I was always told that putting was the most important part of the game because that's where the most strokes occurred. On the surface, it makes sense. If you shot an 85 and had 35 putts, roughly 40% of your score came from your putter. But how many of those putts were tap-ins from 10 inches? Are those shots as influential to your total score as your drives or approach shots?

It turns out it is a lot more nuanced than just counting putts per round or fairways hit. In this chapter, I'd like to clarify a few things and explain how a statistic called strokes gained gives us far more insight into scoring ability.

WHY STROKES GAINED TELLS YOU MORE THAN TRADITIONAL STATISTICS

If you want to understand how golfers separate themselves from one another and get more information on where you need to improve, strokes gained have become the most accurate way to do this kind of analysis.

Mark Broadie first introduced strokes gained to the PGA Tour in 2011. Because the tour uses Shotlink, a laser system to track each shot, it enables them to calculate the value of every single shot. With the advent of GPS tracking systems, and various apps, this information is now available to recreational golfers, and it's tremendously helpful. Fortunately, you don't need to understand how it's calculated; all of the math is done for you!

Why is strokes gained so helpful? Because it gives each shot a numerical value. Golfers know that hitting a drive 275 yards in the fairway is better than 220 yards in the trees. But how much better is it? Strokes gained uses baselines of how many shots it takes a golfer to hole out from various positions on the golf course to achieve these values.

For example, a PGA Tour player has a 50% chance of making an 8-foot putt, or an average of 1.5 strokes to hole out from that distance. Using strokes gained, if a tour player made that putt, you would gain ½ a stroke on the field, and if you missed it, you would lose ½ a stroke.

Every shot they hit is compared against these performance benchmarks as a player completes their round. At the end of their day, they can find out whether or not they lost or gained strokes in each part of the game - tee shots, approach shots, wedge play inside 100 yards, and putting. Additionally, players can see where they stack up against one another over many rounds.

If you gained strokes off the tee (a positive value), you know that you performed well compared to players at a similar level. Conversely, you underperformed if you lost strokes (a negative value) with your putter.

Now let's talk about some on-course scenarios that explain how strokes gained gives a deeper analysis of performance than traditional statistics.

Let's say you were a 10-handicap competing against a friend with an identical handicap. You hit your drive 280 yards in the fairway, and your opponent hit their driver 220 yards in the fairway. Any golfer knows that being 60 yards closer to the hole is an advantage. You'll have a shorter club and a better opportunity to land the ball closer to the hole. But fairways hit could not distinguish between these two shots. That 60 yards in distance is worth something, and strokes gained would tell you the exact value (somewhere about ½ a stroke for a typical golfer).

Or let's say you had a 150-yard approach shot, and you both missed a green in regulation. Your shot landed just short of the green on the fringe, only 30 feet away from the hole - a relatively easy situation. Your friend chunked their 7-iron and only advanced the ball 50 yards, leaving themselves 100 yards from the pin. You have both missed a green in regulation, but there's no question your situation is much easier. Strokes gained would account for those differences in proximity and assign each of those shots the appropriate value based on how many shots it would take to hole out from each position.

As you get closer to the hole, with wedge play and putting, your proximity to the hole continues to dictate your performance. If you were 40 yards from the hole and hit a wedge to 3 feet, you would gain strokes versus a shot that landed 25 feet from the hole. With putting, it's not just whether or not you make or miss a putt. If you had a 50-foot putt and lagged it to 18 inches, that shot would gain strokes versus one you left 8 feet from the hole. And as you make or miss putts from various distances, they are tallied until you get a much clearer picture of your putting performance for the day.

There are plenty of situations where traditional stats can mislead you. On the surface, if you had 29 putts one day, and 32 putts another, you would assume you performed three shots better with your putter on the first day. However, that might not be the case. The starting distances on each putt (influenced by approach and wedge play) can easily distort those numbers.

Let's take two golfers who average 50% fairways each round. At face value, one could assume they have similar abilities off the tee. While that is possible, it is not enough detail to honestly know which golfer is performing better. Here is a theoretical circumstance to illustrate how that is possible.

Golfer A averages 230 yards per drive, whereas Golfer B averages 275 yards per drive. Additionally, when player A misses fairways, they typically end up in 3-4 recovery situations (i.e., in the trees) or incur penalty shots per round. Conversely, Golfer B seldom ends up in a penalty area off the tee and only ends up in the trees 1-2 times per round.

Player B is a far superior driver of the golf ball because they hit it farther and avoid trouble off the tee than player A. However, fairways hit can't take into account all of these variables. It is not enough information. We now know that how far you hit the ball combined with where your ball ends when it does miss the fairway has an incredible influence on a golfer's ability to score.

This is why a player like Jim Furyk can still be one of the leaders on the PGA Tour in fairway percentage off the tee, but using strokes gained, we know he is not one of the best drivers because he can't hit it as far as the competition (who are more accurate than we first assumed).

Calculating the actual performance of each shot relative to other golfers at your scoring level is crucial in determining your strengths and weaknesses in your golf game. You'll see me drive this message home in various ways throughout the book.

HOW GOLFERS SEPARATE THEMSELVES

Understanding how scoring truly occurs in golf, and how players separate themselves from one another is essential in figuring out how to become a better player. Knowing your relative strengths and weaknesses allows you to make adjustments and not waste time honing an area of the game where you are already proficient versus another that could use some more time and effort.

When Mark Broadie's book *Every Shot Counts* came out, he presented his findings on true golfer performance using strokes gained analysis. It's a fantastic book that I consider required reading for any golfer. While there are many notable findings in Mark's research, I believe the following two points to be the most important:

- Putting is not as influential in scoring differential as we first assumed. Broadie assigned 15% importance to putting in determining any player's score. It turns out putting is much harder than we all thought, and it's harder for golfers to separate themselves from one another with the flat stick.
- The long game accounts for roughly 2/3 of the scoring differential. In other words, shots outside of 100 yards (tee shots and approach shots) are the biggest determining factor in why one golfer scores better than another. Broadie concluded that approach shots are where most scoring occurs.

Interestingly, the long game accounting for roughly ⅔ of scoring differential holds up remarkably well whether you are looking at PGA Tour pros or weekend warriors.

When Shot Scope first released their strokes gained analysis of their database of amateur golfers, they were able to benchmark their performance on every shot versus tour players, which you can see in the following image:

Pros vs. Joes

How do recreational golfers stack up against professional golfers in all facets of the game? Shot Scope analyzed their database of golfers and compared each handicap level versus a typical pro golfer benchmark using strokes-gained analysis. The negative numbers indicate players losing strokes to the pros in each category.

	0 HCP	5 HCP	10 HCP	15 HCP	20 HCP	25 HCP
TEE SHOTS	-1.78	-3.34	-3.61	-4.86	-5.75	-7.53
APPROACHES	-2.03	-4.29	-6.11	-8.54	-11.26	-14.23
SHORT GAME	-0.39	-0.97	-1.33	-3.18	-4.06	-5.42
PUTTING	-0.94	-1.42	-2.77	-4.46	-4.48	-4.71
TOTAL	-5.14	-10.02	-13.82	-21.04	-25.55	-31.89

As you would expect, in aggregate, golfers of all handicap levels are losing strokes to tour players. Of course, singular golfers might gain strokes in one category with exceptional play, but on the whole, there's a reason why pros make the big bucks.

As you can see, the clearest trend is that approach shots are where golfers lose the most strokes to the pros and each other. The gap seems to widen as handicaps get higher as well. This indicates an important theme of the value of tee shot distance and proximity to the hole. As skill level decreases, distance off the tee becomes more critical because higher handicap golfers struggle more with longer approach shots. In other words, if you gave a 20 handicap an extra 15-20 yards off the tee, they would benefit more than the scratch golfer or touring pro.

Tee shots take second place in scoring influence. The difference isn't as extreme as approach shots, but they are still very significant. Putting does edge out the short game in just about every handicap level.

Overall, when you combine tee shots and approach shots and divide them by the total strokes lost, Broadie's ratios hold up – even more than the 2/3 he spoke about at certain handicap levels.

THE BIGGEST TAKEAWAYS

Golf is a game of proximity and relative performance. We often get stuck thinking in absolute terms.

For example, we've been told that a 300-yard drive counts the same as an 18-inch putt. In absolute terms, that is correct, but it's a very misleading statement. The expected outcomes of a drive versus an 18-inch putt are far different and don't have the same *relative influence* on your score. You could hit that drive out of bounds, a penalty area, or the trees. As such, your scoring potential on the hole is dramatically reduced. Conversely, if you stripe it 300-yards down the middle of the fairway, you are better positioned to post a lower score. But you're going to make that 18-inch putt close to 100% of the time. The drive and putt don't have nearly the same influence on your score for the day because of the possible outcomes. Of course, that's an extreme example, but it helps illustrate that scoring is far more nuanced.

Every shot you hit on the course is important, but as you get closer to the hole, your opportunity to score and separate yourself from other golfers typically starts to decline. For example, if you had a contest versus a PGA Tour Player to see how many shots on average it would take you to hole out from various distances on the course, this theme would show up quite often. If you started with a putting contest from 20 feet, you could likely hold your own. You and the tour player would two-putt most of the time, and your average score would probably not be that much different. However, if you started hitting shots from 200 yards in the fairway, the tour player would leave you behind in the dust!

If a golfer is looking to have a breakthrough in their game and shoot their lowest scores - I usually tell them a few things:

- Build your game around hitting more greens in regulation. I still believe this traditional statistic has the most value. But what it really means is that I want you to become a better iron player and smarter with your targets. Approach play is the key to your biggest scoring breakthroughs.
- Become more efficient with your driver: keep it in play (it's not fairway or bust), and employ reasonable methods to increase your distance.
- You don't need to be magical with a wedge inside of 100 yards or expect to make a ton of putts. But you do need to be proficient. Avoiding three-putts and having a wedge game that gets the ball on the putting surface most of the time is a formula for lower handicaps.

Yes, that sounds incredibly simple, and it's not going to be easy. I'll help you with all of these goals throughout this book. Overall, tee shots and approach shots will likely make the biggest difference in your scoring for most of you.

But the last thing I want to do is make it seem like your wedge play and putting are not necessary. They're still vital for scoring!!! I see these as quick wins for many golfers, but they have a ceiling.

Generally speaking, if golfers pay more attention to their wedge play and putting, they can experience a faster reduction in their scores. However, that progress will eventually get "tapped out" once an adequate proficiency level is achieved. Over the long term, the most significant gains typically come from outside of 100 yards.

But if you are someone who loses a lot of strokes around the greens with chunks, skulls, and three putts, that can be low-hanging fruit for a handicap reduction. This would become very clear if you were tracking your stats using strokes gained.

And, of course, there is the time element. If you only have a limited time to practice, I often view the short game as a better short-term investment.

All of this will be revisited throughout the book. It has ramifications for your expectation management, strategic decisions, and practice habits. And I do want to reiterate that each golfer is their own unique circumstance. That is why finding your own truths to your game is important, and I'll explore how you can benchmark your performance to see where your game needs the most help.

THE BIG IDEAS

- For years there were many myths on which parts of the game influenced scoring the most, and how golfers separated from one another in performance. The advent of strokes gained analysis and shot tracking has helped clarify how golfers can efficiently lower their scores.
- Traditional statistics like putts per round and fairways hit do not give enough information on performance. Strokes gained gives each shot you hit a numerical value. Taken in aggregate, you can clearly see which parts of your golf game are performing well, and which ones need help.
- Mark Broadie's research has been very influential in determining where scoring truly occurs. For golfers of all levels, roughly 2/3 of scoring differential can be explained by tee shots and approach shots. Approach play is where golfers of all levels can influence their scores the most. Putting is not

as important as we once thought; it explains about 15%
importance of determining any player's score.

- Typically, larger, more sustainable breakthroughs in scoring
  ability will come from approach shots and tee shots.
- Wedge play and putting are usually a way for recreational
  golfers to get "quick wins" in handicap reductions. But
  eventually each player will reach a ceiling where gains in
  performance are marginal.
- Tracking strokes gained performance is a way for each golfer
  to find out the truth in their game, and where they need to
  improve the most.

PART TWO
STRATEGY

CHAPTER 10
THE FOUNDATIONS OF COURSE MANAGEMENT

STRATEGY, also known as course management, is one of my favorite topics to discuss. It's the part of golf that fascinates me the most because it combines multiple disciplines – expectation management, mental fortitude, and numerical analysis. I also love course management because it is a way for golfers of all levels to lower their scores without changing their swing. Everyone has something to gain by sharpening their decision-making skills. Unfortunately, most golfers never learn to navigate the course and optimize their target selection.

In this section of the book, I will outline my main philosophies on course management. Much of this has been learned through painful trial and error. I also have consulted with some of the top minds in the industry, like Mark Broadie and Scott Fawcett, to clear up many misconceptions. I will provide relevant data from recreational golfers and tangible examples to help teach you how to make the right choices.

Learning this information might lead to a significant scoring breakthrough for some of you. For others, it will be a reminder of some key ideas you've already figured out. However, I think there will be something new for all of you. Improving your strategy will reduce your scores by minimizing mistakes and avoiding more double bogeys. You will also make more stress-free pars and the occasional birdie as well.

Fortunately, nothing will be challenging to understand. You may think it's so simple you can execute all of the strategies immediately. But course management is a learned skill. You have to hone it just like your wedge game.

DON'T BE A GAMBLER, BE THE CASINO

I always liken golf strategy to playing poker, or even gambling in general. You have to weigh the odds and try to make rational decisions on every shot, but your emotions make that very difficult to do. Once you learn optimal course management, it becomes a test of psychology and discipline.

In my twenties, my friends and I loved to head to casinos. We'd often joke that the best feeling was when you first got on the floor because the night was filled with so many possibilities. But we all knew the pit in your stomach all too well when the house took all of your money.

One memory in particular always stands out. A friend of mine, probably one of the smartest guys I know (particularly in math), walked to the blackjack table with an envelope stacked with $2,000 and an iron-clad strategy. Thirty minutes later, it was all gone. His experience is probably quite similar to many of yours – when things started going badly, his betting became more erratic and emotional.

The interesting thing about gamblers and golfers is that they behave almost exactly the same way when adversity strikes. How many of you head to the course with optimism about how your round will turn out? More importantly, how many of you know how easy it is to abandon your strategy when things start poorly?

Casinos always win in the long run because the games they design have odds that are stacked against gamblers even if they play with perfect strategy. On top of that, their real edge is how irrational people become when they start losing. While golf isn't 100% the same, many players stack the odds against themselves with their decision-making and inability to control their emotions. The gambler mentality makes a challenging game that much more difficult.

The good news is that you can stack the odds in your favor and start becoming more like a casino in your golf game. You might "lose money" here and there, but you'll be happy with the results in the long run. However, you need to know the rules and apply them.

Overall, there are two crucial elements to becoming a more effective strategic golfer - planning and discipline. Those will be the foundations of everything I discuss.

PLANNING

Many golfers step on the course without any kind of plan. They're winging it from shot to shot, and are mostly playing too aggressively (or conservatively) because they don't have a decision-making system. As you know, golf can throw all kinds of variables your way. There are endless possibilities based on course layouts, weather conditions, and where you are situated. I can't possibly account for all of them, but I can give you a basic framework that can help avoid big mistakes.

If you want to give yourself the best opportunity to score well, much of the work should be done before you even step on a course. For example, it's pretty easy to do your homework with satellite imagery and decide what club you'll be playing off each tee and your targets.

When it comes to approach shots, I will give you a few simple strategies that will be easy to implement and remove a lot of guesswork while you play.

My goal for all of you is that you'll be able to easily choose targets and club selections that will help you each post lower scores on average. Additionally, it will alleviate indecision before each shot so you can initiate your swing more confidently.

Selecting an optimal target doesn't guarantee success. Even the best players can't place the ball where they want to. You're still going to make mistakes. An optimal strategy is a long-term plan, and while you don't necessarily see fractions of a stroke on each hole, they add up to lower scores over time. While planning is important, discipline is even more critical.

DISCIPLINE

"Everyone has a plan until they get punched in the mouth."

-Mike Tyson

No one considers Mike Tyson a philosopher, but this famous quote applies to so many situations, particularly in golf. Every golfer knows what it feels like when things start going poorly during their round. It can occur as early as an errant first tee shot. Panic starts to set in, your heart rate increases, and worst of all, you can't slow down your thoughts.

Smart strategic decisions are easier said than done. I can't tell you how many times I laid out a plan before an important tournament, only to see it fall apart by the 5th hole because of a difficult start. As I have learned over the years, the more and more I can set my emotions aside and remind myself of my process, the better results I see overall.

Throughout the following chapters, please keep in mind that while everything I discuss will be easy to understand intellectually, the real challenge will be having the discipline to stick with it. Your instincts will be to abandon everything I say when you hit a rough patch during your round (side note: all rounds of golf feature a rough patch). You might even curse my name (that's OK). But I can tell you with 100% confidence that if you want to become a better golfer and shoot lower scores, you need to improve your course management.

That is not to say you have to be perfect. Let's say you have been making 10-15 poor decisions each time you play - if you can bring it down to 5-10, you're going to see progress. I can tell you that I will never be perfect at strategy even though I'm the one presenting you with this information. But I have seen improvement over the years by adopting this framework consistently. Smart strategy in golf is like smart investing. Have a long-term view, and avoid the temptation to make decisions based on short-term disruptions.

I will show you how to plan out your strategy, but your job will be to work on the discipline part. I can't do that for you.

THE BIG IDEAS

- Improving your course management is one of the most efficient ways to lower your scores without making any swing changes.
- The "gambler mentality" is where golfers throw away strokes needlessly. You want to stack the odds in your favor over the long run and be the casino.
- Proper strategy is easy to understand, but much harder to implement. Consider it a skill that needs to be honed, just like wedge play.
- Having a plan before you tee off will help make your decisions on the course easier, and give you more confidence when you initiate your swing.
- Eventually, strategy becomes a test of discipline. You will be tempted to abandon your plan when things go poorly in your round.

CHAPTER 11
FIGHTING THE WAR ON DOUBLE BOGEYS

No MATTER what level of golfer you are, one of the keys to improvement is limiting double bogeys (or worse). Many players assume that it's more about making birdies and pars because those scores are more fun. While I want to help you with those too, my focus is more on the bigger scores.

You can see which score separates the lower handicaps versus higher handicaps!

Handicap	Double Bogeys/Round	Birdies/Round
2	1.1	1.9
8	1.9	.8
14	3.5	.4
20	5.5	.2
26	6.1	.1

Source: Shot Scope

The majority of this book is about helping you limit double bogeys. This concept is so important to me that the phrase "fighting the war on double bogeys" is the official tagline of my website Practical Golf.

Double bogey avoidance is crucially important when it comes to strategy.

I'd like to explore a few hypothetical situations to set the table for the rest of the course management section. Each example will contain elements I will explore in the coming chapters and how strategy can significantly impact your score.

THE SUCKER PIN

You have just hit an incredible drive and find yourself in the middle of the fairway with 150 yards to the center of the green. The pin is tucked in the front portion, guarded by deep bunkers. The front of the green is 137 yards, and the pin is just beyond it at 143 yards. Since you hit your 8-iron about 140-145 yards, you decide that is the right club to select. You're thinking birdie!

You hit your 8-iron, and unfortunately, you strike it poorly, and it lands in the bunker. You don't have a great lie, and the bunker is pitched well below the green surface; you're a bit nervous. Sadly, you blade your ball over the green. After chipping it on the green to 15 feet, you two-putt for a double bogey.

Making a double bogey from the middle of the fairway is incredibly frustrating. Let me describe how you could have easily avoided that situation.

The center of the green was 150 yards, and the distance to the back of the green was 162 yards. That means you had almost 20 yards of room to land your ball beyond the pin. Let's say you chose more club in this situation and still didn't strike it that great. You easily could have kept the ball on the putting surface. At worst, you would have a relatively straightforward chip from behind the green. The likelihood of making par would have increased dramatically, and your worst expected outcome would likely have been a bogey. You could have reduced your score by 1-2 strokes by just taking an extra club.

THE HERO SHOT

You have hit your drive into a cluster of trees. When you arrive at your ball, you are still angry about your mistake and aren't thinking so clearly. There is a small opening in the trees, and you desperately want to make par. The green is only 130 yards away, and you figure it is not that hard of a shot.

You decide to go for it and hit a punch shot with your 5-iron with the hope of running the ball onto the green. You quickly find out that trees are, in fact, not 90% air. Your ball ends up in a worse position than where you started.

It ends up being a triple bogey, ouch.

Let's say you had decided to take the easier path, and pitch your ball back into the fairway to leave yourself with a 60-100 yard wedge shot. Your chances of landing the ball on the green from that distance are relatively high, and your expected outcome would likely be a bogey or double bogey at worse. Even if you made the double, you still save yourself a shot in this instance.

MICKELSON-ED

Your approach shot misses the green, and you've got one of those "in-between" lies in the rough where almost anything can happen. You have short-sided yourself, and there isn't much room between the green and the pin. That doesn't stop you from opening up your lob wedge and trying to pull off a Phil Mickelson flop. Your club slides beneath the ball, and it lands about 3 feet in front of you, leaving your-self almost the same exact shot. You take your medicine and chip your next shot 15-20 feet beyond the hole and two-putt for a bogey.

Had you played the high-percentage shot the first time, there would be another stroke that was easily saved.

WHERE GOLFERS ARE SEPARATED

I have watched enough golfers at varying levels to understand what separates those that reach their scoring goals and those that do not. Believe it or not, avoiding double bogeys by making smarter decisions is one of the main separating factors.

While increasing your skill and technique is part of limiting disaster holes, you must meet two general goals with course management:

- Knowing what smart play is based on your skill level and the situation.
- Having the presence of mind to make the right decision.

In the coming chapters, I'll help clarify how to identify what smart choices are. Overall, I want all of your mindsets to be focused on doing everything you can to avoid double bogeys. This is the not-so-secret to becoming a better golfer.

THE BIG IDEAS

- **At every handicap level, double-bogey avoidance is a more significant separator in scoring potential than birdies.**
- **One of the cornerstones of course management is making optimal decisions that will reduce double bogeys.**
- **Aggressive decision-making, particularly on approach shots and greenside wedges, is counterproductive. Often, it results in an increase in score rather than the desired outcome (birdie).**

CHAPTER 12
BETTER GOLF IS NOT ABOUT BIRDIES

WE HAVE DISCUSSED DOUBLE-BOGEY AVOIDANCE, and now it's time to talk about another score - birdie. There is a terrible misconception about birdies amongst golfers, causing players to take unnecessary risks and bloating their scores. Your golf game will be better off if you can shift your mindset on what a birdie represents.

THEY ARE NOT AS EASY AS YOU THINK

Many assume that most professional golfers are birdie machines. Often, we'll see them make upwards of seven or eight of them per round when they play well. However, when you look at their overall statistics for a season, the data suggests otherwise.

The best player on the PGA Tour averages around 4.5 birdies per round. A typical PGA Tour player is averaging approximately 3.5 birdies per round. These are extraordinary numbers! Also, tour players make most of their birdies on Par 5s, where the average score is around 4.65 strokes. They average slightly above par on a Par 3 or a Par 4.

When you start to take a look at ordinary golfers, the birdies disappear rather quickly.

According to a study done by a popular GPS app called The Grint, the amount of birdies made per round starts to drop off significantly as handicaps get higher. Here are their findings:

Handicap Level	Birdies Per Round
1-5	1.5
6-10	.9
11-15	.5
16-20	.3
21-25	.2

I have cross-referenced with several other stat-tracking databases, and these numbers hold up. So while plenty of golfers actively try to make birdies when they're on the course, the odds of making them are pretty low. Sorry if I have burst your bubble!

WHY IS MAKING BIRDIES SO DIFFICULT?

There are a few ways to explain why making a birdie is so difficult and why it shouldn't be your target score. In my opinion, there are two main reasons:

- **It's hard to get it close to the pin:** if you remember from the chapter on PGA Tour stats, most tour players average about 20 feet from the hole with a wedge in their hands from 100-125 yards. For recreational golfers, those numbers are much more significant.
- **Putting is even more challenging:** even if you do manage to knock your approach shot stiff, the odds are stacked against you. A tour pro only makes about 50% of their putts from eight feet. Outside of 10 feet, it gets significantly more challenging.

WHERE ARE ALL THE BIRDIES COMING FROM? TIGER KNEW

If you look at where professional golfers and even low-handicap players are making birdies, it's mostly on Par 5s.

While I don't think there is too much that recreational golfers can learn from Tiger Woods, it is interesting to note how he did most of his scoring during his dominant run. He made sure that he never made unnecessary mistakes on Par 3s and Par 4s. Tiger mostly strategized so that his approach shots were on the fat sides of greens (where you have plenty of distance between the hole and green), and when birdies dropped, it was a bonus because he was such a great putter. He never chased pins that were tucked in challenging spots, particularly in major championships where pars were at a premium.

Tiger used his length off the tee and iron accuracy to make a dispro-portionate amount of birdies on Par 5s. Players who felt the pressure to catch up with him had to play aggressively, make more birdies, and eventually made mistakes.

Tiger's greatness goes way beyond this simple strategy, but he's been quoted multiple times that he was never needlessly aggressive. He had a plan, and he stuck with it. It's no surprise that the two greatest golfers of all time, Jack and Tiger, also had superior course manage-ment skills.

BIRDIES ARE NEVER THE PRIORITY

When things aren't going well, many golfers tend to say, "I've got to make some birdies now." They are pouring gasoline on a fire. That means they will play more aggressively, and usually, our nasty enemy, the double bogey shows up.

All of the information I will present on how to select targets and my overall philosophy on course strategy is not about making birdies. You will set yourself up for them, and occasionally putts will drop for birdie. But my priority is to help you make more pars and bogeys and limit the bigger scores. That is how golfers lower their handicaps.

Overall, it is much easier to prevent larger scores than to make a birdie. Please re-read that last sentence several times; it's that important!

Think of birdies as an occasional bonus for playing smart golf. They will show up from time to time, but it is not a reasonable expectation to consistently make birdies.

THE BIG IDEAS

- **Think of birdies as an occasional bonus. Overall, you should not pursue them; it will create more mistakes than it's worth.**
- **A typical PGA Tour player averages about 3.5 birdies per round, and most of those occur on Par 5s. Recreational golfers seldom make birdies, even scratch golfers!**
- **Birdies are challenging because of a mixture of approach shot proximity and putting difficulty.**
- **It is much easier to prevent larger scores than to make birdies. That is the cornerstone of smart strategic play.**

CHAPTER 13
THERE IS NO TARGET SCORE

EVERY HOLE we play has a suggested score, commonly referred to as par. But I want to explain why starting each hole, or even your entire round, with a target score, can be counterproductive. If you are too focused on where you stand in relation to par, it can force you into making poor strategic decisions. I will propose an alternate mindset that will help you save shots over the long run.

Concentrating on score gets your mind overthinking about results rather than process. Golfers have a hard time not getting ahead of themselves when it comes to scoring. A great start can have you thinking about shooting your personal best. Conversely, a shaky few holes to open up the round gets the mind wandering to just how bad the damage will be on that day.

Overall, I don't think it is productive to enter each hole (or your entire round) with an end score in mind. Instead, committing to evaluating each shot separately and trying your best to make an intelligent decision is more productive.

YOUR SCORE IS A LAGGING RESULT

Every round of golf is a series of independent decisions. That's part of the intrigue of the game. You have to adjust your strategy based on the situation continually. If you tee off on a hole thinking, "I have to make a birdie here to make up for my poor start," you have already shifted your mind into a more aggressive state. In other words, you're making choices for scenarios that haven't even occurred yet.

James Clear, an expert on forming habits, has a great quote that applies very well to golf: "your outcomes are a lagging measure of your habits."

The truth is that your score on each hole, or for the entire day, is partially a lagging measure of the decisions you make on each shot. If you don't have any plan and play too aggressively or conservatively, you're likely to get results that don't make you very happy.

"One shot at a time" is an overused cliché in the game, but the concept has a lot of value. When you start each round or hole, I believe it makes much more sense to tell yourself you will commit to making smarter choices on each shot rather than saying I want to par a hole or break 90.

SHIFTING YOUR IDENTITY

When it comes to course management and scoring, you want to change your identity as a golfer. Many of you like to think of yourself as the player who regularly shoots in the eighties or whatever your target score is. I believe you will see better results if you start thinking of yourself as a disciplined golfer that plays the wise odds on each shot.

Proper course management is a habit. The results will improve if you start focusing more on making optimal decisions with the framework I provide.

A Real-World Example

Let's talk about a real hole to explore how I independently evaluate each shot. It is a short Par 5 that gives me an excellent opportunity to make a birdie. But at the same time, I want to do everything possible to make par at worst. Either way, I want to show you how my target score has no influence on each decision as I make my way through the hole.

The hole has a unique design and presents a few interesting decisions that test two of the weaker parts of my game - fairway woods and bunker play.

On the tee, a series of fairway bunkers spread across the fairway guard the area where I typically land my drives. Additionally, the green is defended by an immense tree that blocks approaches from the left side of the fairway. There are also a series of large bunkers guarding the front and righthand sides of the green.

My goal off the tee is to avoid the fairway bunkers. They have high lips and often result in difficult lies that can make it a challenge to advance your ball. Depending on the wind, and where the tees are situated for the day, I'll have a decision to make. If I feel confident that I can clear the bunkers, I will hit driver. If not, I am laying back with a club that I know can't reach the fairway bunkers.

With my second shot, I am wholly concerned with avoiding the tree on the lefthand side or leaving myself a lengthy bunker shot. So after my drive, I will have to weigh the odds again.

If things have gone well, and I have cleared the bunker with my drive in the fairway, going for the green in two is a straightforward decision.

If I have laid back on my drive, going for the green in two is not the prudent play for me. It's an uphill shot from about 240-260 yards. I would have to hit a perfect fairway wood that rolls onto the green through a gap of the fairway that's about 10 yards wide. It is a very low-percentage play based on my tendencies.

The bunkers surrounding the green are pretty challenging to navigate and can leave you with awkward distances from 20-30 yards. I know that sand play is the weakest part of my short game. My strength is wedge shots from 40-80 yards. If I'm laying up, my goal is to leave myself a yardage that takes the bunkers out of play. I know they start about 40 yards from the green. I also want to avoid the large tree up the left side. Since there is plenty of room to the right, I will favor that side with my target selection. I'll choose the right club depending on my distance and lie.

Usually, I have a straightforward wedge shot into the green if I've hit a good layup shot. My chances of making par or birdie at that point are very high, and I have mostly eliminated the possibility of bogey or worse.

Overall, this is a hole on the course where I make most of my birdies, and usually at worst a par. I don't tee off thinking about either of those scores, though. I am thinking about what I can do to avoid the main trouble on the hole, which are the bunkers and the tree. I know that if I can take those out of play, it will likely eliminate a bogey or worse. I have a plan going in, and I decide on each shot based on the hole layout and my tendencies.

This example wraps up many concepts I will discuss in the course management section of this book, but I hope it provides you with a clear example of how independent decisions can lead to success in any given hole. We are always trying to stack the odds in our favor and avoid big mistakes with strategy. Results like birdies and pars are simply a byproduct of those choices.

THE BIG IDEAS

- **Approaching each hole or your entire round with a target score can be counterproductive. It puts you in a results-oriented mindset when you should be more focused on your habits and process on the course.**
- **Instead of being the golfer who starts their round thinking they want to shoot a specific score, shift your mindset to being the golfer who will evaluate each situation independently and make an optimal decision.**

CHAPTER 14
TEARING OUT THE PAGES OF YOUR GOLF SHOT MENU

HAVE you ever gone to a diner that has a menu as thick as a book? There are more than 100 options, and you're flipping through the pages trying to make a decision but not confident anything will be that good. How could the cooks possibly execute that many dishes well?

Unfortunately, that is what many golfers' games are like. They are continually adding more and more dishes to their menu, and when it comes time to cook, the flavors fall flat.

(in this brilliant metaphor, the dishes are golf shots)

I want to walk you through a few concepts to give specific examples of what I mean. I'll speak anecdotally about my own game and some other ideas, but my main goal here is to shift your thinking.

I want you to become the restaurant that offers just a few dishes but knows how to execute them. I believe it will simplify your decision-making process on the course and ultimately save you shots.

I TRIED THEM ALL

For a long time, I was under the assumption that I had to have a vast arsenal of shots and techniques at my disposal.

Draws, fades, punch shots, flop shots, bump and runs - you know the list.

I never really stopped to analyze my performance, but if I had, I would have noticed I wasn't very good at many of them under pressure. Sure, I could pull them off in the backyard or at the driving range, but the results fell short when I only had one chance to get it right.

Looking back, it is one of the main reasons I had more blowup holes and posted double bogeys (or worse).

I finally understood that if I simplified things and started ripping out all of my menu pages, I would become a much better golfer.

THE ONE TRICK PONY

Several years ago, I went through an extensive evaluation of my swing using launch monitor technology and a swing analysis system called GEARS for an article I was doing on my website. When I asked the instructor what he thought about my somewhat unorthodox swing, his response was, "you're kind of like Mariano Rivera - you've only got one pitch, but you're really good at it."

Of course, he was slightly joking because I'm not nearly as good as a golfer as Mariano Rivera was a pitcher. But it speaks to the notion of simplicity, execution, and results.

Almost every shot I hit on the golf course will be a draw (right-to-left ball flight). My swing is incapable of moving the ball in any other direction. It is almost impossible for me to hit a fade unless I do something that feels very bizarre.

I have one swing. I don't change it at all in almost any situation. It feels mostly the same whether I'm hitting my driver or a 50-yard pitch shot.

So why am I a far better golfer now than I was before? I believe it is because I am fully committed to doing one thing rather than partially committed to doing ten. I am comfortable with what I've got, I mostly know what I can expect, and my head is clearer over the ball because of it.

Rather than speaking in generalities, I would like to go through some specific shots and situations to illustrate what I mean. I hope that you can find a connection to your game.

WORKING THE BALL IN BOTH DIRECTIONS

I don't think recreational golfers need to hit draws or fades on command. The notion that you have to shape your shot based on the fairway or pin placement sounds alluring, but in reality, I believe you're wasting shots if you employ that strategy.

One of the biggest myths out there, and I've fallen victim to it myself at times, is that you'll eliminate one side of the golf course playing a particular shot shape. If you look at most golfers' shot dispersions, they'll miss plenty on both sides of their target no matter what shape of shot they play. You should strive to miss almost equally on both sides - the best players in the world are the same.

My advice is to try and stick with one shot shape as best you can. Many PGA Tour players have made millions of dollars and won major championships with one-shot shape. I think it can work for you too.

PUNCH SHOTS

I play in windy conditions a lot since I live near the water. I also can't execute one of those cool punch shots you'll see on TV during tournaments.

If you're playing a shot into the wind, spin and trajectory are your enemies. A nicely executed punch shot will keep the ball low and reduce the spin on the ball. Despite executing those shots well on the practice tee, I've found I tend to strike it heavy or hook the ball too much in an actual round. It requires muscle memory outside of my normal swing, and I don't find enough practice time to make it work.

Do you know what I do to solve this problem? I use more club. If my standard shot called for a 7-iron, I take a 4 or 5-iron. The lower loft on the club will take care of lowering the spin and trajectory on its own.

There is no need for a fancy solution or a different technique. I can reliably get better results overall with what I already have.

WEDGE PLAY

Part of the beauty of golf is that there is no right way to play a shot. That's also part of its curse too.

Let's say you are 20 yards short of the green, and the pin is in the back. Some would say a true golfing artist would have multiple shots at their disposal - they could bump and run a lower lofted club like 7-iron or loft a wedge back to the pin.

In theory, neither of these shots is particularly challenging to execute. But I would argue that going through an internal debate will invoke enough doubt in your mind to pull any of them off with regularity.

You do need a technique you are comfortable with that can get the ball on the putting surface most of the time (even if it's 20 feet away from the hole). I see so many golfers who can't accomplish this one goal, which wastes shots. Luckily, they are easier to recoup than errant tee shots and approach shots.

I can't tell you what wedge technique is for you. You might need help from a professional to find it. But what I do want you to think about is simplicity. Get good at one kind of wedge shot, good enough that when you stand over the ball, you're almost sure you will strike the ball cleanly enough to get it on the green. If you can get to that point, I guarantee you that your scores will drop.

SIMPLICITY DOESN'T SOUND LIKE FUN, THOUGH?

Whenever I give this kind of advice to golfers, I'll inevitably get some backlash. Some will evoke nostalgic feelings about how the game is supposed to be played with style and artistry. It sounds great, but I've been around thousands of golfers at this point, and I haven't come across too many who actually can play that way.

What I do see is plenty of golfers who are paralyzed by fear and complexity when they stand over the ball because they've got so many conflicting thoughts. That's not a fun way to play this game.

It's hard to have it both ways in golf. I know most of you want to find ways to lower your scores; I believe moving towards simplicity is the right path for almost all of you. Feeling the burden of all of your options is not making you a better golfer.

Start ripping out the pages if you feel your game is like that diner menu with all of those unappealing dishes. Take a hard look at it. Think about what is working and what is making you the most comfortable. Move towards that.

You're inevitably going to face a situation on the course that makes you uncomfortable; that's part of golf. You want to meet those circumstances with confidence. You won't be successful every time, but the trick is to get better at avoiding those big mistakes.

THE BIG IDEAS

- **You don't need a "menu" of golf shots as thick as a book to become a better golfer. Moving towards simplicity and fewer shot types will work best for most players.**
- **When you have so many techniques to choose from, it can create indecision when it comes time to execute.**
- **Try to become more of a one-trick pony. Get very comfortable with a repeatable shot-type that produces functional results.**

CHAPTER 15
GOLF IS A GAME OF PROXIMITY

WHILE IT SEEMS OBVIOUS, the closer you are to the hole, the better your chances are of scoring lower. On some level, golfers have always known this. With advanced statistics, we now know that proximity is even more important than we thought.

The challenge is to blend the desire to get closer to the hole while considering trouble like bunkers, trees, penalty areas, and out of bounds. This chapter will give you some foundational thoughts on proximity as we build closer to the specific framework of selecting targets.

GOLF BECOMES HARDER AS YOU GET FURTHER FROM THE HOLE

Imagine you had a chipping or putting contest with a PGA Tour player. If you are reasonably skilled, the difference in performance would not be that stark. Because you were so close to the hole, the opportunity to separate from one another would be more difficult. For example, you both would two-putt a lot from 30-feet.

However, if you had a contest with your driver or approach shots from 200 yards away, the tour player would blow you out of the water! Their ability to hit their driver much farther (and straighter) would be no match. A typical tour player averages 300+ yards off the tee now, whereas most recreational golfers are still in the 220 - 240 yard range. That difference in distance is worth considerable strokes on each hole. Additionally, on the 200-yard-approach shot, their proximity to the target would be far tighter than a recreational golfer. To be honest, it wouldn't be on the same planet.

We see this across all levels of golfers. According to Shot Scope's database, a scratch golfer has an average proximity to the hole of about 39 feet from approach shots 75 - 125 yards away. A 15 handicap's proximity jumps to 60 feet.

If we moved back to 175 - 225 yards, the separation becomes much more significant. The scratch golfer is 82 feet, and the 15 handicap is now at 166 feet! For comparison, a typical PGA Tour player would average about 40 feet from the hole from that distance, showing a massive separation between the scratch player.

Impact skills become more of a premium as you get further from the hole, which explains these differences. A chip shot just off the green is not nearly as demanding as a 200-yard shot from the fairway. On the 200-yard shot, you'd have to generate a tremendous amount of club-head speed, have proper ground contact, strike the center of the face, and control the ball's start line, trajectory, and curvature. In other words, longer shots are more of an opportunity to showcase the difference between skillsets amongst golfers.

TEE SHOTS

I believe proximity is most influential on your tee shots. If you can advance the ball farther while avoiding major trouble, the rest of the hole becomes easier. You'll have a better chance to keep the ball closer to the hole on your approach shots, wedge play, and putting.

The picture has become pretty clear on posting lower scores with tee shots. Mark Broadie is arguably the lead innovator for this kind of analysis. His advent of the strokes-gained statistic and his book *Every Shot Counts* revealed many insights into how golfers separate themselves by performance in various parts of the game. Overall, his analysis shows that the long game (tee shots and approach shots) explains roughly two-thirds of the difference in scoring between most golfers. Short game and putting explain the remaining third.

Another fascinating takeaway from Broadie's research is that tee shot distance is more important for scoring than accuracy. Interestingly, he found that distance was even more critical for recreational golfers versus professional golfers. An extra 20 yards off the tee is worth more to a 20-handicap golfer than a touring professional. For a PGA Tour player it would be worth 1/10th of a stroke, but for the 20-handicap it could be worth closer to 1/3rd of a stroke. That might not sound like much, but over the course of an entire round, or 10-20 rounds, those strokes add up quite a bit!

While I resisted this information for several years, I'm now in complete agreement based on my testing and evaluation of other data. Playing too conservatively off the tee with shorter clubs can cost you just as many strokes as playing too aggressively. My goal is to show you how to blend the two approaches.

Analysis of data from regular golfers has yielded the same conclusions. There is a clear trend showing that lower-handicap golfers hit the ball farther off the tee (though not prodigious lengths like the pros).

AVERAGE DRIVING DISTANCE BY HANDICAP

	2017	2018	2019
0-5	244.4	244.5	242.6
6-10	231.4	231.5	229.7
11-15	220.5	220.1	219.0
16-20	209.9	209.8	209.0
21-25	201.3	201.6	200.9

Source: Arccos Golf

I'll explore this information further in the tee-shot chapter on strategy. On the whole, how far you hit the ball off the tee has an enormous impact on how well you will score. Think of your distance as a measure of your scoring potential. If this has been a challenge for you, don't fret, I also have practical ways to increase your driver distance coming in the practice section.

APPROACH SHOTS AND WEDGE PLAY

Strategy changes on approach shots. I believe that shifting into a more conservative mode will yield lower scores. The primary goal is to land the ball on the putting surface regardless of the pin position. A golfer's ability to hit a green in regulation is perhaps the most crucial statistic for lowering handicaps. It's one of the few traditional statistics that I believe is still a predictor of scoring. You can see the clear correlation between GIR percentage and handicap level:

Handicap	Greens In Regulation %
0	52
5	38
10	35
15	26
20	21
25	15

Source: Shot Scope

Additionally, if you successfully advance your tee shot far enough, it will take the pressure off of your iron and wedge play.

Distance From Hole	Avg. Proximity to Hole	GIR %
75 - 125 Yards	55 ft	47%
125 - 175 Yards	81 ft	30%
175 - 225 Yards	151 ft	15%

Source: Shot Scope

As you can see, no matter what level of golfer you are, the closer you are to the hole with your tee shot, the higher your chance of landing the ball closer to the hole with your approach shot. This will lead to more greens in regulation and easier wedge shots when you do miss greens.

Proximity to the hole is also crucial with wedge play. With a clear path to the hole and a reasonable lie, almost every golfer will score better from 30 yards versus 80 yards. While some players find these distances awkward, it's easier to land the ball on the putting surface from a shorter distance.

This table from *Every Shot Counts* shows the average number of strokes it takes to finish the hole for golfers of various levels: The expected score is lower for golfers of all levels when they have a 50-yard advantage, even if they are in the rough.

Scoring Group	30 Yards - Fairway	30 Yards - Rough	80 Yards - Fairway	80 Yards - Rough
PGA Tour Player	2.5	2.7	2.7	3.0
80-golfer	2.7	2.8	3.1	3.2
90-golfer	2.9	3.1	3.4	3.5
100-golfer	3.1	3.4	3.7	3.8
110-golfer	3.3	3.7	3.9	4.1

When looking at average proximity from 50, 80, and 110 yards you can see these trends hold up:

Distance	Average Proximity to Hole
50 Yards	35 ft
80 Yards	48 ft
110 Yards	64 ft

Source: Shot Scope

Overall, proximity is an incredibly influential element of scoring potential. The optimal strategic play combines the dispersion of your shots with how far you are from the hole.

THE BIG IDEAS

- **Golf is primarily a game of proximity. The closer you are to the hole, the better your chances of posting a lower score over the long run.**
- **As you get farther from the hole, golfers separate themselves more from one another in scoring potential. You could closely match the performance of a tour player from 30 feet with your putter but would never get close to them with a 200-yard approach shot.**
- **According to research done by Mark Broadie, ⅔ of scoring differential occurs in the long game (tee shots and approaches) versus the short game (wedge and putting).**
- **Proximity plays a massive role in scoring with tee shots, approach shots, and wedge play. No matter what level of golfer you are, being closer to the hole will result in lower scores on average. Therefore, it must be considered when choosing targets and club selection.**

CHAPTER 16
KNOWING YOUR DISTANCES

ALMOST EVERYTHING I discuss on strategy is reliant on golfers knowing two things:

1. Your distance to the green and other important places on the course (bunkers, hazards, doglegs, etc.).
2. How far you hit each club.

If you do not have accurate yardage information on either, you will cost yourself strokes. With technology, it is easier than ever to know your distances. I have explored a lot of options through product testing. I'm going to cover a few ways you can figure out accurate yardage information to make the right strategic decisions on the course.

ON COURSE DISTANCES

To make a confident swing, you need to know the distance to your target. Distance measuring devices take a lot of the guesswork out of finding out how far you are from important places on the course. Luckily, advancements in technology have made this information free or available at a minimal cost. You no longer have to hope to find a yardage marker near your ball.

There are two options available to golfers - GPS and Laser. I'll cover both of them and their strengths and weaknesses.

GPS

I recommend GPS technology for most golfers because it can provide more information. On your tee shots, it can tell you how far it is to reach a dogleg, bunker, penalty area, or other significant points on the course. With approach shots, you can see how far it is to the green's front, center, and back. All of this information is vital for making optimal target and club selections. More importantly, you can access it quickly without wasting too much time.

While GPS might be a little less accurate than laser technology, I have found that it is so close that often the difference is negligible.

There are also a lot of options available with GPS devices. If you're comfortable using your phone on the course, many apps are available that offer crisp maps of every course. Often, they are available for free (18Birdies and The Grint are two that I recommend).

An example of the 18Birdies app

I don't like keeping my phone with me on the course because of the distraction. I prefer using a GPS watch that can quickly show you yardages to areas of interest on the hole. Additionally, handheld devices with advanced features can mount to your golf bag or cart.

Overall, the cost, ease of use, and breadth of information make GPS a more attractive option for most golfers.

There are plenty of options for GPS devices these days

Rangefinders

Laser technology (commonly referred to as rangefinders) are also beneficial on the course. You can lock on to the pin or other points on the course and instantly get exact yardages.

Based on my experience, I would only recommend them for more advanced golfers. There are a few reasons why.

First, and perhaps most important, is that laser rangefinders are mostly used to get yardage information for the pin placement. You now know that I am not a fan of aiming at the pin or using its yardage most of the time. Having the distance to the front, center, and back of the green is more valuable (only a GPS can provide those yardages). Additionally, I believe many golfers fall into the trap of focusing too much on the pin when using a rangefinder. It sometimes can act as a blinder rather than evaluating the rest of the green.

Rangefinders are also limited in what distances they can measure. You can only lock in on targets that are within sight. Changes in elevation and other features of a hole can make that difficult. For example, if there was a penalty area within reach, and you couldn't see it from your current location, the rangefinder would not be able to tell you the distance.

There are now rangefinder models that are starting to blend GPS technology, so you can have your cake and eat it too.

Many of the latest laser rangefinder models are combining GPS capabilities

CLUB DISTANCES

There is usually a significant disconnect between how far a golfer thinks they hit the ball and their actual distances. Players habitually overestimate their typical yardages on each club, leading to poor decision-making on approach shots.

There are two ways to solve this problem without too much hassle - game-tracking systems and launch monitors. If you are serious about improving as a course manager, I recommend pursuing both to find out your club distances.

Game Tracking Systems

There is no better way to determine your average distances with each club than to measure your on-course performance. When the pressure is on, that's when you can collect your most valuable data.

My number one recommendation would be to use a product that passively collects your club data. You can attach GPS sensors to all of your grips, and another device will collect the information (a watch, sensor, or phone). Companies like Shot Scope and Arccos are some of the popular solutions. They all do an excellent job of working in the background without affecting your round too much.

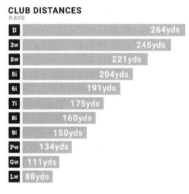

A system like Shot Scope can give you accurate yardages on each club while removing outliers

After playing enough, the software will collect information on how far you hit each club. Most of them will remove outliers and show you your typical performance with each club. For example, you might think you hit your 7-iron 155 yards, but the actual number might be closer to 145 yards. You can make smarter decisions when getting a clear picture of your yardage performance with every club in your bag. More importantly, you can have more confidence in those decisions.

Launch Monitors

With launch monitors becoming more and more affordable over the last few years, these products are popular amongst recreational golfers. In my opinion, some of the most critical information you can receive from them is your carry distances with every club in your bag.

If you want the most accurate data, then it's best to schedule a session on a commercial-grade launch monitor. Many local teaching professionals now own units from Trackman, Foresight Sports, and Flightscope. You can schedule a session to benchmark your club distances. Local golf simulator businesses have sprouted up worldwide using the same technology.

If you are interested in purchasing a launch monitor, plenty of options are available, ranging from $250 - $2000, that cater to recreational golfers. I've found that most launch monitors are pretty good at estimating distances on the lower end. But they are not as reliable as the commercial options I listed earlier. Usually, budget options perform well with shorter clubs like your wedges and for players with slower swing speeds. As distance increases, they start to struggle a little bit.

One product that I've found is the most accurate option for the lower-priced launch monitors is SkyTrak. I've tested it against many commercial options and saw it as precise as 1-3%, but it costs more than many budget options.

A product like SkyTrak can give you accurate distances and visualizations of your shot patterns

Keep in mind that the market is continually evolving, and by the time you are reading this book, things may have changed. You can always check my website for my latest testing and recommendations.

Using a combination of the methods discussed is a foundational element of proper strategy. You can't make the right decisions without knowing your distances!

THE BIG IDEAS

- Knowing your distances to various targets on the course and how far you hit each club is a cornerstone of course management.
- GPS technology is more versatile; it allows you to access more information quickly to hazards, greens, and other points of interest.
- Laser rangefinders are slightly more accurate, but golfers typically only use them for pin locations, which can be a mistake.
- Knowing how far you hit each club in your bag on average is just as important. You can use game-tracking systems on the course to gather data. Also, launch monitors can help you understand your overall tendencies.

CHAPTER 17
UNDERSTANDING SHOT PATTERNS

THERE IS a big difference between where golfers want their ball to go and where it could go. I know, shocking information! Many golfers don't plan accordingly despite understanding that wayward shots are part of the game. No matter your skill level, every shot you hit on the course will have a dispersion pattern. Understanding this concept and how it applies to your targets, club selection, and what outcomes you can expect throughout your round is a foundation of course management.

This chapter will introduce some key concepts about shot distributions that should have you start looking at the golf course differently. Additionally, if you are looking to hone your strategy, I would encourage all of you to figure out your typical dispersions. You can do this quickly using a launch monitor or a shot-tracking system (I'll expand on both concepts in a later chapter).

Golfers get upset and frustrated with themselves all of the time when they hit shots that are within a normal distribution of their shot pattern. Also, many choose targets that are too aggressive and don't account for their dispersion.

Scott Fawcett, who created a popular strategy system called DECADE, put it nicely:

"you're not out there with a sniper rifle; it's more of a shotgun."

If you can accept the following concepts and then use them to make smarter decisions on the course, I guarantee you will save shots.

TEE SHOT DISPERSION

There are two situations where dispersion matters the most - your tee shots and approach shots.

With tee shots, we are primarily concerned with a left-to-right dispersion. For the most part, distance control (long and short) is not as significant of an issue compared to approach shots.

Every club you choose off the tee will have a typical left-to-right pattern. Generally speaking, the farther you hit the ball, the wider the window. A typical pattern is about 55-70 yards with my driver, which I generally hit 280 yards. Many PGA Tour players and elite amateurs have a similar distribution, and I bet that number is larger than most golfers assume.

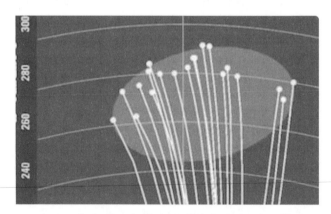

An example of a 68-yard wide driver dispersion in a session with a launch monitor.

For a golfer that drives the ball 220 yards, their dispersion could be 50 yards or less because they have less of an opportunity to hit the ball further offline. Either way, you can think of your tee shot dispersion as more of an oval in a horizontal direction. Even if you are very accurate, this oval is likely broader than you think.

APPROACH SHOT DISPERSION

With our approach shots, another element of dispersion comes into play. Since our goal is to land the ball on the green, we are concerned about left to right distribution and short and long of your intended target.

You can think of your dispersion pattern with your approach shots like a circle, no matter what club you're hitting. For some, it could look like an oval in an angular direction.

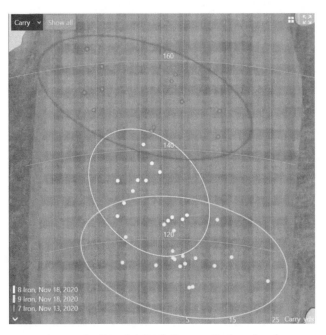

An example of iron shot distributions on a Trackman launch monitor. For many golfers you will see an oval shape favoring shots that miss short/right, on target, and then left/long.

In my opinion, failure to understand patterns with approach shots is one of the main reasons golfers are losing strokes. These shapes are essential to help you choose more optimal targets and keep your expectations in check. Across every handicap level, analysis shows that almost all golfers miss their targets most on the short side of the green rather than left, right, or long.

HOW PATTERNS MOVE AROUND

Every time you select a target, your dispersion pattern will shift. With a tee shot, the further left or right you aim, your imaginary oval will move along with it. So if you get more aggressive and try to land the ball in a tighter window, you have to consider how that change in the target will bring other parts of the course into play (bunkers, trees, or hazards).

A similar pattern will occur with approach shots as you shift your target to the left or right.

Additionally, you have to contend with your distance control. For example, if you are trying to hit the ball 150 yards, your distance outcomes could be as short as 125 yards or as long as 160 yards. The pattern will be concentrated mainly on the shorter side for most golfers because of mishits. As such, your strategy needs to adjust.

Instead of planning for what you want to happen, start thinking about what could happen!

THE TWO WAY MISS

There is a myth that golfers can eliminate one side of the course. I used to believe this too. You'll often hear announcers on TV describing players struggling with a two-way miss as if it is an anomaly. The truth is that every golfer on the planet misses their target on both sides.

Players who typically hit a fade (left to right ball flight) might assume the left-hand side of the course is not in play as much, and vice versa for someone who plays a draw. While some golfers can miss one side of the course more often, you still should choose targets assuming that both sides are potentially in play.

Let's take Dustin Johnson, for example. He is one of the greatest drivers on tour because he combines length and accuracy. Dustin routinely credits switching to one-shot shape off the tee, a fade, as one of the reasons his performance rose to another level. Many assume that means when he does miss the fairway, it's never going to happen on the left side because of the way the ball curves.

The following represents which side of the fairway Dustin ends up when he misses the fairway:

Year	Left Rough %	Right Rough %
2016	15.53	15.53
2017	14.73	16.24
2018	16.34	16.08
2019	18.26	13.09
2020	15.69	13.93

As you can see, the results are almost identical. In 2016 and 2017, he was ranked #1 in strokes gained off the tee, and his distribution was remarkably consistent in both directions. That is hardly eliminating one side of the course!

This occurs because it's nearly impossible for any golfer to control where the clubface is pointing at the impact (known as face angle). We'll explore why this skill is so crucial in the practice section, but know that no matter how your ball curves through the air, you will have to plan for outcomes on both sides of your target.

As I get more in-depth about strategy off the tee and on approach shots, this underlying truth about dispersion will guide many of your decisions.

THE BIG IDEAS

- **Understanding dispersion is a cornerstone of course**

management. No matter where you are on the course, you have to plan for where the ball could end up, not just where you want to go. You're playing with a shotgun, not a sniper rifle!

- Off the tee, we are primarily concerned with left-to-right shot distribution. Great players can have patterns as wide as 55-70 yards.
- With approach shots, distance control becomes more critical. You have to consider your shot distribution in all directions. Missing targets on the short side are where most golfers lose strokes.
- As you change targets, your shot patterns will shift as well. This is one of the primary considerations in course management.
- Every golfer has a two-way miss, no matter how they curve the ball. Working towards missing your targets more equally on both sides is generally a better strategy.

CHAPTER 18
TEE SHOT TARGET SELECTION

CHOOSING the right club and target off the tee massively influences your scoring potential. Your scores will rise dramatically if you cannot keep your golf ball in play. Tee shot performance is where the most strokes are lost for many golfers. Conversely, if you can optimize your decisions, considerable reductions in your handicap are possible.

This is one part of the game where I believe conventional golf advice has been the most counterintuitive (and damaging)! For years, I had tee shot strategy entirely backward. And I will venture a guess that most of you adhered to the same principles I was taught.

In this chapter, I would like to give you a framework that I know can help you lower your scores. You will have your tendencies to consider and perhaps some homework to do. But I encourage you to keep an open mind. A lot of what I am about to say will go against what you have heard in the past.

IT'S NOT FAIRWAY OR BUST

Fairways hit is one of the most misleading statistics in golf. While it could be a good starting point for your performance off the tee, it's not enough information to analyze a golfer's success. True performance is measured by a combination of your distance, whether your drives land in the fairway or rough and how often you end up in recovery situations.

But most golfers plan their tee shots simply by considering the fairway only. While there are plenty of holes where the proper aiming point might be the center of the fairway, there is more to consider.

Tee shots are incredibly influential in scoring. You can give yourself a considerable advantage by driving it farther and keeping it in play. Conversely, your scores can plummet with errant drives that land out of bounds, in penalty areas, in fairway bunkers, or stuck in trees. Becoming a better golfer is more about removing these big mistakes.

So how big of a penalty is it when you miss fairways? Shot Scope did an interesting analysis of their database of golfers of all levels. On average, here is how many strokes golfers typically lose when they miss fairways:

- **Light Rough: .3 shots**
- **Trees: 1.1 shots**
- **Fairway Bunkers: 1.4 shots**

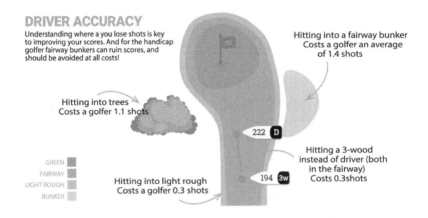

DRIVER ACCURACY

Understanding where a you lose shots is key to improving your scores. And for the handicap golfer fairway bunkers can ruin scores, and should be avoided at all costs!

Hitting into trees
Costs a golfer 1.1 shots

Hitting into a fairway bunker
Costs a golfer an average
of 1.4 shots

GREEN
FAIRWAY
LIGHT ROUGH
BUNKER

222 D

194 3w

Hitting into light rough
Costs a golfer 0.3 shots

Hitting a 3-wood
instead of driver (both
in the fairway)
Costs 0.3shots

Granted, these are averages and based on your playing level or course conditions, these numbers could fluctuate slightly. But they are excellent guidelines to help illustrate the optimal strategy.

Landing your ball in the trees or fairway bunker can be just as punishing as going into a penalty area like a lateral hazard. And, of course, a tee shot out of bounds is the most significant penalty. What surprises most players is that light rough is not as big of a punishment. For lower-skilled golfers, it can be helpful because most courses don't have rough like a U.S. Open, and they can draw those nice lies where their ball is propped up a bit and easier to get in the air.

This distinction is fundamental to understand, and it's why I have changed my definition of a successful tee shot over the years and how I pick my targets. All things being equal with distance, hitting the fairway is the most significant scoring advantage. But golfers of all levels, whether scratch or a 25 handicap, typically only hit 50% or less of their fairways. Distance plays a big role in what separates them, but how often they can avoid the big trouble is often just as important.

So I would like you to shift your thinking on fairways. The bigger priority is keeping the ball in play and giving yourself a clear path to the green on your approach shot with a reasonable lie.

DISPERSION AND TENDENCIES

How far you hit the ball is a relatively easy concept to consider, and it's what most golfers fixate on. But over time, I became more fascinated with dispersion. Intuitively, I began to understand that one of the keys to the game was understanding the two lines that separated your shot patterns from left to right. I knew that they would always be reasonably wide but believed that one of the keys to the game was making them more narrow.

But my ideas were unrefined. There was no such thing as launch monitors or shot tracking devices. I couldn't quantify the value of dispersion because I didn't understand the importance of distance either. So I started to play the game a little too safely as this was the general advice when I was younger.

A conservative strategy helped my approach play tremendously. I stopped chasing pins because I knew I wasn't good enough to control the golf ball. However, it hurt my chances of scoring off the tee. I assumed my dispersion lines were far more narrow with shorter clubs and began to prioritize them. I evaluated every hole looking for an excuse not to hit the driver.

A More Analytical Process

When I started Practical Golf in 2015, I quickly came across Mark Broadie's work with strokes gained analysis. Initially, I was resistant to his findings on the value of distance. I still stubbornly believed that an overly conservative strategy off the tee would lead to lower scores. Interestingly, a lunch meeting in 2017 with my former college coach Rich Mueller, who is now the head coach at Columbia University (where Mark Broadie is a professor), helped change my mind.

Rich showed me how his team improved their performance using strokes gained analysis and Mark's app, Golfmetrics. Then he showed me how he planned all of his players' tee shots for each round using a combination of satellite imagery from golf courses and his players' dispersions that he verified with launch monitor testing. He could map out optimal targets and club selections based on the typical shot patterns.

Rich told me it had improved the players' confidence off the tee and helped their scoring averages. They were able to hit driver where it made sense on a line that mitigated the risk from big trouble and lay back on holes where the landing area between big trouble was too narrow.

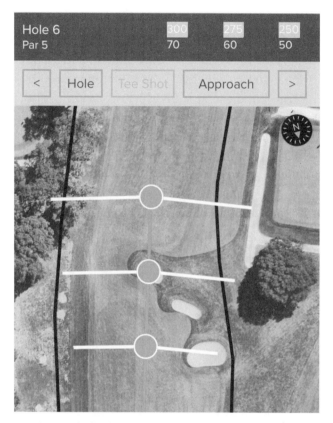

An example of analyzing dispersion patterns. In the DECADE app you can set overlay your expected shot patterns with different clubs off the tee to see your optimal target.

My reaction was, "wow...that makes complete sense!!!" Naturally, I wanted to know where he got the idea from, and he told me it was from a guy named Scott Fawcett. His DECADE course management system was becoming extremely popular amongst college teams (eventually, the NCAA banned his seminar because they deemed it an unfair advantage).

In a nutshell, Scott analyzed shot distribution data from tons of elite players using strokes gained analysis, as well as satellite imagery of golf courses to determine the optimal club selection and aim off the tee. I would urge all of you to search YouTube and watch the video "NGCAA Driving Video" - a lightbulb will likely go off in your head. I also highly recommend his DECADE app.

Having a more refined understanding of your left-to-right shot patterns with your driver and other clubs in your bag that you would use off the tee is fundamental in tee shot planning. Most elite amateurs and professional golfers who drive the ball around 280-320 yards will have a shot distribution of about 60-70 yards wide with their driver, which surprises most people. No matter what shot shape you play off the tee, you will miss some left and some right, and that has to be considered. In other words, you don't have to hit lasers off the tee to score well.

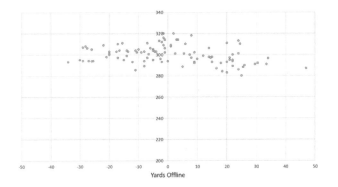

An example of driver dispersion from a top-ranked amateur golfer over multiple Trackman sessions. Notice the width of his shots.

Different golfers have different distributions with the driver. Those that don't hit it as far might have a tighter dispersion, perhaps as little as 45-50 yards. And if driver is a club you struggle with, those numbers could go outside of the 70-yard range. I would encourage you test in order to find out. There are a few ways you can do this.

Shot Pattern Testing Ideas

First, you could use a launch monitor to simulate your shot patterns from companies like Trackman, Foresight Sports, Flightscope, or even SkyTrak. As a baseline, you can hit somewhere around 20-30 shots with your driver and see where your distributions end up. For those who don't own one, many teaching professionals will let you book sessions, or an indoor simulation studio likely will have one of these models. I find this process incredibly powerful, and it's given me a lot of confidence in how I plan tee shots.

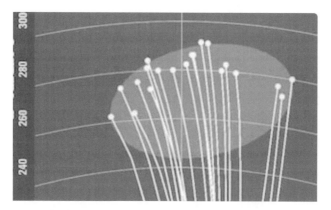

Booking a session on a launch monitor can give you a good indication of your shot patterns with different clubs off the tee

Another method, preferably in conjunction with launch monitor testing, would be to use a shot-tracking system on the golf course. Many apps now will let you manually tag shots with your cell phone. After you play enough rounds, you'll start to gather data on where most of your tee shots end up and get a sense of how wide your distributions are.

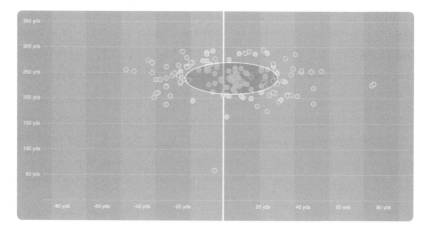

An example of driver dispersion in a shot-tracking app (Arccos)

Last but not least is to map out your local driving range if possible. You can use Google Maps or Google Earth to draw a 65-70 yard wide aiming window. As you hit shots, you can start to see how many are staying within that window. If you can keep it inside of it, that's excellent news.

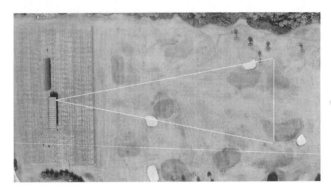

Using Google Earth to map out a target window on a driving range

When you can start establishing baseline numbers of your dispersion with driver and other clubs you might use on tee shots, you can now start making more informed decisions.

PUMPING THE BRAKES AND STEPPING ON THE GAS

A winning strategy off the tee is a little more nuanced than other parts of the game. While each player will have their own tendencies and patterns to consider, all golfers should aspire to the same goal - advance the ball as far as possible while avoiding the big trouble.

The trends are pretty straightforward when looking at what separates higher handicaps from lower handicaps. Better players hit the ball farther off the tee and keep it in play more. I've been fortunate to play with and learn from some talented golfers throughout the years. I can't think of one of them who didn't hit their driver well and prioritize it off the tee.

But every hole is different. While I now believe stepping on the gas pedal wherever possible will lower your scores, there are times when you have to pump the brakes. Problems occur when a player tries to fit their ball in spots that don't make sense. Avoiding big mistakes is almost as important as how far you can hit the ball. The balance is crucial.

In approach play, we have a much smaller target to consider, and because of that, my advice to you will become far more simple. But when it comes to tee shots, you have to do a little more homework on the course layout to make better decisions. There is a distance element - how far are bunkers, penalty areas, and other big trouble? Also, there is the width of the hole to consider and match your expected shot patterns.

There is still a large margin of error you can expect. No matter how skilled you are with your driver and how smart your targets are, mistakes will still occur. But if you can start playing more rounds where you finish with the same ball you teed up with on the first hole, you know things are heading in the right direction!

Overall, if you want to play your best golf, I fully agree with Scott Fawcett's philosophy, which states you start each hole thinking driver first, and then you have to find a good reason not to hit it. Not the other way around. If anything, I was searching for evidence to the contrary for years. But after doing my own testing, seeing the data from plenty of other golfers' performance, and understanding strokes gained analysis, I am in complete agreement.

Aiming Away From Trouble

One of the great takeaways from Mark Broadie's book, *Every Shot Counts*, is how to choose optimal targets off the tee when there is trouble on one side of a hole. Broadie used data from real-world golfers and computer simulations to calculate the optimal target on a 400-yard par four that had out of bounds up the right side and only rough up the left side.

He found that picking a target in the center of the fairway led to the *highest* possible score for a golfer of just about any level. Why? Because a certain percentage of those tee shots would go out of bounds, and the penalty is so severe that it would bring down their average score over time even though it only occurred 7-15% of the time.

Interestingly, he found that aiming up the left side would save golfers of all levels strokes over time, even for pros. How far left depends on skill level. For example, an 8-handicap might aim up the left edge of the fairway, whereas a 20-handicap might need to aim in the rough. The scoring advantage might only be fractions of a stroke each time, but those fractions equal multiple strokes over the long run. This is how you stack scoring odds in your favor and reduce your handicap.

The worst penalty in golf is out of bounds, and your target should be adjusted away from it. But when you encounter less punitive areas like trees, a lateral hazard, or fairway bunkers, you don't have to adjust as much. Again, this does depend on skill level. The more accurate you are, the less you should aim away, so you will have to use some judgment on your end. But making adjustments away from trouble where it makes sense will help lower your scores in the long run.

Here is a common scenario that many of you might face on the course:

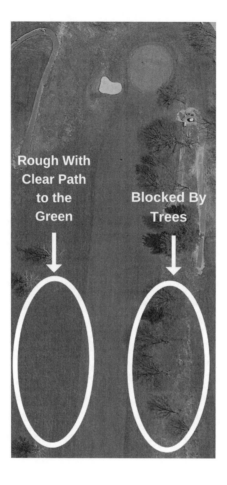

This is the #1 handicap hole at Port Jefferson Country Club. It's a long par 4 with a narrow fairway. Additionally, a large series of trees lines the righthand side. You have virtually no chance of landing the ball on the green if you miss to the right.

However, the left side of the hole is almost completely wide open. I've highlighted the landing zones to illustrate the difference.

Despite the fairway being narrow, I believe it still makes sense to adjust your aim more to the left. Your lowest expected score on a hole like this will mostly be dictated by how often you can avoid the trees. Landing the ball in the lefthand rough is a minor penalty in comparison, and you don't have to contend with a fairway bunker.

Taking Less Club

Certain holes feature designs where it does not make sense to hit your driver. There are a few scenarios where this occurs, depending on the courses you play.

A classic example is where a fairway narrows and is surrounded by trouble on both sides. Architects love to entice golfers to fit the ball in small windows sometimes, and if you take the bait, your scores will suffer in the long run. Whether it's trees, fairway bunkers, or a hazard, these narrow areas need to be considered. Your shot pattern will now end up in the fairway less often, and your average score for the hole will increase because the penalty for missing the fairway in these areas increases dramatically. It usually makes sense if there is an opportunity to lay back in a safer area.

Example #1

The 5th hole at St. George's Golf & CC is a Par 4 that measures 350 yards. At about 210 yards from the tee box, a series of bunkers begins to pinch the fairway. Additionally, deep fescue lines the left side of the hole, and surrounds each set of fairway bunkers. If you land in the fescue, you can easily lose your ball. Or if you do find it, it becomes hard to advance it more than 50 yards depending on the lie.

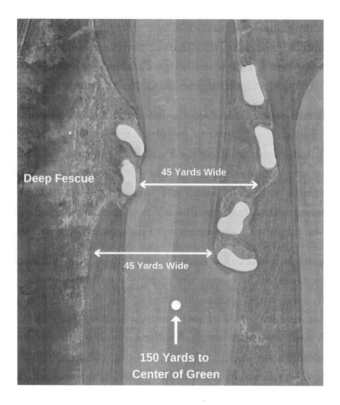

So now that we've established the major trouble, we can start thinking about whether or not it makes sense to challenge it.

The first two fairway bunkers on the right will come into play with tee shots traveling roughly 210-230 yards. The landing zone shrinks to about 45 yards wide between the fescue on the left, and the bunkers on the right.

If you can fly your tee shot more than 230 yards, then you will be faced with a similar landing window with the two fairway bunkers on the left.

However, if you choose to avoid the bunkers, and lay back, you have virtually a limitless window to land your tee shot. The next hole shares a fairway (the satellite image has not updated - there is no rough on the righthand side anymore), and you can safely aim away from the fescue on the lefthand side.

For almost every golfer, I would suggest laying back off the tee, and aiming further to the right to avoid the fescue. With a 200 yard tee shot, you can leave yourself a 140-150-yard approach to the green, and significantly reduce your chances of avoiding the big trouble.

If you chose to thread your tee shot between the first, or second series of bunkers, most players would only end up with an approach shot of 100-150 yards. The closer proximity to the hole is worth a fractional amount of strokes. But ending up in the bunker, or the fescue, could cost you well over a full stroke. In this instance, the math doesn't pay off for more aggression off the tee. The only players I would suggest hitting driver would be those who could carry the far lefthand bunker, which is 260 yards from the tee box.

Example #2

The 4th hole at Old Westbury Golf & CC is another Par 4 that measures 350 yards. At about 230 yards from the tee box, a water hazard on the right and fairway bunkers on the left come into play.

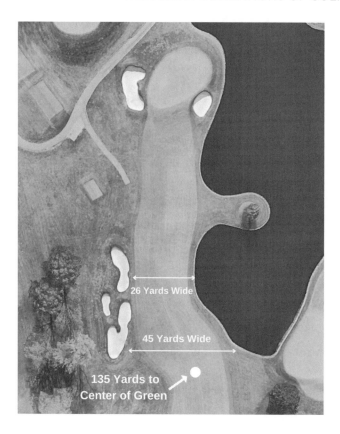

The fairway narrows even more between the water hazard and bunkers at about 260 yards from the tee box. So as a player gets more aggressive off the tee with club selection, the landing area becomes more narrow. However, you have the option to leave yourself a 135 approach shot with a shorter club.

This is another example where I believe it makes no sense to take on the trouble. Trying to get closer to the hole brings the water and bunkers into play, and only offers a marginal gain in proximity to the hole. I would suggest taking a club you know has no chance of reaching the water or bunkers, and you can step up to the tee with a clearer mind knowing you don't have to contend with them.

Another example is an extreme dogleg. Let's say you had a hole that was a dogleg left with a very abrupt turn. Going through the fairway on these holes can often result in a penalty area. This hole might still be a driver for a golfer who draws the ball. However, if your preferred shot shape is a fade, you might want to take a club that removes the possibility of going through the fairway and into a penalty area.

Rethinking Safety Clubs

There are certain holes where hitting a driver is a mistake. If you have done your homework and determined that there is too much trouble in play by hitting it further, it might make sense to use a fairway wood, hybrid, or iron. However, many golfers will default to safety clubs because they place too much value on hitting fairways.

For years, I lived in fear of my driver. I looked for any opportunity not to hit it off the tee and defer to shorter clubs which I assumed were much straighter. But I made two errors in judgment:

1. I did not factor in what the loss of distance was costing me.
2. I overestimated my accuracy with shorter clubs off the tee.

I know many golfers fall into the same category - I will give you further analysis on both points.

Distance Costs Strokes

Proximity to the hole on approach shots is easily one of the most influencing factors in scoring, especially amongst recreational golfers. If you gave a PGA Tour player an iron shot from 180 yards in the fairway, they would outperform a 15-handicapper substantially because their approach play is far superior. In other words, being farther away from the hole becomes more of a penalty for less-skilled players.

So you have to consider as soon as you start taking a shorter club off the tee, you are already losing strokes. How many strokes will depend on how far you are away from the hole and your overall skill level.

If you hit your driver 230 yards in the fairway versus a 3-wood of 200 yards, your average score on that hole could be close to a third of a stroke lower over the long run by hitting the driver.

What's even more interesting is that hitting the ball into light rough is not as big a penalty as most would think. On average, light rough will cost an average golfer upwards of .3 strokes, so it is equivalent to about 30 yards in distance. A tee shot in the light rough of 230 yards would be the equivalent of 200 yards in the fairway in the prior scenario. Basically, it is a wash for most players.

These numbers will fluctuate depending on skill level and proximity to the hole. Still, it's important to understand that laying back 20-60 yards off the tee can cost you substantially in terms of scoring potential.

This is a common decision to make when you face a difficult driving hole and you cannot aim away from trouble. You might have trees lining both sides, a narrow fairway, or bunkers on both sides. The question becomes can you lower your scores by laying back with a shorter club for accuracy?

For those that instantly default to the shorter club because it makes you feel safer, I want to challenge that decision and have you think a little more critically.

How Safe Are Shorter Clubs?

You're probably thinking, "well, I will hit the fairway more with the shorter club." That may be true, but you also have to consider the difference in performance between your driver and other clubs you might use off the tee. Hitting a fairway is only a premium in scoring if you can do it substantially more with another club than a driver.

A common decision golfers face is whether to hit their driver or 3-wood off the tee. The popular belief is that the 3-wood will find more fairways than the driver, but what if that wasn't necessarily the case?

There will always be differences in distances to consider. On average, golfers of all levels will lose somewhere around 15-30 yards between their driver and 3-wood. Interestingly, when you look at fairway percentages with each club, they aren't all that different:

Handicap	Driver Fairway %	3-Wood Fairway %
2	60%	61%
8	52%	53%
14	46%	48%
20	41%	42%
26	34%	33%

Source: Shot Scope

This is not a good tradeoff. Losing upwards of 30 yards in distance and not hitting more fairways is not a recipe for success!

A lot of this has to do with club design. Modern drivers have larger faces with plenty of forgiveness. Since drivers are such an important product in the golf industry, manufacturers employ rocket scientists (I'm not kidding) to make them perform as best they possibly can.

However, 3-woods are designed differently. Their primary purpose is approach shots and not off the tee exclusively like the driver. As such, they have much smaller faces and less forgiveness. So the combination of a long shaft, smaller face, and less forgiveness creates an issue for many golfers.

Trade-offs in club design necessitate fairway woods having much smaller faces than drivers.

You have probably heard the word MOI or Moment Of Inertia before. It is used to describe how forgiving a club is on off-center strikes. When a golfer misses the center of their driver or 3-wood, the clubface will twist open or closed. The result is twofold - the ball will travel further offline and lose distance.

Drivers typically have 2-3 times the amount of MOI compared to a fairway wood. That means when a golfer fails to hit the sweet spot, a driver can help the ball travel farther and straighter compared to their 3-wood. When you factor in the smaller face of the fairway wood, and players who generally struggle to strike the face consistently, it's not a surprise that a driver can produce straighter shots (or equivalent) off the tee.

However, each golfer will have their tendencies, which are important to explore. You might find that your driver is too wild off the tee compared to shorter clubs. If that were the case, then I would suggest using some of the advice I'll give you in the practice session to mitigate the issue. Others might find more surprising results, that their shorter clubs don't provide that much more accuracy to overcome the loss of distance.

I always encourage golfers to gather their own data. Everyone's game is different, and it can influence your decisions off the tee. There are a few ways to do this.

Throughout the years, I've done my testing with launch monitors to compare my biases off the tee with my driver versus shorter clubs.

Interestingly, when comparing my driver performance versus a 3-wood, I found I hit slightly more fairways with the longer club! Even though I am a fairly skilled ball striker, the off-center strikes from my fairway wood proved to cost me too much distance and accuracy. I have proven that my driver will gain me about 30 yards on average with a similar dispersion pattern to my 3-wood, which I factor into my tee-shot strategy.

I also have tested my driver versus a 4-iron on a launch monitor. In an experiment where I hit 30 shots with each club under no pressure, I tracked how often I could hit a 25-yard fairway, which would be considered a difficult target.

With the 4-iron, I hit 57% of my fairways. When the ball landed in the fairway, it traveled about 210 yards, and in the rough, it was about 200 yards. Also, my entire dispersion from left to right was about 48 yards, which is larger than I expected.

Naturally, I hit fewer fairways with my driver. It dropped to 43%, with a total dispersion of about 65 yards. But I was gaining more than 60 yards of distance on most shots.

Based on the math, hitting a 4-iron to hit more fairways would not be a good decision for me. I've also had plenty of other golfers perform similar tests with launch monitors or who have tracked their shots on the golf course, and they too find that their shorter clubs were not as accurate as they first thought. It can be a real eye-opener! But I would love for you to do your own testing and keep track of your shots on the course to see what results you will find.

CHASING ANGLES

No matter how skilled you are, you cannot place the ball where you want with enough regularity to expect to hit small targets. This concept is just as important in tee shots as it is for approach shots. A playing partner might tell you that you want to land your tee shot on the left side of the fairway to gain a better angle with your approach shot. However, adjusting your aim to that side of the hole will shift the distribution of your shot pattern. Yes, you might be able to execute some of your tee shots in the exact spot sometimes. But it's more important to consider if that target brings trouble into play. Is there a fairway bunker closer to that side or a hazard?

To be a successful course manager, you need to evaluate each shot independently. As I stated earlier, the primary intent with a tee shot is to advance the ball as far as possible while avoiding major trouble. The latter is usually most necessary for scoring jumps in recreational golfers. When you start looking ahead to an approach shot before you even know where your tee shot lands, I believe you will start making mistakes that can put you in challenging positions.

Better Angles Don't Always Work

There is a persistent myth that having the correct angle into a green, mainly based on pin placement, will yield a lower expected score on any hole. For example, if a pin is on the left side of the green, you'll often hear that you want to have an approach shot from the right of the fairway. In theory, it makes perfect sense. However, I've got some interesting data to show you that might change your mind.

PGA Tour players are exceptional ball strikers. But I have shown throughout several parts of the book that even they have limitations. The image below is a visual representation by statistician Lou Stagner of about 90,000 shots hit on the PGA Tour with pins on the left-hand side of the green, and the right. The numbers represent whether players are gaining or losing strokes by landing the ball in certain parts of the fairway or rough based on the pin position.

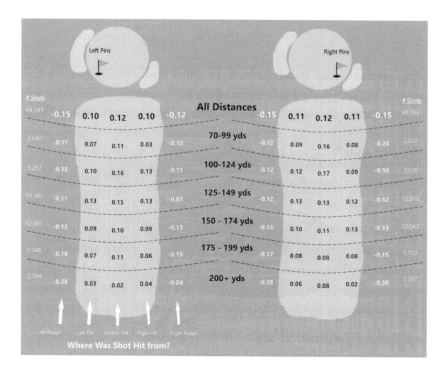

For example, from 125-149 yards, a player who lands the shot in the right rough to a pin situated on the left side of the green is losing .07 strokes to his competitors (indicated by the negative number).

While the image might be a bit confusing to some of you, let me summarize some of its key findings:

- The biggest gain in scoring is landing the ball in the fairway regardless of its position. It is about a 1/4 of a stroke advantage versus being in the rough.
- There were no distinct changes in scoring when having an approach shot from the opposite side of the pin position.

So if PGA Tour players can't gain any advantage with a better angle into a pin, why should you?

Course management is about playing the odds over time. If you continually chase angles that bring trouble into play off the tee, you will lose more strokes than you gain in the long run. Even if you successfully position your tee shot with a better angle into the green, you are not gaining the advantage you think you are. I will explore why in the next chapter on approach shots. Overall, if you want to shoot your lowest scores, aggressive angle chasing should not be part of your plan!

ONE-SHOT SHAPE

As you have likely gathered by now, I value simplicity on the golf course. I genuinely believe that the more variables and decisions you can remove from this game, the more confidently you will play and the lower your score will be. This is why I encourage golfers to pick one shot shape off the tee and stick with it.

There are a few reasons I believe this is the proper strategy off the tee and even for approach shots. The most important thing is your golf swing and having conflicting thoughts. To hit a draw and fade on command, you will need to shift your club path and where the club-face is pointing at impact. These changes are challenging for most players and end up being more trouble than it's worth, in my opinion.

When a golfer switches their club path from a fade pattern to a draw pattern or vice versa, it usually can confuse their clubface angle at impact. This can often lead to the clubface pointing too far in the opposite direction, which results in the dreaded "double-cross." For example, this would occur when you are set up to hit a fade and hit a pull hook. These shots result in lost balls, penalties, and recovery situations because they travel so far offline.

Another myth in golf is that if you hit a fade, you will eliminate the left side of the golf course, and a draw will eliminate the right side. The truth is a little more complex. Great drivers of the golf ball typically will miss their target equally, or close to it, on both sides. How the ball curves through the air doesn't necessarily matter. If anything, I would tell a golfer who misses 80% of their targets in one direction that they are not choosing their targets optimally and need to adjust.

The good news is that most holes do not have an extreme design to favor one-shot shape. You can play great golf and score well with one shot shape off the tee - Dustin Johnson has done quite well hitting a fade off the tee almost all of the time!

Certain designs, especially doglegs, can get extreme, though. My suggestion would be not to change your shot shape to accommodate the hole - I believe you will make yourself more vulnerable to a big mistake, which is the primary outcome we are trying to avoid on tee shots. Instead, you can evaluate the distances to the big trouble, and if taking less club off the tee makes sense with your preferred shape, then do it. Scores usually go up when golfers try to force a "square peg in a round hole."

LAYING UP YARDAGES

When I was learning the game, a conventional piece of course management advice was to lay up to your favorite yardage. The theory was that golfers would hit better shots when they had a full swing into the hole from around 80-100 yards versus partial wedge shots from 30-50 yards. Now that we know more specifically how much proximity to the hole plays in scoring, I would urge you to abandon that strategy. Getting closer to the hole will result in lower scores for most golfers because your proximity to the hole will decrease. This is a blended scenario for tee shots and playing a Par 5, where you decide how close to leave your third shot.

Scoring Group	30 Yards - Fairway	30 Yards - Rough	80 Yards - Fairway	80 Yards - Rough
PGA Tour Player	2.5	2.7	2.7	3.0
80-golfer	2.7	2.8	3.1	3.2
90-golfer	2.9	3.1	3.4	3.5
100-golfer	3.1	3.4	3.7	3.8
110-golfer	3.3	3.7	3.9	4.1

How many shots it takes players of various levels to finish a hole from different wedge distances and lies. Closer to the hole wins! Source: Mark Broadie

Even in real-world situations, the numbers have held up. Shot Scope looked at proximity to the hole averages for golfers from 50, 80, and 110 yards. You can see that closer was better as well:

Distance	Average Proximity to Hole
50 Yards	35 ft
80 Yards	48 ft
110 Yards	64 ft

So whether you are playing a short Par 4 or laying up on a Par 5, being closer to the hole is almost always better. I will throw in two caveats, though.

It does not make sense to get closer to the hole if you take on significantly more risk. If you choose between a 100-yard layup or a 50-yard layup, and there is only light rough and fairway, it's a bit of a no-brainer to go closer. However, if there is a water hazard or series of bunkers at around 50 yards, it does not make sense to take on this trouble for closer proximity. I would defer to some of the rules I've mentioned earlier in this chapter, which primarily suggests laying back or aiming away from penalty areas and bunkers if possible. Proximity is only an advantage if you avoid the trouble!

The second caveat has to do with the dreaded "Y" word. I often get a lot of pushback from golfers when I tell them to avoid laying further back. Many assume they are more accurate with a wedge in their hands from 100 yards versus 40 yards. If most of them put this to the test, they would find out they are wrong. However, some golfers struggle mightily with partial wedge shots - trust me, I've been there. If this problem is so bad for you, then yes, it could make sense to avoid these distances with your layup shot. But I urge you to mitigate this problem through practice rather than avoid it entirely.

THE BIG IDEAS

- Successful tee shots are more about keeping the ball in play and avoiding trouble than hitting fairways. Fairway bunkers, trees, penalty areas, and out of bounds cost golfers far more strokes than hitting it in light rough. The number one priority should be to advance the ball as far as possible while giving yourself a clear path to the green on your approach shot.
- Understanding the typical width of your dispersion with different clubs you use off the tee is valuable information. You can use this data to analyze courses before you play to pick targets based on where trouble is situated.
- Start each hole thinking driver first, and if it makes sense, use a club less than driver to avoid big mistakes. There is some nuance on when to step on the gas pedal and pump the brakes.
- If there is major trouble on one side of the hole, and just rough on the other side, you can aim away from it to save strokes. How much you adjust your target will be based on your skill level.
- Be careful when assuming shorter clubs (fairway woods, hybrids, irons) are "safer" off the tee. Once you decide to

pull a club less than driver you are already costing yourself strokes because you will be further from the hole. You must prove to yourself that those clubs are significantly straighter to offset the loss of distance. Many times they are not! This is a common decision to make on difficult holes where you cannot aim away from trouble.

- Resist the temptation to think ahead to your next shot. If you are trying to gain a better angle into a green with your approach shot, and that target brings you closer to trouble, you will lose more strokes than you will gain in the long run.
- Pursuing one shot shape, and getting very good at it, is the better strategy for most players. If you try to curve the ball in both directions based on the layout of the hole, you will likely have more big misses due to conflicting swing thoughts. Boring is good!
- Closer to the hole is better. Trying to leave yourself a specific yardage off the tee, or on a third shot to a Par 5, costs strokes. The only caveat would be for golfers who struggle mightily with partial wedges.

CHAPTER 19
APPROACH SHOT TARGET SELECTION

COMPARED TO TEE SHOTS, approach shot strategy is more basic and straightforward. It is so simple that I could tell you what to do in one sentence, and most of you would lower your scores. However, like any coach, I am changing your ingrained habits. All of your experiences in golf have likely made you too aggressive with your targets, and it's costing you valuable strokes. But you will need to be convinced otherwise.

If you stick with me for a bit, I will persuade you why a far more simple, conservative strategy will lower your handicaps. Additionally, you'll step up to each shot with more confidence and less indecision - two factors that will help improve your ball striking. Approach shots are where scores are influenced the most, so I consider this one of the most important chapters of this entire book!

YOU NEED TO FORGET ABOUT THE PIN

Many golfers default to aiming at the pin with their approach shots, but I will show you why ignoring the pin will save you strokes.

There are a couple of factors at play here:

- No golfer on the planet has enough control over the ball to land it close to the pin consistently.
- Putting difficulty makes it harder to take advantage of close shots.

Overall, aiming at the pin all of the time will cost you far more strokes than it will save you.

Let's Talk Proximity Again

When it comes to approach play, the statistic that surprises most golfers is proximity to the hole from 100-125 yards. When we watch golf broadcasts, the announcer usually says, "he's got the green light here; he's going for the pin." And then, when the ball lands 15-20 feet from the hole, the follow-up is usually, "well, he will be very disappointed with that one!"

According to Shotlink, the best PGA Tour player from 100-125 yards can land the ball 15 feet from the pin on average. The median is about 20 feet, and the worst performance (they are still world-class) is around 27 feet. It's hardly a birdie-fest from those distances.

Now let's look at normal golfers and how they perform. I will even be generous and include shots from 75-125 yards to give them a little proximity advantage over tour players.

Handicap	Average Proximity To Hole
0	39 Feet
5	42 Feet
10	49 Feet
15	60 Feet
20	67 Feet
25	74 Feet

Source: Shot Scope

As you can see, no matter what level of golfer you are, I can guarantee you that you cannot land the ball inside a 15-foot window on average around the pin. Even 30 feet would be exceptional. Perhaps you can do it from time to time, but it's not realistic throughout many rounds.

Additionally, as you move further away from the hole, proximity skyrockets as handicap level increases. Remember, golfers separate themselves more from one another as shot distance increases. Pin hunting from 175 yards is even worse than with a wedge in your hands.

Let's look at proximity to the hole from all distances by handicap level:

75 - 125 Yards:

Handicap	0	5	10	15	20	25
Avg Prox	39 Feet	42 Feet	49 Feet	60 Feet	67 Feet	74 Feet

125 - 175 Yards:

Handicap	0	5	10	15	20	25
Avg Prox	45 Feet	61 Feet	70 Feet	88 Feet	107 Feet	114 Feet

175 - 225 Yards:

Handicap	0	5	10	15	20	25
Avg Prox	82 Feet	109 Feet	123 Feet	166 Feet	192 Feet	236 Feet

Source: Shot Scope

These numbers should give you some much-needed perspective!

What Happens When You Pin Hunt

Golf course architects and course superintendents have a common goal in mind. They want to lure you into making the wrong decision.

As you know, pin locations are variable depending on the day. Some of them will likely be situated around trouble, no matter what course you play. Whether it's deep rough, bunkers, or a steep dropoff in elevation – you need to resist the temptation.

The concept is quite simple. Your shot pattern will follow whenever you shift your aim around the green. As you move your target closer to areas of trouble, your odds of landing the ball there increase.

Avoiding Short-Sided Misses

One of the main reasons golfers waste strokes with approach shots is because they put themselves in difficult situations when they miss a green. Usually, the scenario is called a short-side miss. It's defined as missing a green on a side closest to the pin. Here is a hypothetical visual representation:

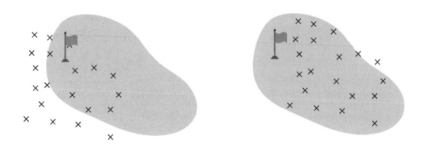

On the left, a golfer chooses the pin as their target which results in a substantial portion of their shots missing the green in a short-sided situation. By choosing a more appropriate target closer to the center of the green and with more club, the same shot pattern now shifts with more balls landing on the putting surface, and more importantly, limiting short-sided results.

It's much harder to save par or even make bogey from a short-sided situation because there is such a small window to land the ball. Golfers often get aggressive to make up for their mistakes and fail to get the ball on the putting surface. While very skilled wedge players can save themselves from these situations more often, ordinary golfers tend to struggle even more with short-sided misses.

If you aim at pins, you will likely increase the times you miss a green on the short side. I can assure you larger scores will follow. Conversely, if you can land it on the "fat side" more frequently and have plenty of green between you and the pin - it is much easier to make a par. More importantly, you will avoid more double bogeys (our main goal). It's easier to prevent double bogeys than making a birdie with approach shots.

The Payoff Isn't There

The icing on the cake is putting. Let's say you are world-class at wedge shots and could keep pace with PGA Tour players. That would mean you could land the ball somewhere around 15-20 feet from the pin on average from a distance of 100-125 yards (in the fairway).

If you remember our putting make percentages, you would only hole about 15-23% of your putts if you could putt like a PGA Tour player. A scratch golfer would one-putt around 14-21% of the time. A more realistic situation would be the performance of a 90-golfer, who would only hole around 6-11% of those putts.

Here again are one-putt percentages from different distances and handicap levels:

Distance	Tour Pro	Scratch Golfer	90 Shooter
3 Feet	96%	93%	84%
5 Feet	77%	66%	50%
8 Feet	50%	41%	27%
10 Feet	40%	33%	20%
20 Feet	15%	14%	6%

Source: Mark Broadie

Going further back, it's even harder. From 150-175 yards in the fairway, PGA Tour players land the ball anywhere between 22 – 35 feet from the hole.

This is why birdies are so hard to come by, especially on a Par 3 or Par 4. The combination of proximity to the hole and putting difficulty make it a strategy not worth pursuing.

Aggression Doesn't Get Rewarded

Hopefully, I've built a convincing case by now. If a pin is tucked towards the edge of any green, and you're aiming there, you are making a poor strategic decision.

Over the long run, you will miss more greens and put yourself in challenging situations that are hard to recover from. Additionally, the chances of landing your ball close to the pin and making the putt are much lower than you think.

No matter what level of golfer you are, "pin avoidance" can save you strokes. I know coaches who teach strategy to professional golfers and top-level college players who have improved their players' scores by convincing them not to aim at pins. I've seen major championship winners who admitted that going for the pin most of their career prevented them from winning more. Resisting the pin is a universal concept that can help all golfers.

Also, teaching pros have even done experiments where they remove the pins from the course for one day. Everyone I have spoken to who has done this exercise reports that most golfers shoot better than their handicaps on those days. Why? Because they choose a very safe target that gives them the best chance of landing on the green!

As usual, the biggest challenge with strategy is discipline. Nothing in this chapter is hard to understand, and you have likely heard this advice before. What separates good strategic players from poor ones are those who can adhere to the plan throughout a round, no matter how great or bad they are playing. Interestingly, performing poorly or very well might make the pin a more enticing target. You could think it is a way to keep a great round going or make up ground on a day that has gone poorly.

No matter the situation, if you can resist the urge to pin hunt, you will save strokes!

AN EASIER SOLUTION

Luckily, I have a straightforward strategy that all of you can embrace on the course. Tons of readers from my website have reached out to me after adopting this approach, telling me that their handicaps have dropped significantly. There are no gimmicks here; it works.

I want you to aim at the center of every green and play closer to the back yardage.

That's it! I know that it's not a sexy approach to the game, but it considers most of the common mistakes golfers make on the course and fixes them.

Allow me to build the case for you...

"The Center of the Green Never Moves"

Many great players have used some variation of this quote over the years. It speaks to the fact that the center of the green is never a wrong target. It's course management 101. No matter the design of any green, if you aim at the middle, you allow your dispersion patterns to land on the putting surface more often. More importantly, you'll find yourself short-sided less often.

Remember, wherever you are aiming, a certain percentage of your shots will miss on both sides. Your primary goal is to land the ball on the putting surface with any approach shot. If you can do that, your expected score on the hole drops dramatically. More greens in regulation equal lower scores - it's a guarantee.

Handicap	Greens In Regulation %
0	52
5	38
10	35
15	26
20	21
25	15

Source: Shot Scope

Additionally, this method takes a lot of guesswork out of your planning process. Every time you step up to the ball, you know what your target is. It won't take more than a few seconds to figure out where the middle of the putting surface is. Having this kind of routine and committing to it will give you more confidence on the course.

The More Important Decision

With approach play, your shot distribution from back to front, or "north and south," is far more important. This variable is mostly determined by club selection and strike quality. Also, it is where golfers of all levels lose most of their strokes.

When shot-tracking companies started popping up years ago, I was very interested in seeing some of the more significant trends they were noticing amongst golfers. I had suspicions on several topics. Where golfers were missing their approach shots was one area in particular I wanted to know more about.

Back in 2016, I spoke with the CEO of GAME GOLF, one of the pioneers in this category. After collecting millions of shots, I asked him their key takeaways. His immediate response was that almost every golfer misses greens on the front side most of the time.

Several years later, Shot Scope released similar findings. Looking at handicap level, you can see how stark the differences are between missing greens short vs. long:

Handicap	0	5	10	15	20	25
Greens Short %	26%	35%	41%	51%	58%	67%
Greens Long %	6%	6%	5%	6%	4%	5%

There are many explanations why most golfers miss their approach shots in front of greens and rarely miss long. I believe the main culprits are the following:

- Golfers don't have accurate information on how far they hit each club in their bag on average. For example, if a player knows when they hit their 7-iron perfectly, it goes 155 yards, they'll pick that club whenever that yardage comes up.
- It is more common to mishit a shot than flush it over the green.
- Lack of accurate yardage information for their targets.
- Choosing clubs based on pin placement.
- Not taking into account the influence of wind and elevation change.

Nobody Is Great at Front Pins

One of the most common scenarios where golfers make mistakes are on front pins. In a sense, you're already short-sided if your goal is to keep the ball close to the hole. It makes no sense to take on these targets. You are just increasing your chances of missing your shot well short of the green.

What's even more interesting is that professional golfers fall for the same thing! DECADE Golf analyzed how PGA Tour players performed when the pin position changes from the front of the green to the back:

Distance to Hole	Front Pin (GIR %)	Back Pin (GIR%)
100 to 119 Yards	78%	82.1%
120 to 139 Yards	75.4%	78.9%
140 to 159 Yards	70.1%	77.2%
160 to 179 Yards	57.5%	71.6%
180 to 199 Yards	49.5%	63.6%

As you can see, tour players hit more greens on average with a back pin versus a front pin. Even they fall victim to chasing pins, and as a result, they find themselves missing more greens.

So if you're tempted to take on a front pin, remember that the odds are stacked against you. You'll miss more greens short and increase your average score over the long run.

The Back of the Green

Most of the shots you hit will not be perfect strikes. Even pro golfers don't hit every shot on the sweet spot. You want to give yourself enough of a cushion so that you can still land on the green even with a less than perfect impact.

On top of that, most golf course architects know that players miss greens on the front side. Shot Scope analyzed satellite imagery and player performance and found that 72% of danger is in front of the green (usually bunkers or water). Missing long is not as penal on most holes.

Considering everything, I believe most golfers should ignore the yardage to the pin. Instead, you should focus more on the yardage closer to the back of the green, or at minimum the center of the green. This will require the use of a GPS device.

Placing more emphasis on the yardage in the darker section will give you more of a cushion with approach shots.

Making this choice repeatedly will allow you to hit more greens in regulation and lower your scores. It sounds too good to be true, but this is one of the most basic secrets of course management.

Why You Will Want To Abandon this Strategy

Aiming to the center of the green and taking more club sounds easy, but it's not. The hardest thing in golf is to keep executing a plan despite seeing results you are not happy with. If you employ this strategy, you will not hit every green. You will still hit plenty of errant shots that miss short, left, right, and even longer. That's golf.

However, if you stick with it and add two or three more greens in regulation per round, it will quickly drop your handicap by multiple strokes.

You will be tempted to chase pins when things aren't going well, but you will just be pouring gasoline on the fire. You cannot force birdies and pars; they happen by giving yourself enough chances to make them through smart target selection (and of course, quality ball-striking). So if you're on board with the center/back strategy, you have to commit to it.

A FEW CAVEATS

I firmly believe this strategy will work for most golfers reading this book. I've heard from countless players who have lowered their handicaps using this method over the years. But of course, I can't account for every player and every hole out there. While I believe the center of the green is usually a good target, there are a few instances where the back yardage might not make sense:

- If there is significant trouble behind the green (penalty area, bunkers, etc.)
- More skilled ball strikers can use yardages closer to the middle of the green more often. However, always avoid playing to the front of the green yardage even if the pin is there!
- As you get closer to the hole, particularly inside of 100 yards with your wedges, you can adjust your target a little closer to the hole. But always aim away from the pin, and closer to the center of the green - avoid being short-sided at all costs!

Also, there are ways for you to get more customized advice if you keep track of your stats. My suggestion would be to start with the center target and back yardage and then track your results to see if they need to be refined. I'll explore that concept in a different chapter.

Overall, without making too many modifications, I'm confident this simple strategy with your approach shots will make a big difference in your scoring. The challenge for many of you will be the discipline part.

Approach play strategy is quite simple. Do everything you can to give yourself the best chance of landing the ball on the green and avoid the temptation to chase pins. A safer, conservative strategy will save you strokes in the long run.

THE BIG IDEAS

- **Approach shot strategy is far simpler than tee shots. Using a basic, conservative system will have you step up to the ball** more confidently, and it will lower your handicap in the long run.

- Aiming at the pin is a losing strategy. It will cost you more strokes than it saves you due to being short-sided more often. Additionally, the combination of putting difficulty and average proximity to the hole, makes it a suboptimal decision.
- "The center of the green never moves" is an easier strategy to adopt that will help you hit more greens in regulation and lower your scores. You have to allow for your lateral dispersion to play out over a larger part of the green.
- Across all skill levels, golfers miss most of their targets short of the green. This discrepancy gets larger as handicap level increases.
- One common mistake is choosing your club based on the distance to the pin. This is especially harmful to scoring potential when pins are closer to the front of the green.
- Adjusting your target based on the yardage closer to the back of the green will give you more of a cushion. Golfers rarely hit their irons, hybrids, and fairway woods too well, and it will allow for mishits to still have a chance to land on the putting surface.
- Aiming to the center of the green and taking more club will save you strokes over the long run, but it can be frustrating in the short term. You will still miss plenty of greens and feel tempted to abandon this strategy!
- Adjustments can be made based on skill level, wedge shots, and extreme features surrounding the green.
- Keeping track of your stats is another way to verify the effectiveness of this strategy or if you need to make small adjustments.

CHAPTER 20
RECOVERY SITUATIONS

I WANT to talk about one of the most critical and overlooked strategic situations - the recovery shot. It is never fun to hit your tee shot into the trees, deep rough, or a fairway bunker. However, you can save strokes easily. Whatever level of golf you are playing, the information I'm about to give you is crucial, and it can save you multiple shots per round. As usual, the challenge will be sticking with it.

DEFINING A RECOVERY SITUATION

It all starts with an errant tee shot. For the sake of simplicity, I'm going to describe a recovery situation as:

- Not having a clear path to the green (in the trees).
- Having a lie that prevents you from realistically reaching the green (fairway bunker or deep rough).

If you miss the fairway, still have a clear path to the green, and your lie in the rough is manageable - that situation does not apply to this discussion.

AVOIDING "TILT"

Dealing with a recovery situation is usually like fighting against the inner gambler inside of all of us. Often, when golfers hit a poor tee shot, our instinct is to play more aggressively to make up for our initial mistake. It's very similar to poker players when they go "on tilt."

Tilt is defined as the following:

> *Tilt originated as a poker term for a state of mental or emotional confusion or frustration in which a player adopts a less than optimal strategy, usually resulting in the player becoming over-aggressive.*

If you've played any other kind of casino game like blackjack, you likely know the feeling. You'll start to bet more aggressively to make up for your losses and lose even more money. It's not a pleasant feeling!

In recovery situations on the golf course, we get upset and frustrated with our initial mistake and start to think about what we can do to make up for it. Suddenly, that small opening in the trees starts looking bigger and bigger. Golfers assume that their only way to keep their round going is to "go for it" and make the aggressive play.

Unfortunately, your mother was right - two wrongs don't make a right. It is tough to calm your emotions and think clearly when you make a mistake off the tee. I'll show you why getting your ball back to safety will save you strokes in the long run.

80% BOGEY

Earlier in the book, I shared some PGA Tour statistics with you. I always find they help readjust your expectations on the golf course. One statistic that stands out from Mark Broadie's Book *Every Shot Counts* is how PGA Tour players perform in recovery situations.

If a PGA Tour player hits their tee shot in the trees, they make bogey about 80% of the time. On TV, we see heroic shots that result in birdies and pars, but on the whole, the best golfers on the planet can't do that on average.

Usually, this statistic surprises most golfers (it shocked me the first time I read it). It highlights how challenging it is to make par in a recovery situation.

THE CORRECT DECISION

If you can shift your thinking from "what can I do to make par here" to "what can I do to make a bogey," - I can guarantee you that you will lower your scores on average. Every round of golf you play is likely going to have recovery situations. No matter how skilled you are or how well you are playing, a tee shot will eventually miss your target by a large margin.

If you find yourself in recovery situations too often, then you are likely making poor strategic decisions off the tee. Or you need some help with your swing mechanics. I will address both of those situations in separate chapters.

So how do you solve the recovery situation? The answer is straightforward. You need to select the shot that gives you the highest probability of getting the ball back to safety. I would define safety as having a clear shot to the green in the fairway (or even light rough). Your goal is to get the ball on the green with the next shot and two-putt for a bogey. Remember, if you make a bogey, you are keeping pace with PGA Tour players.

That could mean punching the ball sideways back into the fairway or advancing it as far as you can without bringing trouble back into play. Your number one goal is to avoid compounding the initial mistake you made off the tee. Going for the low-percentage shot will bring double bogey (or worse) into play, and those are the scores that hold you back from improving.

I want to reiterate that this sounds very simple in theory. I can assure you that you will be tempted to abandon the smart strategy and go for the aggressive play in the heat of the moment. That's OK if you do; I'm not asking for perfection. But if you can start making smarter decisions more often, you will see progress in your scores. Perhaps that positive feedback will lead you to a place where you will rarely go for the hero shot in a recovery situation.

Remember this chapter the next time you hit your tee shot into the trees. Keep saying to yourself, "bogey is my friend."

THE BIG IDEAS

- Recovery shots are one of the most misunderstood scoring situations. Golfers of all levels can separate themselves by making smart decisions. Instead of thinking about saving par, shift your mindset to saving bogey.
- After an errant tee shot, it's very common to go "on tilt." However, choosing the more aggressive strategy will likely compound your initial mistake and result in a double bogey (or worse).
- PGA Tour players make bogey 80% of the time in recovery situations. What you see on TV is not real; keep reminding yourself of that statistic!
- The correct strategy is to advance the ball as far as possible while making sure your next shot will have a clear path to the green. Sometimes, this means punching out sideways.

CHAPTER 21
SHORT GAME TARGET SELECTION

GOLFERS TYPICALLY DO NOT GIVE much thought to course management with their short game. I want to explore a few concepts with your wedges and putter that I know can quickly save you shots with minor adjustments in target selection.

WEDGE PLAY

With a wedge in your hands inside 100 yards, it can be tempting to get more aggressive and land the ball closer to the hole. Try to remember the lessons you learned from some of the earlier chapters. It is not reasonable to expect to land the ball within a 5-foot or even a 10-foot circle from just about any distance.

Let's review our typical proximity distances once again:

10-20 Yards:

Handicap	0	5	10	15	20	25
Avg Prox	10.8 ft	11.6 ft	13.2 ft	16.2 ft	16.8 ft	18.6 ft
Up & Down %	57%	48%	41%	30%	30%	25%

20-30 Yards:

Handicap	0	5	10	15	20	25
Avg Prox	13.4 ft	14.6 ft	18.2 ft	22.6 ft	22.8 ft	26.1 ft
Up & Down %	42%	38%	26%	18%	16%	14%

30-40 Yards:

Handicap	0	5	10	15	20	25
Avg Prox	16.3 ft	22.5 ft	23.4 ft	27.6 ft	28.2 ft	30.1 ft
Up & Down %	27%	22%	22%	16%	15%	12%

You have to prioritize this question on any wedge shot, "what can I do to make sure I get the ball on the putting surface?" Everything else is secondary. Golfers throw away so many strokes around the greens, biting off more than they can chew.

I will explore a few hypothetical situations to illustrate my point. Overall, your intentions likely need to change.

Short-Sided Hero

There will be plenty of times where you miss your approach shots in a short-sided situation, and there won't be much room between you and the pin. Like recovery shots, golfers are tempted to get more aggressive to make up for their initial mistake and try to save par. This is usually where our nasty adversary, the double-bogey shows up.

The aggressive play is to try to land your ball where the green starts, or even just before it:

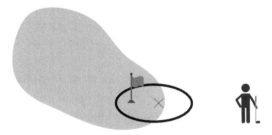

If your target is just on the green, your shot pattern (indicated by the oval) will now shift to having some portion of your shots failing to make it to the putting surface

Intention is everything with wedge play. If you are trying to land your ball just on the green, you shift your shot pattern. A certain amount of balls will land short of your target and not even reach the green. So while you are focused on the best outcome, which is landing your shot in the perfect window, you have to consider what happens when you fail to execute.

The proper play that will lead to lower scores in the long run, is to choose the safer target. Like our recovery situation in the trees, we want to do our best to guarantee a bogey and avoid the double bogey.

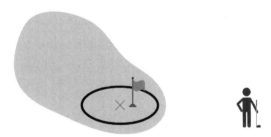

Adjusting your target past the hole will help ensure that most of your shots will end up on the putting surface

Shifting your landing target closer to the hole, or even past it, is the better choice for almost all golfers. You can still leave yourself a putt from 10-20 feet, which will lower your chances of making par, but virtually guarantee a two-putt for bogey.

Trying To Leave Yourself a Specific Putt

Sometimes when the slope of a green is more dramatic, golfers get ahead of themselves and start thinking about the kind of putt they want to leave themselves with wedge play. A common piece of advice you'll hear is that you should try to leave yourself an uphill putt instead of a downhill one for par.

I believe this is a flawed strategy for two reasons:

1. By trying to leave yourself below the hole, you have already shifted your shot patterns further away.
2. Downhill putts aren't substantially harder.

In *Every Shot Counts*, Mark Broadie analyzed the probabilities of making putts from different slope scenarios. For example, here are the expected outcomes for a PGA Tour player on a downhill putt versus an uphill one:

Putt Distance	Downhill Make %	Uphill Make %
3 Feet	96%	96%
5 Feet	75%	80%
8 Feet	48%	53%
12 Feet	30%	33%
15 Feet	23%	25%

As you can see, there is a slight advantage to being below the hole, but it isn't substantial - even for great putters. On sidehill putts, there are slight advantages for certain breaks. A right-handed putter will make more shorter putts that break from right to left than from left to right.

Broadie concluded that distance to the hole is the most critical factor in putt difficulty with all that being considered. Pursuing a 10-foot uphill putt versus a 6-foot downhill putt will not yield lower scores in the long run. In other words, get the ball as close to the hole as possible.

So let's say a golfer misses a green below the hole and has a relatively straightforward uphill chip shot. They will face a downhill putt for par if they go beyond the pin. I believe you are making a mistake by consciously trying to leave yourself an uphill putt for par. Your expected shot patterns will shift further away from the hole.

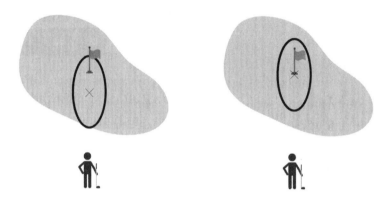

Moving your intended target away from the hole to leave yourself an uphill putt will result in having a larger frequency of longer putts

In an optimal scenario, you would leave yourself a somewhat equal distance from above the hole and below the hole rather than a higher frequency of longer, uphill putts.

PUTTING

I have stated several times throughout the book that improving your putting generally looks like the following for most players:

1. Increasing your chances of making putts inside of 10 feet.
2. Avoid three-putting by leaving yourself closer to the hole on longer putts.

As it pertains to strategy, this is a combination of analyzing the slope of your putts and judging the speeds of the green.

I will not cover green-reading because I think there are much better resources. I have used a system called AimPoint to read my putts for the last several years, and I have encouraged followers of Practical Golf to learn the basics of AimPoint Express. Additionally, the following books can be helpful: *Dave Pelz's Putting Bible, Unconscious Putting* by Dave Stockton, *Every Shot Counts* by Mark Broadie, *Your Putting Solution* by James Sieckmann, and *The Lost Art of Putting* by Gary Nicol/Karl Morris.

Overall, I believe once you become more proficient at reading greens, you must shift your focus almost entirely to speed control. I will offer one piece of strategic advice that I know can save you strokes. It's a mistake I have seen countless golfers make and one that I made for years.

Don't Make the Hole Smaller

The diameter of a golf hole is 4.25 inches. I often wonder how much different and potentially more enjoyable the game would be if someone had decided in the beginning to make it 10 inches. Either way, we are stuck with this tiny hole for better or worse, which is why making putts is so difficult.

Many of you understand this concept intuitively, but as the ball approaches the hole with more speed, its ability to drop into the cup becomes smaller. For example, if you hit an 8-foot putt with too much speed to the right-hand portion of the hole, it would violently lip out. Conversely, if the ball made contact with that same part of the cup at a much slower speed, it would drop into the hole.

Tiger Woods is arguably one of the best putters ever inside of ten feet. Anyone who watched him play during his peak years noticed how he confidently rolled birdie and par putts into the center of the cup with tons of speed. Unfortunately, this is a losing strategy for the rest of us because none of us have the face control that Tiger had.

Golfers get into trouble when they hit putts harder to try and make them. Quite often, it's done on shorter putts when we feel like we have to "jam" it in the hole. But in reality, you are making the hole smaller and smaller with more speed.

This image from Erik Barzeski, the co-author of a great book entitled *Lowest Scores Wins,* is an extremely helpful visualization. You can see how the size of the cup changes based on how far past the hole the ball would have come to rest:

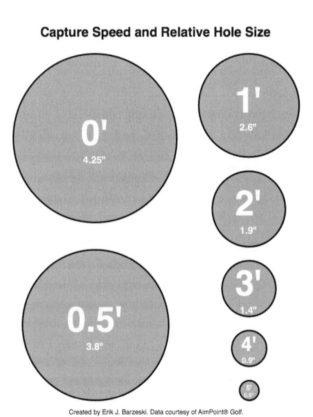

Created by Erik J. Barzeski. Data courtesy of AimPoint® Golf.

The more speed you apply to a putt, the smaller the hole becomes

For example, a putt hit with the perfect speed that would drop into the hole on its last revolution would not change the size of the hole at all. But you can see the cup getting smaller and smaller as speed increases. A putt that would end up four feet past the hole shrinks the "capture size" of the hole from 4.25" down to just less than an inch.

So if you feel like you need to hit a putt harder to make it, you are likely increasing your odds of missing it. On top of that, your next putt coming back will be further from the hole, raising your chances of three-putting.

So what is the solution? I believe that no matter how far you are from the hole - five feet or fifty feet - your intention should be to apply the proper speed. It has been debated the optimal distance you should leave yourself on the second putt; most agree it's somewhere between 12 to 24 inches. Either way, if you intend to apply way more speed than that, your performance on the greens will likely decline.

THE BIG IDEAS

- Prioritize this question on any wedge shot, "what can I do to make sure I get the ball on the putting surface?" Everything else is secondary. Don't bite off more than you can chew! It is not a reasonable expectation to land the ball within a five or ten foot circle every time.
- When you are short-sided, you must take your medicine. Trying to land the ball on the beginning of the green, or even before it will bring larger scores into play more often than you will save par. There is nothing wrong with landing the ball past the hole and making sure you will make bogey at worst.
- On more straightforward wedge shots where you have more green to work with, your goal should be to get the ball as close to the hole as possible. Trying to leave yourself an uphill putt versus a downhill one will result in longer putts overall.
- Your goal on any length putt should be to apply the proper speed so that the ball will come to rest somewhere between 12-24 inches past the cup. Applying more speed to putts, especially shorter ones, in an effort to make them only makes the cup smaller. You will miss more putts, and end up three-putting more often.

CHAPTER 22
CUSTOMIZING STRATEGIC DECISIONS

I FIRMLY BELIEVE that all of the strategic advice I've given you up until this point can help you shoot lower scores. However, everyone's golf game is unique. There are exceptions to every rule, and I cannot possibly account for all of the differences in your games.

If you want the best chance to go on the golf course with an optimal strategy, I recommend keeping track of your statistics and shot patterns. Not only will it help you make better decisions, but this exercise will also enhance your practice methods (which we'll cover in the next section of the book).

Over the past several years, significant technological breakthroughs have made it easier to keep track of your shots and analyze your performance. If you can take a deep dive into your game and see what is going on during your rounds, you can customize your strategy.

PLENTY OF OPTIONS

While the technology market changes quickly, you have a plethora of stat tracking options at your disposal when I first wrote this book.

My primary recommendation is to use a GPS system that automatically tracks your shots. They are pretty easy to install (usually, it means screwing a small sensor into the end of your grips). Using GPS technology, it automatically sense when you hit shots around the course - the information uploads to an online dashboard where it's intuitively presented to you. The two companies I would recommend are Shot Scope and Arccos.

There are also mobile apps that you can operate from your phone. While you have to enter your shots manually, they still provide detailed analysis. For more advanced players, I highly recommend using the DECADE app or Golfmetrics. Another solution would be from a popular GPS app called 18Birdies.

A BIRD'S-EYE VIEW

As I've mentioned before, strokes gained analysis is a far more accurate method to track your performance than traditional statistics like fairways hit and putts per round. It gives each shot you hit a numerical value, and then you'll be able to see a top-level analysis of your strengths and weaknesses relative to other golfers.

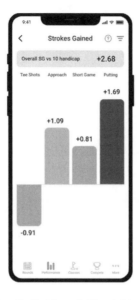

In this example from the Shot Scope dashboard, this golfer is comparing their performance to a 10 handicap. Since they are losing strokes off the tee, this is an area where they can do further analysis.

Using strokes gained is a great starting point, but then you'll have to dig a little deeper. For example, if you were a 15 handicap comparing your game to a 10 handicap and losing the most strokes with approach shots, you need to find out why. The next place to look would be your shot patterns.

Another alternative is to assign a handicap to each part of your game to see where you are over-performing and under-performing in recent rounds. In this example, the golfer's overall handicap is a 1.1. The strength of their game is driving, indicated by a plus 1.9 handicap. However, with the putter they are performing like a 5 handicap, indicating a weakness (Arccos dashboard)

SHOT PATTERNS

I've spoken a lot about how you can use your shot patterns, or dispersion, to make better target and club selections. Many golfers have no idea what their shot distributions look like with each club. With shot tracking systems, you'll be able to see visual representations of your dispersion patterns in aggregate form, by the club, or by shot distance. It's a treasure trove of data that you can use during your preparation. So if you don't have access to a launch monitor, your on-course shot patterns can be just as valuable.

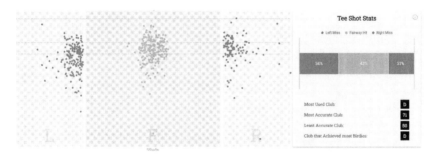

Looking at this golfer's tee shot patters, they are displaying a slight tendency to miss to the left (Shot Scope dashboard)

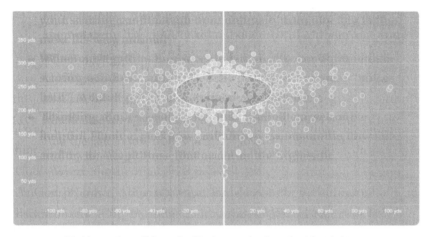

The bigger misses off the tee for this player tend to favor the right side (Arccos dashboard)

Anecdotally, I've discovered the following by tracking my shots:

- I was more accurate than I thought with the driver, and it gave me the confidence to use it more.
- I found that I missed my targets on almost every club equally on both sides. This prevented me from making poor decisions that were based on wrong assumptions.
- Most of my misses on approach shots were short of the green; I very rarely missed long.

You might come to similar conclusions that I did or find something else. Either way, it becomes easier to make customized decisions when you have a bird's eye view of your shot patterns.

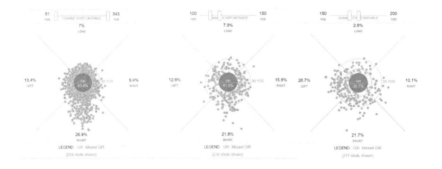

In aggregate (left) this golfer shows a fairly even distribution of misses from left to right, but 27% of shots missing greens on the short side. As you get further from the hole we start seeing a clear pattern emerging to missing on the left as they get 150-200 yards from the hole (Arccos dashboard)

As you analyze your strokes gained data and dig into your patterns, you have to ask yourself if they result from strategic mistakes, or perhaps it's something in your swing that needs to be addressed. If you notice you are missing the green on the short side, one of the most straightforward patterns to fix is just to take more club!

Or you might notice that you are consistently missing fairways on one side with your driver. One solution is to adjust your aim slightly, left or right. However, upon deeper analysis, you learn this is because you have an excessive curve on your tee shots, which would have to be addressed through practice methods.

Overall, you want to play detective and keep asking yourself questions when you notice patterns. Is this something you think you can solve through a better target and club selection, or is it something to do with your skill as a ball striker?

KNOWING YOUR REAL DISTANCES

One of the main benefits of using stat-tracking systems is finding out how far you hit the ball. As I've discussed in previous chapters, most players overestimate their distances with most clubs. It leads to poor decisions on approach shots and can cost you plenty of strokes during your round.

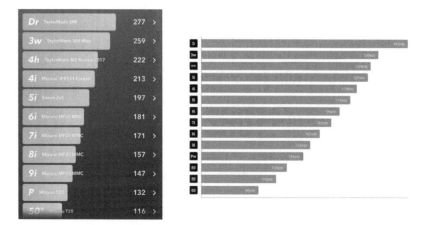

An example of typical distance by club in Arccos (left) Shot Scope (right)

Most of these systems take into account your best and worst shots as outliers. For example, your range of distances with your 7-iron could be 80 to 165 yards based on severe mishits, or shots you strike perfectly. Using their methods of calculating, you will be given a typical distance for each club, which could be around 145 yards based on those numbers.

Once you enter enough rounds, you can start to see distance data for each club. Not only can you choose the right club based on the target, but you'll have even more confidence that you're making the right decision.

Additionally, you can choose clubs on tee shots knowing that you can avoid bunkers and other hazards.

EQUIPMENT DECISIONS

Another benefit of keeping track of your on-course performance can apply to your equipment. For example, many years ago, I had purchased a 3-wood off the rack without testing its performance. After using it a couple of seasons, I knew something was off because it seemed to be more volatile than other clubs in my bag.

After tracking the club for 30 rounds, I noticed that my distances were all over the place, and my left-to-right dispersion seemed more significant than it should be. So I tested the 3-wood on a launch monitor with a clubfitter who saw it was wrong. The main culprit was that it had way too much spin. When I changed to a more appropriate 3-wood, I gained about 25 yards in average distance, and my dispersion tightened significantly.

Having data on all of your clubs can help you make more informed decisions on equipment. Whether it's evaluating driver distance or choosing the proper lofts for your wedges, I have found the information to be invaluable.

THE BIG IDEAS

- Tracking your shots and analyzing statistics is the best way to customize your strategy.
- Strokes gained analysis can give you a top-level view of your game and where you need to focus your efforts. Once you find deficiencies, the next step is to dig deeper and find out why.
- Analyzing your shot patterns from different distances around the course can help reveal patterns. Do your best to find out if you can fix them through strategic decisions. If it's more of a deficiency in your ball striking, then that needs to be addressed through practice.
- Learning how far you hit each club will help you make better decisions and be more confident.
- Tracking can also reveal issues with your equipment. If you see patterns that seem unusual, it's possible that club might not be suited for your swing.

CHAPTER 23
HOW TO STUDY A COURSE BEFORE YOU PLAY

A CORNERSTONE of course management is preparation. Making more decisions about your club selection and targets before the start of the round will allow you to play more confidently. Indecisiveness can lead to poor execution. If you want to give yourself the best opportunity to score well, it makes sense to prepare beforehand.

Studying a course before you play is a more advanced technique but undoubtedly worthwhile. Coming up with a plan before your round is especially crucial for courses you've never played before. Ultimately, it will give you more "mental freedom" when you play.

Let's explore how you can do some homework before your round to optimize your strategic decisions.

SATELLITE DATA IS A GOLFER'S BEST FRIEND

Satellite imagery has revolutionized many industries. For golfers, it provides crystal clear images of golf course layouts that were only available previously through laborious note-taking. In a matter of seconds, you can load up any golf course in the world and start analyzing each hole.

Two tools that are the most helpful, in my opinion, are Google Maps and Google Earth. Google Earth is more advanced, but Google Maps has incorporated many of its features over the past few years. You can now measure distances between various points on the course and see most layouts in 3D to understand the topography and elevation changes on a course. If you want the most information possible, you can't go wrong with either.

An example of using 3D imagery from Google Earth to illustrate the contour of a hole. You can see how extreme the fairway slopes from right to left and is downhill.

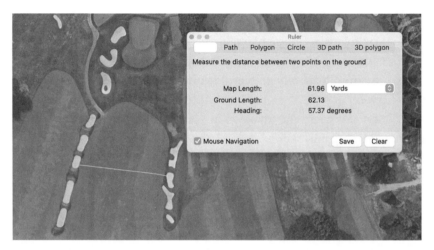

Measuring how wide the landing zone is between bunkers

Additionally, other golf-specific apps and websites allow you to research courses beforehand. Two of my favorites are Blue Golf (www.bluegolf.com) and the 18Birdies App, which you can use on your phone.

Overall, having a birds-eye view of the course and measuring distances to multiple points of interest (penalty areas, bunkers, trees, etc.) is valuable information for a golfer.

There are a few ways to research with satellite imagery. I'll explore my favorite options and explain how they will provide the foundation for choosing targets in the coming chapters.

THE BIG TROUBLE OFF THE TEE

Avoiding penalty areas, trees, fairway bunkers, and other spots on the course that put you in a recovery situation is a surefire way to lower your scores. Knowing your distances to these areas of the course and the overall design of the hole can help you make smarter choices before you play.

For the most part, the big trouble is vital for your tee-shot decisions. Our primary goal is to avoid significant problem areas off the tee while advancing the ball as far as possible. To simplify your analysis, you should try to answer these two questions:

1. Is the trouble mainly on one side of the hole? Can I aim away from it?
2. Does taking less club make more sense to limit distance to avoid a big mistake?

For example, if you see that a fairway is heavily guarded by trees and fairway bunkers on the right side of the hole, it makes more sense to aim further left. You'll still allow yourself to hit the fairway, but you will increase your chances of avoiding the trees and bunkers. If you happen to land in the rough left of the fairway, remember it's not that large of a penalty. So you can make a note before you play to hit driver on the hole, but aim on the left side of the fairway.

Other times, there might be penalty areas such as water or out-of-bounds in play if you hit the ball too far. If you find that choosing a driver could potentially put you in those parts of the hole, taking less club to limit your distance makes sense. Measuring the distances to these areas of interest on a tool like Google Maps is invaluable.

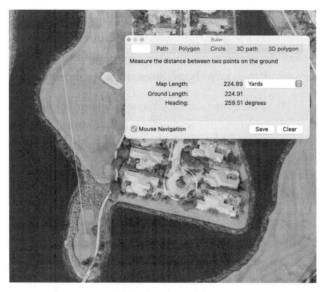

Measuring how far the water starts to come in to play off the tee box.

Of course, we want to hit more fairways with our tee shots. But taking a look at satellite imagery and evaluating the design of each hole can help you decide if it makes more sense to aim away from the big trouble or take less club off the tee by measuring distances to various hazards.

I find it's easiest to make small notes for yourself for each tee shot. It can be as simple as what club you will hit and aiming in any particular direction. Going through this exercise for a new course can save you plenty of shots before you even play.

LAYUP SHOTS

My primary recommendation is to plan out your tee shots before you play. This is a worthwhile analysis that won't take much time for most golfers. If you want extra credit points, you can study a few other things.

Many course architects will challenge golfers with their layup shots on Par 5s (or even a Par 4). This could mean placing bunkers in the middle of the fairway or having water in play. These points on the course should become apparent when you look at satellite imagery. The math says that golfers should try to get the ball as close as possible to the hole with their layup shots on Par 5s. However, it is not worth it if you take on additional risks.

Measuring the layup yardage on a Par 5 that gives the safest landing zone to avoid bunkers.

Let's say there is a bunker in the middle of the fairway or even a penalty area with water. If you measure that it begins about 80 yards in front of the hole, it will make sense to lay back if you don't believe you can clear it with your second shot. These are small notes you can add before you play, as well.

APPROACH SHOTS

Choosing targets on approach shots is far more straightforward. As discussed in a previous chapter, the majority of you will lower your scores by merely aiming at the center of every green and taking more club than you think. However, there are always exceptions.

I recommend looking for anything out of the ordinary when looking at green complexes. Most holes have trouble in front of the green, but that's not always the case.

If you see that there are penalty areas or excessive bunkering in any direction of the green, it's worth taking note of those instances. There could be water behind the green. Then it would make sense to adjust your yardage downward to avoid the penalty of missing there.

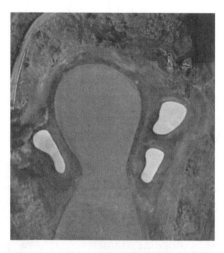

An example of a green with trouble behind it. You can see trees and a native area. When looking in 3D it becomes clear there is a steep drop-off as well when you go long.

Overall, you want to improve your target or club selection to do your best to take those significant problem areas out of play. I should note that those circumstances will be a minority. I strongly urge you to stick with the basic approach-shot strategies I will cover.

DON'T WRITE A NOVEL

Taking notes on a course can be a reasonably quick exercise before playing. Once you get used to it, the analysis shouldn't take more than 10-15 minutes. I don't want you to think you need to show up to the course with an entire yardage book of notes.

I recommend mainly focusing on your tee-shot decisions. If you have any holes where it doesn't make sense to aim down the middle of the fairway with your driver, then you can make a small list of notes to bring with you. Also, note if you will hit a club other than the driver.

If anything else strikes you out of the ordinary on layup shots or approach shots, you can make notes on those holes as well. Overall, if you are playing a course that you are unfamiliar with or want to opti-mize your decisions on a course you play regularly, this is a very productive activity. Using the framework I have given in previous chapters will allow you to step on the course with more confidence since many important decisions will already be made.

THE BIG IDEAS

- **Studying a golf course before you play is a great way to improve your course management. Making as many decisions as possible before you tee it up will give you more freedom and decisiveness while you play.**
- **There are plenty of options available to you now using satellite imagery. Using a tool like Google Earth, you can view a course from above or even ground level using 3D views.**
- **You want to establish the big trouble on holes with tee shots and how far it is from the tee box. Can you avoid it by**

aiming away, or in some instances, by taking a club less than a driver?

- Taking note of layup areas on a Par 5 or even a Par 4 is also essential. Your overall goal is to get as close to the hole as possible and make sure you are not taking on additional risk by bringing fairway bunkers or penalty areas into play.
- You can also examine green complexes to see if any holes have extreme design features.

CHAPTER 24
FACTORING IN THE ELEMENTS: WIND, TEMPERATURE, HUMIDITY, AND ALTITUDE

ONE OF THE features of golf that makes it such an interesting, sometimes random game, is that we play out in the elements. Based on the weather forecast, a course can completely change from one day to another. We need to adjust our targets to accommodate these factors from a strategic perspective.

This chapter will cover "the big four" - wind, temperature, altitude, and humidity. There are a lot of persistent myths about how each can alter distance and trajectory, and I'll provide you with some rules that you can take out to the course. I'll also thank Marty Jertson and Chris Broadie from PING; their research in this area has been extremely helpful.

YOU CANNOT CONTROL THE WIND

Golf is sometimes a bigger fight against Mother Nature than the course or even ourselves. When the wind is blowing more than usual, it's essential to understand that you have to give up a certain amount of control. There are rounds where the wind will come from a constant direction and be more predictable. Other times, it might seem to be swirling all over the place. No matter what the case is, your golf ball will be at the mercy of its randomness.

I will give you some sound rules that can help save strokes when playing in the wind but try to remember that you cannot control what happens once you contact the ball. For example, you might choose two extra clubs when hitting a 15 mph headwind. It might be the correct decision at the moment, but all of a sudden, the wind can stop blowing while your ball is in the air (and your ball lands 20 yards past your target). That's golf!

Headwinds

In my experience, most golfers struggle most when hitting into the wind - also known as a headwind. As mentioned in an earlier chapter, almost every player tends to miss greens on the short side, and headwinds contribute to this pattern. Overall, golfers underestimate the effects of headwinds and are not choosing enough clubs. A headwind will alter the distance of your shot more than a tailwind.

The following image from PING highlights how much wind can alter the carry distance of a moderately high-launching drive.

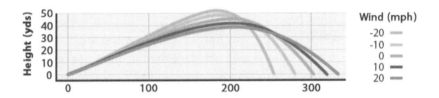

You can see that the headwind hurts distance more than a tailwind helps:

Wind (mph)	Carry Distance (yards)
-20	243.9 (-44.9)
-10	268.2 (-20.6)
0	288.8 (0)
10	305.6 (+16.8)
20	319 (29.8)

When hitting into the wind, you have two adversaries - launch angle and spin. Frequently, they work together against you. So whether you hit the ball higher or with more spin, a headwind will affect ball flight more. Both situations can result in the golf ball "ballooning." The ball seems to climb higher and higher into the air, then it hits an imaginary wall and lands well short of your intended target distance. I am sure you are aware of how frustrating it can be.

You cannot fight a headwind; you must succumb to it. Almost every golfer tends to swing harder and try to pierce their ball through the wind by sheer force. Usually, swinging harder with the same club adds either more loft or spin and sometimes both - the opposite of what you need to do.

So how do you keep the ball lower with less spin? It's pretty simple, take more club! Instead of using an 8-iron, use a 6-iron. A lower-lofted club will naturally launch the ball on a lower trajectory with less spin. There's no need for a fancy punch shot, as some suggest. I don't recommend altering anything in your swing. It lowers your chances of producing a solid strike, which is crucial in a headwind.

I have found the following formula from Andrew Rice, a top 50 instructor, to be helpful when hitting into the wind:

- **5 mph = 5% of the total distance + 5 yards**
- **10 mph = 10% of the total distance + 5 yards**
- **15 mph = 15% of the total distance + 5 yards**
- **20 mph = 20% of the total distance + 5 yards**

These numbers are a great rule of thumb for the majority of golfers. For example, if you had a 5 mph headwind and your target was 150 yards, you would calculate the following:

$$150 \times .05 = 7.5 \ yards$$
$$7.5 + 5 = 12.5 \ yards \ extra \ distance$$
The shot would play 162.5 yards

One way to gauge the speed of the wind is to check the local weather forecast before you tee off. If you want to get more advanced, you could purchase a wind meter to learn how different speeds feel. Please remember these are guidelines, and you don't have to be exact. Don't bring a calculator out on the course!

One last thing to understand about headwinds is that they will typically increase the dispersion of your shots. Whatever curvature you play will be exaggerated. Draws might turn into hooks, and fades might turn into slices. So it is pretty normal to adjust for a larger dispersion pattern, especially for your tee shots.

Tailwinds

While tailwinds also present a challenge, I have found that they will have far less impact on your carry distances. Speaking with PING engineers, they've found that tailwind tends to help less with carry distance as swing speed decreases.

On the whole, tailwinds will add distance to your shots but not influence total distances as much as headwinds. Depending on how much the wind is blowing behind you, taking less club might make sense, which will add some height to your shots.

The following formula from Andrew Rice can help estimate club selections when hitting shots downwind:

- **5 mph = 2% of the total distance**
- **10 mph = 3% of the total distance**
- **15 mph = 5% of the total distance**
- **20 mph = 7% of the total distance**

In our headwind example, 5 mph of wind added 12.5 yards of distance to a 150-yard shot, making it play 162.5 yards. But a tailwind would only add 3 yards of distance (2% of 150 yards), making the shot effectively 147 yards.

Tailwinds tend to "knock the ball down" and send it on a lower trajectory. This can certainly help increase the distances of your tee shots, but it's worth noting that if you play on firmer surfaces, the ball will release more once it lands. Additionally, tailwinds will reduce the left-to-right dispersion of most of your shots, thereby minimizing curvature.

HUMIDITY

Golfers routinely overestimate how much influence humidity can have on ball flight. You'll hear that the ball won't travel as far in humid, "heavy air."

Higher humidity actually lowers air density, making the ball fly further. But the result is almost negligible. According to research from PING, changing humidity from 0% to 100% would make a 280-yard drive only .9 yards further.

However, you should be concerned about moisture on your golf ball. Whether you are playing a morning round with a lot of dew on the course that can cover your ball or in light rain, it influences ball flight quite a bit. Iron shots can travel as much as 5 yards shorter and drives about 15 yards shorter due to an increase in spin rate. Conversely, moisture on the ball and clubface can reduce spin with wedges. So do your best to keep your clubface clean in wetter conditions! You can't wipe your ball down, so you need to be aware of the potential loss in distance on longer clubs.

TEMPERATURE

Big changes in temperature can influence how far you hit your clubs. There are three primary factors to consider:

- As temperature increases, air density decreases. Generally speaking, warmer temperatures will allow the ball to fly farther.
- Your swing speed will also change based on temperature. You will likely wear additional layers in colder conditions, and your muscles won't be as loose. As it gets warmer, your speed

will likely increase because you will have fewer layers and looser muscles.

- Temperature also affects the elasticity of the golf ball. Colder golf balls have less ball speed compared to warmer ones. So don't leave your golf balls in your trunk overnight if the temperature drops significantly!

Keep in mind that all three factors will work together and vary from player to player. For example, you might be able to preserve your swing speed in colder temperatures if you do a proper warmup before you tee off.

A good rule of thumb is that extreme temperature changes, let's say 30-40 degrees Fahrenheit, could add or subtract as much as ½ - 1 full club of distance. However, going from 65 degrees to 75 degrees will be much less noticeable.

So when playing in an early spring round versus the middle of summer, you might need to take an extra club into greens or expect your driver distance to travel somewhere around 10 yards less. The temperature has enough influence to consider, whereas humidity levels have a negligible effect.

ALTITUDE

Last but not least, the altitude of where you play must be considered. The density of the air is heavily dependent on altitude. As elevation increases, shots fly farther but with a lower peak height.

Moving from sea level to Denver, Colorado (5,280 ft) can increase the carry of a drive by as much as 11 yards.

So if you are traveling to areas above sea level, it's important to consider changes in altitude could make your ball fly a little further than it usually would, even as little as 1000 ft.

THE BIG IDEAS

- Wind is the most significant influence on ball flight. On days where it is gusting more, accept that you will have less control over the golf ball. You must succumb to the wind rather than fight against it!
- For most golfers, headwinds will alter distance and trajectory more than tailwinds.
- You need to launch the ball lower with less spin when playing into a headwind. Instead of swinging harder with the same club selection, just take more club! Only advanced players should consider trying to play punch shots.
- Headwinds also tend to increase the left-to-right dispersion of your shot patterns.
- Tailwinds will add some distance to your shots and tend to flatten the trajectory. But you will not need to adjust club selection as much as headwinds. Additionally, they usually tighten your left-to-right shot patterns. Be careful in firmer conditions, as the ball will run out more.
- Extreme temperature changes can alter your shots as much as ½ - 1 full club. The density of the air, clothing you wear, ball elasticity, and how loose or tight your muscles are all contribute to these variables.
- By itself, air humidity has no negligible effect on trajectory or distance. However, any moisture on the golf ball (morning dew or rainfall) can reduce your distances. Do your best to keep your clubs dry before each shot.
- Going from sea level to higher altitude can add distance and lower the trajectory of your shots. Be aware of these changes if you are traveling.

PART THREE
PRACTICE

CHAPTER 25
THE MOST IMPORTANT INGREDIENT FOR SUCCESSFUL PRACTICE

THERE IS nothing more frustrating than spending hundreds of hours practicing your golf game every year and not seeing any meaningful results. While there is plenty of information on the golf swing, golfers are never really taught how to practice effectively.

Throughout the past seven years, I've had the opportunity to communicate directly with thousands of golfers through my website, Practical Golf. Players from around the world have come to me with their frustrations. Through a lot of research, experimentation, and personal failings - I've concluded that practice is one of the most misunderstood parts of the game.

I will give you plenty of ideas to make your practice sessions more productive. I want to provide you with a new perspective on the concept. My goal is to give you a framework to use. It's up to you to do the actual work, which should be fun.

As an introduction to practice, I'll explore common mistakes. I'll also present some concepts that I believe are the pillars of successful practice.

ZOMBIE RANGE SESSIONS

The most common complaint heard on any golf course is, "I was hitting it so great on the range, and then I was terrible on the course. I don't get it!" It stems from arguably the biggest mistake that golfers make. Most players think that merely showing up to the driving range will make them better golfers. Unfortunately, that couldn't be further from the truth. Plenty of golfers are getting worse because of how they practice!

In my opinion, the biggest culprit is something I call zombie range sessions. Golfers show up to the range and start rifling through their bucket. They don't take any time to think about what they are doing, pick a target, or give themselves more than five seconds between swings.

In most cases, players are just reinforcing bad habits. They are not learning anything new, internalizing feedback, or challenging themselves.

You've heard it before – if you do the same old, you get the same old.

THE MISSING FACTOR

Practice can be a valuable tool for improvement. But there has to be one crucial factor in making it worth it.

I'm talking about *intent*.

One of the main differences between highly-skilled golfers and the rest of the pack is that they practice with intent. They show up to the practice range with specific goals and a plan on how they will spend that time.

However, your practice plan doesn't have to be complicated or feel like doing tedious chores. It should be fun and challenging so that you stay engaged.

WHAT DOES INTENT LOOK LIKE?

Throughout the practice section of this book, I will show you plenty of ways to add intent to your practice sessions. Here are a few introductory examples.

Having a Target

This sounds almost too simple, but many golfers fail to identify a target before each shot. Most are hitting balls "out there." Don't do that! Without a goal, you can't evaluate your performance and pay attention to feedback. Also, you are failing to recreate conditions you will face on the course (another cornerstone of effective practice).

Every shot must have a specific purpose, and you can't get much more fundamental than your target.

Experimentation

One of the great ways to increase your golfing skill is to experiment with minor changes in your technique to manipulate the golf ball. I recommend devoting a small portion of each practice session to experimentation.

What do I mean? Here are some examples:

- Try to hit a big sweeping hook.
- Move the ball around in your stance to see how it can affect your shot shape and trajectory.
- Try to hit your 6-iron 75 yards.
- Hit your sand wedge to the same target with three different trajectories.

The golf course can throw so many variables at you, and being able to adjust is vital. More often than not, we don't get perfect lies on flat surfaces. Golf is about adaptation. Hitting these shots will help you become more creative, but more importantly, I believe it will help you become a better ball striker with your normal swing.

A lot of my practice as a junior golfer was spent experimenting. At the time, I didn't know it. I thought I was having fun and playing. As an adult golfer, this kind of practice is one of the more fruitful versions of intent that you can add to your preparation.

Challenging Yourself

One of the great ways to make your practice more effective and engaging is to challenge yourself with skill games. Not only will it make things more fun, but this is how you simulate the pressure of playing an actual round of golf.

There are hundreds, even thousands of games out there you can try. For many golfers, games can be the missing puzzle in their development.

Building Skill

Building long-lasting skills are fundamental in your quest to become a better golfer. However, the golf world obsesses over technique.

Whenever we watch golf broadcasts, we're shown slow-motion videos of pro golfers, and they talk about the various technical positions each player goes through during their swing. However, what we cannot see is their skill.

If you listen to my podcast, The Sweet Spot, you know that we constantly talk about skill development. Being able to strike the center of the face, control where the clubface is pointing at impact, and have proper ground contact are all skills. Great golfers all share these but use different techniques to achieve them.

You'll see that many of the practice methods I explore will focus on skill development rather than the technical elements of the golf swing. These are universal concepts that golfers at every level need to hone. How you swing the club (your technique) is very personal. There is no right way to do it. This leads me to my next point…

Technical Changes

Millions of golfers are on an endless journey to make swing changes. They often receive random swing tips from strangers or friends that won't help them improve. That is why I tell anyone that if they want to make meaningful changes to their golf swing, it's best to work with a qualified teaching professional.

If you are working with a golf instructor, you'll likely have some homework on some swing changes. You need to do the prescribed work during your practice sessions to see results. Taking the lesson is the first part; putting in the work is critical.

Doing your swing homework certainly qualifies as intent and can be a core component of your range sessions. However, I wouldn't recommend taking shots in the dark with swing changes. If you read an article or watched a YouTube video that tells you to swing a golf club a certain way, it likely will not resonate with your particular swing.

Overall, working on technique during a range session is essential. But you want to make sure it's the right kind of work for your golf swing.

WITHOUT A PLAN, YOU CAN'T EXPECT MUCH

If you want to become a better golfer and have time to practice, your best chance of success is to make that time mean something. You don't have to spend three hours at the range to see improvement. You want to work smarter, not harder.

A lot of that starts with the idea of intent. What are you looking to get out of each practice session? How will you give each shot meaning?

I'll help answer those questions in this section of the book with various practice methods. Some of them will resonate with you; some of them might not. You can choose a few that make sense to you, and if you stick with them, I am confident you'll see results.

THE BIG IDEAS

- **Every golfer knows the frustration of not being able to bring your range performance to the golf course. A lot of this has to do with practice habits.**

- Most golfers default to "zombie range sessions." They rifle through their bucket of balls without any kind of meaningful engagement.
- The missing ingredient for successful practice is often intent. Without intent, you can't expect to improve.
- This section of the book will cover many of the pillars of effective practice: experimentation, challenging yourself, skill-building, technical work, and collecting the proper feedback.
- You don't need to spend countless hours practicing. Being efficient is more important.

CHAPTER 26
BLOCKED VS. RANDOM PRACTICE

WHEN YOU SHOW up at the range and hit the same shot to the same target repeatedly, it's pretty easy to build some false self-confidence. You'll get into a groove that wouldn't be possible on the golf course. When we play golf, we only get one chance to hit a shot, and often there are several minutes between each attempt. This disconnect between practice and live action is where golfers fall into a common trap.

Most golfers have spent too much time on blocked (repetitive) practice. While repetition has its merits, I want to explore why introducing variation to your training can help take you to the next level in your game.

THE DIFFERENCE BETWEEN BLOCKED AND RANDOM PRACTICE

Most of you are very familiar with blocked practice; it's what most golfers are doing. A simple definition would be practicing the same skill repeatedly. An example would be if you were at the range and hitting your 7-iron to the same target without making any changes.

Random practice introduces some changes in each shot. Let's say you had a lob wedge in your hands, and you hit targets that were 75 yards, 25 yards, 50 yards, and then 40 yards. Each time you had a new goal, it would force your mind and body to go through a calibration process. Another example would be changing the club on each shot - you could hit a sand wedge, 7-iron, and driver.

In my experience, the vast majority of players are spending way too much time on blocked practice. Many golfers don't even know what random practice is and what kinds of benefits it can provide.

WHY BLOCKED PRACTICE HAS COME UNDER FIRE

Over the last several decades, plenty of research has emerged in sports and other disciplines that question the efficacy of blocked practice. One of the main arguments is that repetitive practice might lead to better results during training sessions but fails to transfer long-term skills to "game situations." Many of you probably know the frustration of hitting great shots at the driving range and being wholly demoralized when you can't recreate that success. I believe a lot of that has to do with how you practice.

Additionally, blocked practice can work against many golfers because they merely ingrain bad technical habits. If you are struggling with a slice and keep hitting balls repeatedly without making any changes, how can you ever expect to fix it? Perhaps taking a lesson and getting some new drills or experimenting with trying to hook the ball could fix the issue. But you would never know until you made some change.

Without getting too deep into the woods on the topic, it's believed that randomized practice helps transfer skills more effectively because it challenges you to solve more problems. When you hit a driver 30 times in a row, you are probably not paying too much attention. It requires a lot of mental discipline to concentrate while you do something repetitively. However, if you had to change your club and target each time, your mind would have to readjust and adapt to the new challenge. Many believe that variation is training your brain to perform better under pressure.

ENGAGEMENT IS THE MOST IMPORTANT FACTOR

It's impossible to know precisely the right amount of blocked practice and randomized practice that will lead to your best results. I believe both have their merits for improving your golf game. No matter what you are doing, engagement and concentration is the most critical factor in my estimation.

If you have a plan for each shot and focus throughout the process, you give yourself a better chance of improving your skills. I believe that introducing random practice to your routine can help with that process. But that doesn't mean you should throw repetitive practice out the window!

In this entire section of the book, I will give you examples of both. My recommendations will help provide more meaning and challenge you more during training, whether it's blocked or random. I want to stop you from "going through the motions" and use your time productively.

WHAT DOES PRODUCTIVE BLOCKED PRACTICE LOOK LIKE?

Let's say you were hitting your 8-iron to the same target 20 times in a row. Here is a list of things you could be doing to increase your engagement:

- You went through the same pre-shot routine before each shot that you would use on the golf course.
- Each time you step up to the ball, you pay attention to your setup. Is your posture the same? Are you gripping the club any differently? Where is the ball positioned in your stance? Where are your eyes focused?
- There is a specific technique you are trying to work on. Perhaps it's a rehearsed drill that your instructor gave you to address a swing flaw.
- You are focused on your target entirely before you hit the shot. Afterward, you pay attention to the result. Which direction did

you miss? Do you think about why that might have occurred and what you can do on the next shot to adjust?

Those are just a few examples, and there are probably hundreds of different ways you could come up with to give meaning to a blocked practice session. I don't want to inundate you with too many ideas because focusing on one thing at a time will likely work best for you. For many golfers, merely concentrating on the target and noting where the ball ended up could enhance their performance.

Overall, repetitive practice does have its merits if you are correctly engaged and paying attention to the proper feedback. My number one hope for you is to prevent those zombie range sessions where you mindlessly hit balls without giving much thought to what you are doing. You are lowering your chances of increasing your skills.

WHAT DOES PRODUCTIVE RANDOM PRACTICE LOOK LIKE?

I don't want to give the impression that random practice is the solution to all of your golfing woes - because it isn't. Even if you change your target every time you hit a golf ball during practice, there is still a chance that your mind and body are not adequately engaged in the process. However, I believe variation gives you a much better chance of simulating the conditions you will see on the golf course and preparing you more effectively.

After all, golf is a random game. How often do you get the same shot on the course over and over again? Every round you play, you are constantly faced with randomness. You'll get different lies in the rough, uneven stances, the wind will keep shifting, or perhaps a tree will be in your way, and you need to find a way around it. Your preparation should take that into account and introduce some variability.

Here are some examples of random practice, and these are many of the topics I'll explore in the coming chapters:

- Playing performance games that simulate the pressure and variation of a real round.

- Choosing one target and hitting four different clubs to the correct distance.
- Experimenting with varying shot shapes and trajectories.
- Trying to strike different parts of the clubface consciously.
- Cycling through different yardages and targets with your wedges inside of 100 yards.

The best part about all of these methods is that they are usually more fun for golfers. If you try some of them out, you'll probably start looking forward to the practice range rather than feeling like it's an obligation.

Overall, there should be a healthy mix of repetitive and variable practice methods. No matter what you are doing, you want to have a plan and be engaged. The coming chapters will show how you can do that with many ideas.

THE BIG IDEAS

- **Blocked practice involves repetition of the same skill over and over without any kind of interruption. Most golfers default to this method without knowing.**
- **Random practice introduces some kind of change on each repetition. Some research indicates that it is more effective at building long-term skills and improving performance.**
- **No matter what method of practice you choose, engagement and focus are critical factors for success.**
- **Introducing randomness to your practice sessions can increase your enjoyment and challenge you to build longer-lasting skills.**
- **A healthy mixture of both methods can make your practice sessions more meaningful.**

CHAPTER 27
IMPACT TRAINING

SIMILAR THEMES EMERGE when the instructional world talks about fundamentals in the golf swing. Topics like posture, grip, alignment, and swing plane get a lot of attention.

The truth is that all of these are variable and require the proper matchups. There is no right way to grip a golf club or align your feet at address. The combinations of golf swing techniques are endless. What works for your swing might not work for someone else's. However, one fundamental is not negotiable or variable, and I don't think it's talked about enough. I'm speaking about impact location.

Where you strike the ball on the face of the club is perhaps the most essential skill any golfer can develop. It's a skill that needs to be grown over time, which means paying attention to your current impact tendencies and improving them. The more I've learned about how golf clubs are designed and ball flight physics, the more I believe in impact training. No matter what level of golfer you are, I firmly believe this kind of practice is a must. It applies to every club in your bag.

WHY IMPACT LOCATION IS SO IMPORTANT

Golf is a game of proximity – we pick a target, make a swing, and hopefully land the ball within a reasonable distance of where we aimed. The closer you are, the better opportunity you have to post a lower score.

It all sounds easy, right?

Where you strike the ball on the face of the club will significantly influence your ability to reach your targets on the course. There's no question that golf club technology has come a long way, and clubs are more forgiving than ever on off-center strikes. But the fact remains that the closer you can strike the ball to the sweet spot (also known as the center of gravity), the more optimal your ball flight will be.

There are several reasons why missing the center of the clubface can be so penal on the course.

Something called gear effect becomes an issue with your driver, fairway woods, and hybrids. Looking at the club horizontally, if you strike the ball closer to the toe of the club, it will impart a hook spin, and if you make an impact closer towards the heel, the ball will tend to slice more (for a right-handed golfer). I'll explore this concept further in-depth during the driver practice chapter, but here are two examples of how impact location can alter ball flight:

Striking it lower on the face reduces launch angle, ball speed, and increases spin. These all limit distance potential.

The first swing launches at 6.2 degrees (very low), spins at 2606 rpm (high for my swing), and carries 213 yards.

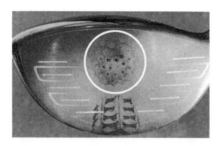

Striking it closer to the center of the face, or just above, helps maximize distance potential.

The second swing launches 14.3 degrees, with 2078 rpm, with a 257-yard carry.

Those are extreme examples, but you can see how missing the club-face's center robs me of 40 yards of distance (and accuracy).

While gear effect isn't an issue with your irons or wedges, strike quality greatly influences outcomes. When you miss the center of the face, you'll see reductions in ball speed, different launch angles, and spin rates. Mishits make it harder to hit greens in regulation with irons, one of the most significant determinants of scoring ability. One typical result is missing the green short of your target.

Additionally, with wedge play, mishits alter your ability to control trajectory and spin - two critical components of distance control.

DIAGNOSING YOUR TENDENCIES

The first step in improving your impact location is understanding your current tendencies. Some golfers tend to strike it more towards the heel, others more towards the toe. And yes, plenty don't have any pattern at all, and they seem to hit it all over the face.

Either way, most players have no idea where they are striking it on the face, and they should take some time to find out.

There have been several methods that have been popular through the years. Some golfers purchase impact stickers, but they don't allow clean contact with the face of the club and can alter your ball flight. I've used dry-erase pens to mark the back of the golf ball, and it will leave residue on the clubface where you made an impact. However, I've found myself getting lazy and not wanting to keep marking my ball before every shot.

I have settled on the easiest method for irons and woods, which is using foot odor spray like Dr. Scholl's. Years ago, some golf instructors realized that it was the perfect material. Another alternative is dry shampoo.

During your practice sessions, start diagnosing your impact tendencies with various clubs in your bag. When I'm not swinging well, I drift closer towards the club's heel and lower on the face with my irons and woods.

Also, you want to note how the shot feels at impact before you look at the face. You'll start to learn what specific impact feels like in your hands so that when you're on the course, you'll begin to understand where you are missing your shots on the face (with the goal of self-correcting).

IDEAS FOR PRACTICING IMPACT LOCATION

There are two main reasons I like practicing with impact location intent:

1. It gives your practice session more meaning and structure.
2. Focusing on impact allows your swing to self-organize a fix that doesn't require you to think about all of the moving parts it took to get there.

I never tell all golfers that impact training can fix everyone. However, many players are amazed at how much progress they can make once they figure out their impact patterns. The real magic comes from consciously starting to strike different parts of the clubface.

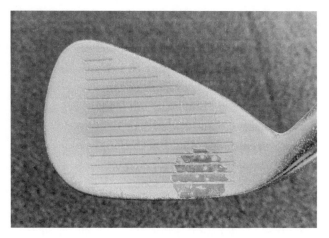

A low heel strike

If you notice a bias towards one side of the face, I like using my "fight fire with fire" approach. For example, when I am struggling with heel strikes, I exaggerate a miss on the outside of the toe. Sometimes I'll even set up with the ball on that side of the face. Interestingly enough, when I try to strike the toe, it moves my impact from the heel to the center of the face.

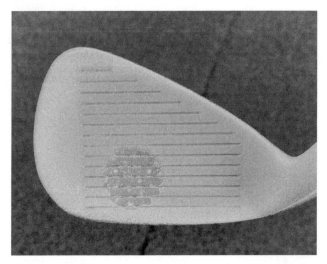

An example of trying to hit closer to the toe intentionally

You can also experiment with small changes in your setup to see how it changes your strike location – like standing closer or further away from the ball.

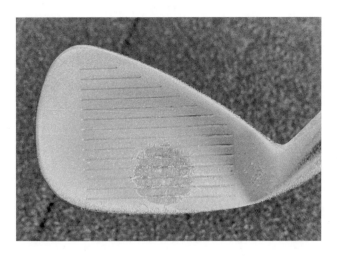

Another experiment I love to do is altering tee height. Start adjusting your tee in low, medium, and high positions. See how it changes your impact location on the driver's face (or other clubs you use off the tee). Your goal is to reduce strikes towards the bottom of the face and get them more towards the center or above it. Finding the correct tee height for your swing could help add 20 yards to your drives. No, I'm not kidding!

Changing tee height can influence your vertical impact location dramatically

Using physical barriers like tees can help improve your impact location. A good drill is to set two tees slightly wider than the width of your club – try clearing the gates with your practice swings and then while trying to hit a ball. Or you can experiment with a tee on one side of the ball, depending on where your misses are. My podcast co-host, Adam Young, also has great resources in his Strike Plan available on his website.

Lastly, you can challenge yourself to strike different parts of the club-face on purpose. Consciously try to hit the club's heel, center, and toe separately. If you're looking for bonus points, you can try Andrew Rice's drill, where you separate the driver's face into four quadrants and try to strike each one separately.

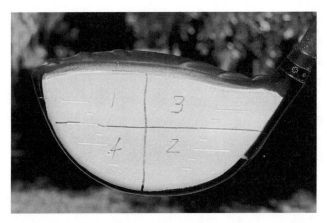

An advanced drill from Andrew Rice challenges golfers to strike each quadrant of the driver face

YOU'LL LIKELY BE SURPRISED

I think you'll be surprised what kind of results you'll see if you try any of these ideas or a mixture of them. Your goal as a golfer is to increase your ability to access the clubface center. When you are struggling, you want to find ways to self-correct.

All of you reading this are at different levels of ball-striking ability. Still, as always, my advice is to seek incremental improvement. Even if you succeed at hitting as little as 1-3 shots per round closer to the sweet spot, it could substantially reduce your scores.

Strike is king!

THE BIG IDEAS

- The golf world loves to focus on technical fundamentals such as grip, posture, alignment, and swing plane. While these are all important, there is no correct answer for all players.
- Learning to strike the center of the clubface closer to the sweet spot (center of gravity) is a fundamental skill that all golfers should work towards. Center strikes will lead to an

increase in distance and accuracy with every club in
your bag.

- Impact training should be an element of each kind of
practice you perform - it's one of the most critical methods.
- The first step is to use a method like spraying the face of
your club with foot spray and keeping track of where you are
making contact with the face. Look for any tendencies
towards one part of the face. Your goal is to learn what
different strikes (toe, center, heel) feel like without looking.
- There are two primary methods to train impact - learning to
strike different parts of the face on command and doing the
opposite of your current patterns. You can pursue a mixture
of both with all clubs.
- Strike is king - make impact practice one of your top
priorities!

CHAPTER 28
EXPERIMENTING WITH YOUR INNER CHILD

AS A JUNIOR GOLFER, I spent hours "playing" during my practice sessions. I'd hit all kinds of shots in the yard, experimenting with how I could manipulate the ball. At one point, I built a small driving range in my bedroom by draping a blanket over my closet. That experiment quickly ended when I hit an errant shot through the wall! At the time, I didn't know it, but all of the things that a child does during imaginative play were helping build my skills as a golfer.

Years later, as an adult, I don't have the free time or the playful mindset I did as a kid. But I've realized that I still need to embrace that creative and whimsical spirit in my golf game to keep improving. Most adult golfers struggle with similar limitations in their practice methods. In this chapter, I want to explore how experimentation, or 'play,' should be a part of your training.

EXPERIMENTATION CHECKS OFF MANY BOXES

There are several foundational practice concepts that I've come to believe in:

- Acquiring skills, rather than focusing so much on technique.
- Giving meaning to each shot.

- Adding randomness and variability.

Experimentation satisfies all of those requirements. It's also one of the most overlooked practice methods in the golf world. Almost no one talks about it.

The whole point of experimenting is not necessarily to build a new arsenal of shots or techniques to bring on the course. As you've gathered from the strategy section, I want you to do the opposite! Experimentation is more about expanding your skillset.

Some of the methods I suggest might seem a bit out there to you. You won't necessarily be repeating these shots on the golf course, either. However, if you give them a try, they will likely build your skills as a ball striker and problem solver. Becoming a better player requires a bit of artistry and creativity that most golfers don't prepare for.

One way I like to think of it is that you will start building multiple reference points in your golf swing. If you can begin to feel what certain extremes are with various impact fundamentals, it can allow you to improve your stock shots. Additionally, when things go awry on the course, you will be able to self correct more often.

WHAT DOES EXPERIMENTATION LOOK LIKE?

You can get very creative on your own, but here is a list of ideas to get you started in the right direction:

- Pick a target and try to hit several clubs to that distance. For example, choose the 125-yard practice green and hit your fairway metal, 5-iron, 7-iron, and 9-iron.
- Work the ball in both directions, and vary your trajectory. Try to hit a high slice or a low sweeping hook. Change the clubs you use and vary your ball position and swing technique to see what works best.
- Choose a target 10 yards away - try to hit the same wedge with a low, medium, and high trajectory.

- Spray your clubface with foot odor spray; try to consciously strike different parts of the face (heel, toe, low, high).
- Give yourself different lies in the rough and then try multiple wedge techniques to see how the ball reacts.
- If you can, practice hitting full shots from various lies on the course (sidehill, uphill/downhill, fairway bunkers, different lies in the rough). See how the ball reacts while making minor adjustments in your technique or setup.

Hopefully, those examples can get you started. I'm sure many of you will come up with ideas of your own. One suggestion would be to address a deficiency in your current game. Think about an area of your game that makes you uncomfortable and focus your experimentation there.

Another recommendation is to read Adam Young's book, *The Practice Manual.* He expands on this topic, motor learning, and plenty of other pillars of successful practice quite a bit. I consider it required reading for just about any golfer looking to improve. Listeners of our podcast, The Sweet Spot, will often hear us discuss this topic quite a bit.

HOW MUCH TIME SHOULD YOU DEVOTE TO EXPERIMENTATION?

I don't think there is a hard and fast rule for how much experimentation you should add to your practice sessions. Like anything else I discuss, I think a healthy dose is beneficial, but avoid going to extremes. For those who don't do any practice that resembles experimenting, devoting as little as 10% of your time can yield tangible results. Additionally, beginner and intermediate players can likely benefit from an even bigger investment of time.

It also might make sense to add experimentation to the end of a block practice session. Let's say you were working on your wedge game with 25-30 shots; you could devote the last five or six shots with some out-of-the-box thinking.

Or, if you are someone who has more time to practice and is doing it multiple times a week, one of those sessions (perhaps a shorter one) could be devoted to experimenting. I'm confident this method will help add some fun to your practice and make you a more well-rounded ball striker.

THE BIG IDEAS

- Devoting a portion of your practice sessions to experimental practice is a helpful exercise. Try to engage your playful, inner child.
- Trying to hit shots that you would not necessarily use on the course will help build your overall skill level.
- You can mix experimentation with other methods to challenge yourself and break the monotony of repetitive practice.

CHAPTER 29
"FIGHTING FIRE WITH FIRE" PRACTICE METHOD

I LOVE USING the word functional pertaining to the golf swing and ball-striking. So many golfers suffer from extremes when it comes to impact fundamentals. Whether it's their swing path, how they present the clubface, or the club's trajectory as it approaches the ball, many players need to move from extreme territory back to functional territory.

Golf can be a remarkably counterintuitive game. We're taught to perform the same technique repeatedly. As I mentioned in the blocked practice chapter, sometimes that repetition can ingrain poor swing habits. But what if going entirely off the script and doing the complete opposite of what you usually do can make you a better player?

I want to introduce you to a practice method that I think can add value to your sessions. It's not something you have to do all the time, but adding small doses of it can provide many benefits, especially when you are struggling with controlling your ball flight. I like to call it the "fight fire with fire" method. You'll notice this approach will become a recurring theme throughout the practice section - I strongly believe in it!

HOW OPPOSITES CAN FIGHT EXTREMES

Several years ago, I was invited to play in the Goslings Invitational Tournament in Bermuda. Before the tournament began, we had a pro-am on Monday. I was paired with two athletes I had watched on TV for years, and another golfer who (as luck would have it) was a follower of Practical Golf.

I was a little more nervous than usual before the round. I felt a lot of pressure to play well that week because the guy who invited me (now a close friend) used one of his invites on the premise that I was supposed to be a pretty good player. Also, I had never played golf with any celebrity before, which threw me for a little bit of a loop.

Unfortunately, after not having played in over a month, my swing was really out of whack. Typically, if I'm struggling, it will be hooking the ball. That day it was far worse than usual. I hit duck hooks for the first six holes and was utterly dumbfounded. Luckily, my teammate, a former Cy-Young Award winner, carried me in our match with 330-yard drives and birdies.

I decided to do the only thing I could think of with embarrassment mounting – try to hit a huge slice. So before each shot, I used a drill that a friend of mine had given me years ago. I pointed my feet towards the target and rehearsed an extremely exaggerated out-to-in swing path. Perhaps I looked foolish, but it worked like magic and saved the rest of the round (and week).

In reality, what the drill was doing was shifting my swing path. What felt like a huge slice swing was moving my extreme club path back to a functional state.

UNDERSTANDING YOUR TENDENCIES

Many golfers say they want more consistency. But in reality, most players are remarkably consistent with how they deliver the golf club. This could be any of the following categories:

- Club path (out-to-in or in-to-out)
- Impact location (toe or heel bias)
- Turf Interaction (controlling the low point of the club)
- The loft of club at impact (adding loft or delofting)

A lot of players I watch are consistently fighting extremes. I'm no different. For example – I draw the ball, deloft the club, have a shallow angle of attack with irons, and have a heel-bias clubface strike. When any of these impact factors get extreme, I have to intervene during my practice sessions or on the course.

I've found that doing the exact opposite, or "fighting fire with fire," can help neutralize the problem.

The best place to start is knowing your tendencies. You can measure your impact location, work with a teaching professional, use a shot-tracking system, or even use a launch monitor (with the help of an instructor) to understand the inclinations in your swing.

HOW YOU CAN FIGHT FIRE WHILE YOU PRACTICE

Luckily, this practice method is pretty simple. The goal is to get you to do a little self-exploration and get outside of your comfort zone. Broadly speaking, I want you to do the exact opposite of what you seem to struggle with.

Here are a few examples:

- If you're striking it too close to the club's heel, consciously try to hit the toe (measure with foot spray).
- Are you struggling with a nasty slice? Try to hit the biggest hook imaginable.
- Is your ball flight typically too high? What can you do in your setup and golf swing to keep the ball lower?
- If your shots are starting in one direction (push or pull), see if you can start the ball in the opposite direction on a series of shots.

- Do you hit your iron shots fat? Try consciously striking the ground several inches in front of the ball during practice.

While I can't account for all of your results, I think many of you will see some exciting things happen when you do this. Going back and forth between practicing extremes and then trying to hit the ball "normally" might reduce many of the problems you have in your swing.

Overall, I like this kind of practice because it helps build your skill. Too many golfers try to fit into some model swing and make their technique look a certain way. However, what's most important is your inherent skills as a ball-striker – not what it looks like.

Also, this form of practice will allow you to start finding fixes for swing flaws that arise while you play. If you can learn to identify when your impact fundamentals are getting extreme and neutralize the issue, you will be gaining one of the most critical golf skills.

THE BIG IDEAS

- **Becoming a better ball striker is often about fighting extremes in your swing. Learning to bring all of the impact fundamentals together into functional territory is one of the game's great challenges.**
- **Understanding what your tendencies are is crucial.**
- **A powerful practice method is to try to do the exact opposite of your faults. For many, this can neutralize the core issue.**

CHAPTER 30
TEMPO TRAINING

ONE OF THE great joys as a golfer is to marvel at the swings of the best players. Legends of the game like Ernie Els and Fred Couples come to mind because of their smooth, effortless swings. It looks like they're not even trying. But they are trying and swinging the club at speeds that ordinary golfers couldn't dream of.

Then how does it look so smooth and easy? A lot of it has to do with the timing of their swing and the relationship between their backswing and downswing. It turns out that tempo is one of the best secrets of the golf swing. Also, I believe practicing tempo is one of the most effective tools for any golfer.

You'll often hear advice like "slow down, and swing smoothly." In theory, it makes sense. But it's not about swinging slower - I've come to believe that's one of the worst pieces of advice anyone could give to a player. It's more about finding a repeatable timing to your swing and training it.

I want to tell you a little story about how I discovered the concept of swing tempo, why it can be so powerful, and effective ways to practice it.

THE CONNECTION BETWEEN THE GREATS

If you look at still images of the best golfers in the world, you'll see different techniques. Their hands are in various places throughout the swing. Some take the club way past parallel at the top like Bubba Watson. Others have very short backswings like John Rahm. Despite thousands of golf instructors' best efforts, there is still no right way to swing a golf club from a technical standpoint. That's the beauty of this game; there is more than one way to get it done.

But what if I told you that most of the all-time greats did have something in common? You'd probably be interested in finding out what it is and trying to copy it.

It turns out it's their swing tempo.

JOHN NOVOSEL AND TOUR TEMPO

In the year 2000, John Novosel was editing the swing of a professional golfer for an infomercial. As a small test, he measured how many frames it took for the golfer to get to the top of their swing and then to the bottom. The calculation arrived at precisely a 3 to 1 ratio. He wasn't moved by this initially. The prevailing wisdom about tempo was that each golfer had their unique timing, and nothing unified them from player to player.

He then looked at Tiger Woods' swing from the 1997 Masters. It also had the same ratio, 3:1. He became a little more curious and started analyzing the swings of all of the best players in the game's history - Jack Nicklaus, Gary Player, Arnold Palmer, Sam Snead, Tom Waston, and Byron Nelson. They were all 3 to 1. It was as if he had discovered the Rosetta Stone of golf.

In 2004 he published his findings in the best-selling book *Tour Tempo*, and then again in 2011 with *Tour Tempo 2* (which offered an update with the short game). He also has created various training aids, the most popular being his series of tones that golfers can use to help hone their tempos. I did not stumble upon John's findings until around 2016. I'm thrilled I did because understanding the concept of tempo has made me a better ball striker and plenty of readers of Practical Golf as well.

THE PHYSICIST

For several years, a playing partner of mine was a former physics professor at Yale. His name is Dr. Bob Grober.

Bob, as you would imagine, is a brilliant guy. He also happens to be a phenomenal golfer. Bob played collegiate golf at Vanderbilt. When he realized that he wouldn't turn professional, he devoted himself to physics.

He has done some fascinating work throughout the years, combining his love of golf with physics. Lucky for me (and a HUGE coincidence), Bob published an academic study on swing tempo in 2012 after conducting experiments at the Yale lab and with various teachers and students across the country. It is the only scientific research that has been done on a golfer's swing tempo to date. The paper is entitled "Towards a Biomechanical Understanding of Tempo in the Golf Swing." If you are interested, you can find the full version by doing a Google search. I'll have to warn you, it features some heavy math, but it's fascinating.

Dr. Grober studied the tempos of three groups: touring professionals, teaching professionals/low-handicap amateurs, and average players. Looking at the data, Bob proved what John Novosel first found out almost ten years prior. The touring pros had an average ratio of 3:1. They were within a tight range of each other, meaning that their swings were very repeatable.

Not surprisingly, the last group of average players exhibited far more significant differences in their ratios. They were all over the place. He concluded that the best golfers at their core have a remarkably uniform "biomechanical clock." In many ways, John Novosel's findings were validated.

WHY ISN'T TEMPO MORE IMPORTANT IN THE GOLF WORLD?

John Garrity was the co-author of both Tour Tempo books. He has been a veteran of *Sports Illustrated* for more than 30 years and has covered golf for most of his professional life. He was kind enough to speak with me on the phone, and I gained some interesting information from him.

Many teaching professionals had courted John to co-write instructional books through the years. Sports psychologists and swing pros would routinely contact him to see if he was interested in collaborating with them. Every time he would turn them down because he felt it was more of the same swing tips that had been regurgitated for years.

When John Novosel first contacted Garrity about the Tour Tempo books, he assumed he was another guy who claimed he had the golf swing figured out. Since they both lived in Kansas City, he agreed to take a lunch meeting with Novosel. After 15 minutes of seeing his research, he knew that he wanted to collaborate with him because it was something different that no one had explored before.

I asked John Garrity why the 3:1 ratio was not more popular in the golf world. The book was a fantastic success when it first came out and instantly became the best-selling sports book that year on Amazon. If players were so successful using the tones, why isn't every golfer listening to them on the driving range right now?

John believes that the findings were taken seriously at the professional level. Several famous teachers approached him while he was covering PGA events, and they congratulated him on the work that he and Novosel had done.

While he can't prove his theory completely, he believes that many pros had begun to speed up their swings by using the tones. Players registered at a 27/9 ratio were now moving down to a 24/8. Those who were previously at a 24/8 had moved down to the 21/7. Novosel and his team proved this by analyzing their swings using television footage, and they felt that it could not be a coincidence.

Now many young touring pros are measuring lightning speeds of 18/6. Garrity believes that once the players figured out they could speed up their swings while maintaining the proper swing tempo, they started to add considerable distance while maintaining control.

Personally, I believe that the golfing establishment has not embraced John Novosel's findings because he is an outsider. If David Leadbetter or Butch Harmon had figured this out, you would see more teachers trying to perfect their student's tempos using the tones.

HOW TO PRACTICE YOUR SWING TEMPO

Alright, let's get down to specifics. There are a few different ways to practice your tempo and measure it. I should caution you that this isn't magic, and it won't work for every golfer. That being said, it's been an invaluable practice tool for me, and many readers of my website have told me how powerful it's been for their golf swing.

The first step is working with the tones from the Tour Tempo app (you can find it on most app stores through your phone, which costs $24.99).

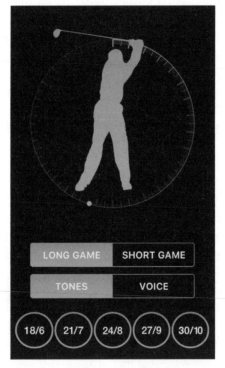

The Tour Tempo App

The app uses a series of beats to represent your swing's beginning, top, and impact. They are all timed in a 3:1 ratio (backswing to downswing). There are also several different speeds ranging from slow to fast. Although pro golfers take much less time to complete their back-swings and downswings, they can still maintain a consistent ratio between the two. Recreational players can still have the same ratios but take more time overall because they are not swinging at the same speed.

Depending on the current tempo of your swing, it might make sense to start with the slower beats and work your way to one that feels more comfortable. It may feel awkward at first. My recommendation is to remain patient.

I like this form of practice because it helps fix the timing of your swing, and it allows you to stop obsessing about the mechanics involved. Many golfers (myself included) notice that focusing on the tempo beats enables their swing to self-organize naturally.

The most common fault I see amongst recreational golfers is a back-swing that is way too slow. It usually results in them trying to guide the club, and a ton of bizarre movements occur along the way. When many of those golfers were able to quicken the timing of their back-swing, a lot of those moves disappeared because they were not actively trying to steer the club. Another typical benefit is that their swing speed will increase, and they can hit the ball farther.

If you want to take your tempo training a step further, you can validate your results to see where you stand. Tour Tempo does have an addi-tional app that will allow you to video your swing and track your tempo by looking at the frame rates.

I have found a couple of other methods that are a little easier but will require further investment. Currently, Garmin has two GPS watches with a tempo training feature - the Approach S60 and Approach S62. A helpful feature is that it also tracks your tempo on the golf course. I have often seen that my backswing gets much slower during rounds, and being able to adjust over the years has led to better results.

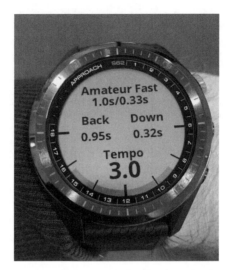

The Garmin S62 Approach Watch in Tempo Mode

There were plenty of swing analyzers on the market that also measured swing tempo for a while. However, many of them are no longer in business. One that is still currently on the market is from Blast Golf.

If you can verify your swing tempo, you should practice with the beats and then without. You want to see how the results are transferring over. First, take notice of what your current tempo is. Many of you will likely see that your ratios are a bit random. When I started training, I would see ratios from around 3.8:1 (my backswing was too slow) down to 3:1.

Experiment with different speeds and keep track of your ball flight. For some, 27/9 might be appropriate. Others might find better success with faster intervals around 21/7. There is no right or wrong tempo or speed. You are looking to get a more repeatable timing in your golf swing. After years of tempo training, I have settled on having a 2.8:1 - 3:1 ratio in my swing and using the 21/7 beats. You don't necessarily need to have 3:1 as your exact goal; I would settle on a tempo that you can repeat consistently, leading to better ball flight results.

Another benefit of tempo training is in your short game. There are also a series of beats in the 2:1 ratio with finesse wedge shots and putting.

Golfers who experience the dreaded yips and various other problems can experiment with these to get their minds off the mechanics and free their bodies to execute.

Overall, I believe tempo training is one of the best-kept practice secrets for golfers. I highly recommend it if you want to add structure and meaning to your practice sessions.

THE BIG IDEAS

- **All great golfers have various techniques - none of their swings look the same. John Novosel discovered that most of them have similar timing, though, and the ratio of their backswing to downswing is usually around 3:1.**
- **Tempo training can be a powerful method for a golfer of any level. It gets their mind off mechanics, increases swing speed, and improves their ball striking consistency.**
- **Experimenting with different tempo ratios and settling on a speed that gives you the best ball-striking results is an excellent practice method. If you can, verify your tempo through video frame rates or a separate device to keep track of your progress.**

CHAPTER 31
GATHERING THE PROPER FEEDBACK

SINCE GOLF IS a game that continually changes and presents us with variables each time we play, it is crucially important to pay attention to the proper feedback during practice. Without feedback, you can't make the necessary adjustments to get back to my favorite phrase, functional territory. While practicing, many golfers either aren't paying attention or don't know what to look for, and hopefully, I can point you in the right direction.

So what should you pay attention to while you practice? Look no further than impact fundamentals and ball flight. If you are aware of what to look for, you can work backward, make adjustments during your practice sessions, and eventually, on the golf course.

Focusing on this feedback is far more productive than aimlessly making swing changes. In other words, stop worrying so much about the aesthetics of your golf swing. I want you to pay more attention to variables like impact location, ground contact, start direction, curvature, and the trajectory of your ball flight. Your focus here will be far more productive than worrying about how the top of your backswing looks on camera.

I'm going to cover quite a bit in this chapter, and for some, you might need to re-read it several times. But I genuinely believe that if you start to understand many of these concepts, you will begin to coach yourself more effectively and hone your skill.

IMPACT LOCATION

No matter what club you are using, where you strike the ball on the face is perhaps the most important feedback you can receive on any shot. As loft decreases, impact gets more critical, especially with hybrids, fairway woods, and your driver (gear effect becomes more of an issue).

You'll notice that I discuss impact quite a bit in the practice section because it's pretty important. If you can learn to access the center of the face, closer to each club's sweet spot, you will allow the golf club to do what it's designed to do.

Being mindful of your impact location on each shot is often the most crucial piece of feedback. Most golfers have no idea where they are striking it on the face. And it's as easy as spraying the face with foot spray or marking the golf ball with a dry erase pen. After a while, you'll be able to diagnose your impact just by feel and sound.

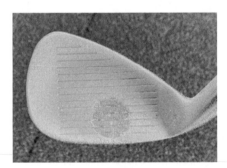

Most importantly, learning to self-correct impact location will make you a better ball striker and lower your handicap.

GROUND CONTACT

Evaluating ground contact (also known as turf interaction) is tricky. It's one of the most critical impact fundamentals but usually the hardest to get proper feedback. Ground contact influences scoring tremendously with your fairway woods, hybrids, irons, and wedges. We all know the pain of chunking a 7-iron from the middle of the fairway and watching the ball travel 20 yards in front of you. But if you can't diagnose your tendencies while you practice, it becomes challenging to make the proper adjustments.

Ideally, we want to strike the golf ball first and then the turf. When grass and debris get caught between the golf ball and the face of the club, it reduces the ability to generate the proper amount of spin. As such, your ball flight will suffer.

There is a pervasive myth that golfers need to take enormous divots to become better wedge and iron players. It's just not true. Golfers should strive to avoid extremes by initiating ground contact too far behind the ball or too far in front. That is usually the most significant battle. The depth and size of your divots can vary based on many other factors, and there is no one-size-fits-all.

Ground contact feedback is much easier if you have access to a grass driving range. It's more straightforward to feel, see, and hear. You can use some enhanced techniques, like spraying a line across the ball position with foot spray or even placing a tee beside your ball. Then you can keep track of your divot patterns in relation to the initial position of the golf ball. Though divots can be misleading, it's still mostly good feedback on overall ground contact patterns.

Using a tee as a reference point can give valuable feedback on divot patterns

Using foot spray can also give you a visual reference point

But I'm sure most of you do not have access to grass driving ranges. They are harder to maintain, cost more, and seem to be dwindling over the years. So many of us are stuck with an imperfect solution - artificial turf.

Driving range mats do not provide accurate ground contact feedback. You could strike the ground several inches behind the ball and still hit a decent shot. But if you were out on the course, you'd likely chunk it, and the ball would land well short of your target.

Skilled golfers can get better at knowing if they are making ball first contact on artificial turf, but it's more of a struggle for intermediate to beginner players. However, I found a product called the Divot Board. It is one of the few training aids I recommend to almost every player.

It's a small mat that you can use at the range or at home that gives crystal clear feedback on where you made contact with the ground.

The Divot Board is an excellent product to get ground contact feedback when practicing on artificial turf

I'd recommend it to any golfer looking to improve their ground contact, and there are similar products on the market, though I have found their visual feedback is not as clear.

Another method used by many teaching professionals is to place a towel several inches behind your golf ball. If you contact the towel, you'll know you have hit too far behind the ball. Depending on your skill level, you can adjust how close or far it is positioned.

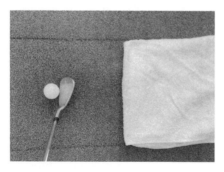

Overall, paying attention to ground contact, especially with your irons and wedges, can lead to significant scoring breakthroughs. It's a skill you need to work on consciously.

FACE TO PATH RELATIONSHIP

I will warn you; this will probably be the most complicated part of the entire book. You might need to re-read this section several times. But I believe knowing why the golf ball starts in one direction and how it curves through the air is essential. Managing the relationship between your club path and face angle at impact is a battle that never ends in golf. I believe having better information will help you diagnose your impact conditions. Looking at your ball flight, and working backward, can help neutralize issues you are having.

I will do my best to keep this as simple as possible!

Face Angle

Face Angle is the direction the clubface is pointed (right or left) at impact and is measured relative to the target line.

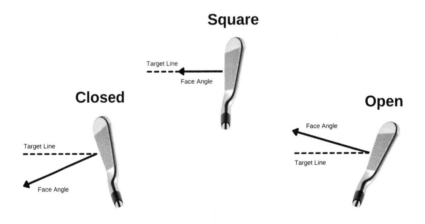

Throughout the past 25 years, I've likely hit hundreds of thousands of golf balls. I didn't fully understand why the ball started in a specific direction and curved in another for most of that period. Like many of you, when I initially took up golf, I was given information that turned out to be incorrect. Over time, as I became a better ball striker, I started to understand ball flight laws intuitively. And once I finally learned them, a lightbulb went on. When people ask me what it took to become a scratch golfer, my simple answer now is, "I learned to control the face of the club at impact."

A lot of scoring in golf is determined by your lateral dispersion. On tee shots, if you're missing too far to the left or right, you are losing golf balls, ending up in recovery situations, and costing yourself tons of strokes. The same is true for approach shots - missing the green in either direction gets penalized by bunkers, rough, and the undulations of the course. Tightening that dispersion and removing many of those "uh oh" shots was the key to lowering my scores. In other words, I was learning to control my face angle more effectively.

Where the clubface is pointing at impact (closed, open, square) is the most significant influence on where the golf ball starts. We used to think the path of the club was responsible for where the ball initially started. Now we know that club path plays a much smaller role.

As loft decreases, face angle becomes even more influential on start direction. But no matter what club you are hitting, it will have roughly 65% - 80% influence on the ball's initial direction. So if you hit a massive block to the right or pull to the left off the tee, you can know that face angle was the main culprit.

The other reason why face angle is so important is its relationship to the path of the club at impact. No matter what direction your club is traveling through the impact zone (in-to-out or out-to-in), you have an opportunity to create a functional curvature of the ball by controlling the face angle. You can think of it as the glue that holds things together at impact.

You are going to hear me say over and over again that avoiding extremes is the key to hitting better golf shots. This concept is perhaps most important when it comes to clubface control. It's almost impossible to see significant reductions in scoring without having better control over face angle. In other words, you are working towards avoiding a clubface that is either way too open or closed at impact.

Like impact location, having face angle awareness and training this skill is crucial. One of my favorite practice methods is experimenting with face angle and start direction. You can take a lower-lofted club like your driver, or even a mid-iron, and see if you can start the ball to the right, left, and then straight down the target line. Cycling back and forth between these will help build reference points in your golf swing. Eventually, if you get skilled enough, you can start making adjustments when you see specific patterns in your ball flight.

For example, when I notice I am missing most of my targets to the right, I know that I need to find a way to get the clubface a little more closed at impact. Or the opposite could be true, and when I'm pulling shots to the left, now I need to get the face a little more open. Because I have trained this skill, I can make these changes more effectively to mitigate the problems I see.

Most golfers don't even consider this skill or pay attention to this feedback while they practice. You should place a significant amount of emphasis on your clubface awareness!

Club Path

Another crucial impact condition that gives the golf ball its marching orders is the club path. It is defined as the direction of the clubhead at impact relative to the target line. Like face angle, there are three possibilities - in-to-out, out-to-in, and zero.

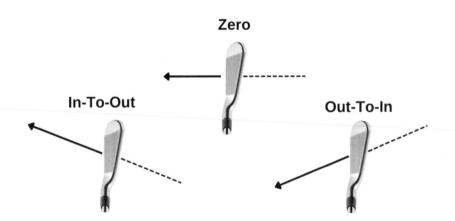

Club path is primarily responsible for the curvature of the golf ball. Your path will need to be out-to-in to hit fades (hopefully not slices) and in-to-out for draws for a right-handed golfer. A straight shot down the target line would require a club path of zero.

Speaking with many instructors through the years and observing golfers myself, a golfer's club path tends to be more consistent compared to face angle. The curvature of their shots usually follows one pattern. But how much the ball curves and where it starts, is all due to the relationship between face angle and club path. This is perhaps one of the most important concepts to understand.

The Anatomy of a Straight Shot

I find it is best to start the discussion with straight ball flights. If you wanted to hit a perfectly straight shot, your face angle would need to be square to the target, and the club path would need to be zero.

Straight Shot

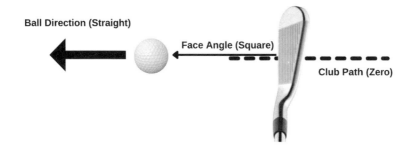

I have only watched one golfer in my life hit perfectly straight shots in person; his name is Adam Scott. He is arguably one of the best ball strikers in the game's history, so I don't believe it is a viable strategy to pursue a straight ball flight. In my opinion, it is too difficult to have perfect control of the face angle and club path on every swing.

If you have been playing golf long enough, you've likely witnessed shots that travel straight to the right of your target or left of it without any curvature. We usually refer to them as a push or a pull. In most cases, your club path and face angle were perfectly aligned.

Push

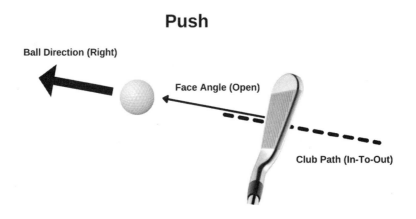

For example, if your club path and face angle were 5 degrees to the right of your target line, you would hit a shot that goes precisely in that direction. And the opposite would be true for a closed face and club path that were perfectly aligned. So when you see these shots on the practice range or the course, they are excellent indicators of your club path.

Pull

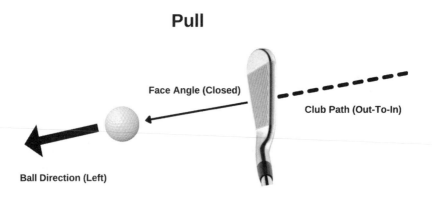

Fades and Slices

Here is where things get more complicated. As the face angle and club path begin to move away from one another, we start to see the ball curve more and more. Since most golfers struggle with slicing the ball with their driver, let's start here.

The anatomy of a slice usually starts with an excessive out-to-in swing path. Many instructors would say anything beyond 6 degrees is where you begin to get into "extreme territory."

So let's say you swing your driver 8 degrees out-to-in relative to your target line. This club path will primarily be responsible for the left-to-right curvature of the golf ball. We now must combine face angle to see where the ball will start and how much it will curve through the air.

Many golfers are told to square their club face to the target at impact, but let me show you why this can be a bad idea. In this scenario, if you presented the face at impact perfectly square to your target line, now we have two problems:

1. Because the difference between the path of the club and face angle is so significant, you will have more curvature on the ball moving from left to right.
2. Since the clubface angle is primarily responsible for where the ball starts, especially with your driver, your shot starts slightly left of your target (swing path has a minor influence on start direction) and curves further to the right.

And here we have a classic slice:

Slice

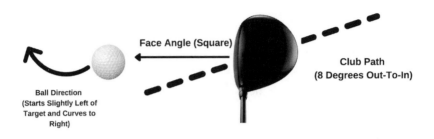

Face Angle (Square)

**Club Path
(8 Degrees Out-To-In)**

**Ball Direction
(Starts Slightly Left of
Target and Curves to
Right)**

Target Line

As the separation between club path and face angle becomes more extensive, the bigger the issue. For example, if you kept the swing path 8 degrees out-to-in, and started presenting the clubface even further to the right at impact, now you will have shots that start to the right of your target and slice even more. Yikes!

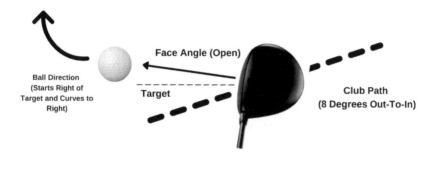

Face Angle (Open)

Ball Direction
(Starts Right of
Target and Curves to
Right)

Target

Club Path
(8 Degrees Out-To-In)

Target Line

So how do you turn a slice into a controlled fade? For the sake of simplicity, I'll give you two options for this theoretical golfer. Though the answer can be a blend of both:

1. Reduce the extremity of the swing path.
2. Get your clubface pointing between the target and club path.

To hit functional fades, the face of the club must be pointing some-where in between the club path and the target line. If you keep your swing path of 8 degrees out-to-in, your clubface would need to point somewhere left of your target but right of the swing path. That will allow the ball to start to the left of the target but curve back towards it.

Functional Fade

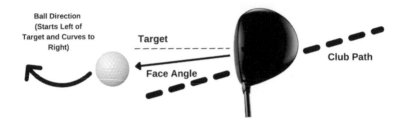

Ball Direction (Starts Left of Target and Curves to Right)

Target

Club Path

Face Angle

Target Line

Many would say that to have more control over the ball, you would need to reduce the extremity of your swing path. For example, learning to swing closer to 4 degrees out-to-in would reduce the left-to-right curvature of the ball. Either way, your clubface will still need to be pointing somewhere between the club's path and target line to hit a functional fade.

Many slicers try to do the opposite to fix the issue. They will try to swing more to the left, thinking they will start the ball further left of their target. Unfortunately, this pours more gasoline onto the fire - and we now have a banana slice. As someone who struggles with an excessive swing path in the opposite direction, my philosophy is to try and neutralize issues.

A good rule of thumb is to have somewhere around a 2:1 ratio of your club path and face orientation with lower lofted clubs. So if the path of your driver is 6 degrees out-to-in, having the face 3 degrees open relative to the club path would give you a nice fade that starts left of your target and curves back. But to be honest, you don't need to worry about the numbers. I'd rather you have a more intuitive understanding when watching your ball flight.

Draws and Hooks

You can take everything I just said and reverse it for hooks and draws. When you have an in-to-out path, your club face will need to be closed in relation to the path to put a right-to-left curvature on the ball.

This image represents how a golfer would hit a hook off the tee that starts somewhere around the target but quickly turns to the left - noting the significant separation between the club path and face angle.

Hook

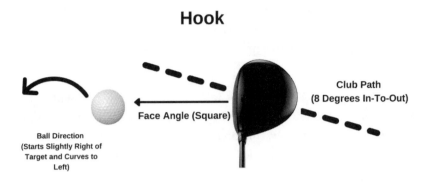

Club Path
(8 Degrees In-To-Out)

Face Angle (Square)

Ball Direction
(Starts Slightly Right of
Target and Curves to
Left)

Target Line

To turn that hook into a draw, the golfer must learn to present the club-face somewhere between the club path and the target line.

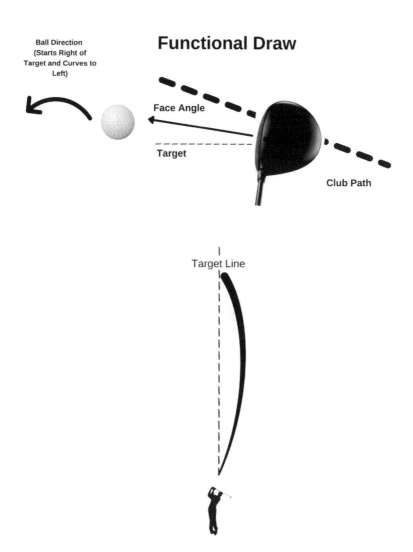

Functional Draw

Ball Direction
(Starts Right of
Target and Curves to
Left)

Face Angle

Target

Club Path

Target Line

One Exception (the nastiest ball flight)

I encourage you to keep re-reading the prior section to understand how the face/path relationship works. If you are a more visual learner, you can even go to YouTube - search for "The Royalty of Shot Shape." It's a great video from Andrew Rice explaining these concepts using chess pieces.

The dreaded pull-hook and push-slice are the most problematic shots on the course. They wreck scores. But when you see them, they are often confusing to diagnose and sometimes contradict the conditions for fades and draws. Hang on tight, and read this part slowly.

Let's go back to our golfer with the out-to-in swing path. In most instances, this will result in a curvature in the opposite direction (left-to-right) because the face of the club is usually pointing somewhere to the right of the club path. However, there is one scenario where you can hit a hook with an out-to-in club path. It's when the face of the club points to the left of the club path.

Here is an image explaining how you can hit a pull-hook with an out-to-in club path:

Pull Hook

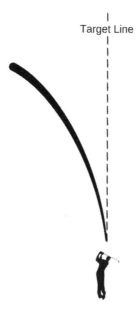

And the reverse is true for a push-slice, a shot that starts right and curves even further right.

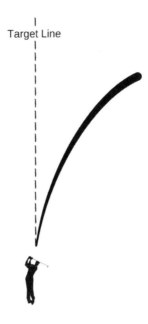

Target Line

So if you start seeing pull hooks or push slices on the course, it can be confusing because it doesn't necessarily indicate what your club path always is. The easiest solution I can give you is that it's primarily a face-angle problem. Your clubface is pointing way too far to the left if you are hitting a pull hook. And if you see a push-slice, your clubface is pointing way too far to the right. This is why controlling where your clubface is pointing at impact is such a vital skill - it can avoid the big mistake swings.

Sometimes, these shots result from a golfer trying to do the opposite shot shape of what they are used to. For example, my natural shot shape is a draw. I am very comfortable swinging in-to-out and presenting the clubface somewhere between my target and swing path. However, when I try to shift my club path in the opposite direction to hit a fade, it can confuse me so much that the face angle points way too far to the left. So instead of hitting a nice fade, I get a pull hook. We often refer to this shot as the "double-cross." It's one of the main reasons I don't advocate golfers trying to play two different shot shapes on the course, which you will hear me talk about several times throughout the book.

DELIVERED LOFT AND ANGLE OF ATTACK

One of the great myths in golf is that you need to "hit down on the ball to make it go up." Many players believe (especially with irons) that they require a very steep angle of attack. It simply isn't true. I spent hours on the driving range as a kid slamming my irons into the mat with this advice. When I got on to the course, it made me chunk the ball more with irons.

The honest answer is far more straightforward. The loft of your club at impact is primarily responsible for making the ball go up in the air. How steep or shallow your club approaches the ball will somewhat influence it, but how you deliver the club's loft is far more critical.

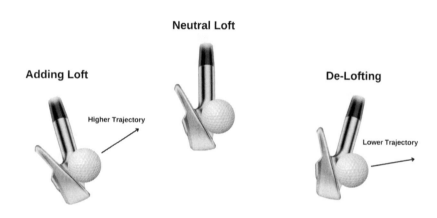

However, the loft on your golf club is just a starting point. The golf ball has no idea what club you're using; it responds to its loft orientation at impact. Let's say I have a wedge that is 56 degrees; I can either add loft at impact and turn that into a 60-degree wedge or remove loft and deliver 50 degrees of loft.

There are a few ways to do this. For many, moving the ball back in your stance will reduce delivered loft, and moving it up in your stance will do the opposite and add loft. Additionally, how your hands are oriented at impact and the resulting shaft lean will also influence delivered loft. If your hands are ahead of the ball at impact, the club's shaft will lean forward and deloft the face at impact. Conversely, you will add loft if your hands are behind the ball.

While this book is not about the golf swing, knowing this information and experimenting with things like ball position and where your hands are at impact can be beneficial to fixing some of your ball flight issues. For example, many golfers add too much loft and have their hands behind the ball at impact. Learning to have neutral or a slight forward shaft lean can help them "compress" the ball more at impact and hit more powerful iron shots. As you will see in the coming driver practice chapter, ball position can help launch the ball higher for more distance.

**Reverse Shaft Lean -
Adding Loft**

Neutral Shaft Lean

**Forward Shaft Lean -
De-Lofting**

Your hand position, and the corresponding shaft lean can heavily influence how you deliver the loft of the club, which will help determine the trajectory and quality of your shots.

It's up for debate whether a player should deliver the golf club in a neutral position or with some amount of shaft lean. However, going in the opposite direction, where your hands are behind the ball at impact, is something all golfers should avoid. This is not a functional impact position - you will add too much loft, and plenty of other impact fundamentals will suffer. If you feel like you are hitting shots that are way too high, then filming your golf swing head-on and seeing where your hands are in relation to the golf ball at impact might be even more valuable feedback. This problem is quite common.

Just know that you don't need to do anything excessive to make the ball go up in the air; the golf club will take care of most of it!

You won't see me talk about attack angle much in this book other than how to practice with your driver.

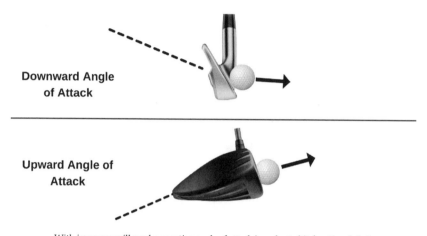

With irons you will need a negative angle of attack in order to hit functional shots. However, golfers with slower swing speeds should be cautious about getting too steep. Conversely, with your driver, working towards an upward angle of attack can unlock a lot of distance potential.

When it comes to your irons and wedges, many golfers believe they need to have a very negative angle of attack to spin the ball more and help it into the air. This just isn't true. Striking the ball closer to the center of the face and how you deliver the club's loft will take care of that mostly. If anything, most golfers need a more shallow descent because their swing speeds are slower than the pros.

SWING SPEED

I have changed my mind a lot on swing speed. For years, swing speed was an afterthought, and something that we assumed was fixed and couldn't be changed. You were either naturally gifted with a lot of swing speed, and if you weren't, you just had to go on the course with what you had.

I now view swing speed as a skill no different from controlling where you strike the ball on the clubface or how you manage the face-to-path relationship. We have a much better understanding of what creates speed and how to train for it.

There are a few ways to explore swing speed. In the wedge game, where distance control becomes more important, your ability to dial-up or dial down your swing speed is crucial. Many of us refer to this as "feel." If you have a wedge shot from 35 yards, you will have to apply a different swing speed than 70 yards.

With approach clubs, where you are taking a full swing, swing speed becomes more fixed. I still believe adjusting your swing speed to add distance or take some away depending on the situation is valuable, but it won't need to vary nearly as much with finesse wedge shots.

With tee shots, the upper limits of your speed become more important. You can think of swing speed as potential. A golfer who can swing their driver 110 mph has more potential to score lower than a golfer who swings it 90 mph. The former can drive it close to 280-300 yards or more, and the latter will be closer to 220-240 yards. That difference in distance is worth significant strokes.

However, it doesn't always work out that way. The golfer with more swing speed can be so wild off the tee that it is not a scoring advantage. And players with less speed can make up scoring in other parts of the game like their iron play or putting. But if you can learn to increase your swing speed the right way, many good things generally happen. You will have shorter clubs on approach shots, thereby improving your proximity to the hole. Also, your ability to hit higher iron shots that land softly on the green or get the ball out of difficult lies in the rough increases.

I will explore how to train for increased swing speed in a separate chapter, but it is an important piece of feedback that should be considered.

PUTTING FEEDBACK ALL TOGETHER: WHERE IS THE BALL ENDING UP?

It might sound almost too basic, but you have to pay attention to where your golf ball finishes relative to your target. This is the final piece of feedback. Along with how the ball flies through the air, your impact location, and ground contact, this helps tie everything together.

Depending on which club you are practicing with, the types of feedback you pay attention to will change. Driver practice won't look the same as wedge practice. For example, ground contact is not an issue when teeing up your driver but becomes far more critical with wedge practice.

Essentially, when practicing, you want to go through a mini checklist after each shot and ask yourself the following questions:

- Where did the ball land in relation to my intended target?
- How was the strike? Did you access the center of the face? If not, can you diagnose which part of the face the ball made contact with?
- How was ground contact? Did you achieve ball first, then turf interaction? Did you make contact with the ground too far behind or in front of the ball?
- How was the curvature of the shot? Was it excessive or functional?
- Where did the ball initially start? Did it match up well with the curvature of the shot and reach your target? Or did you start it too far left or to the right?
- How was the initial trajectory of the shot? Did it seem too low or too high?

All of this feedback help create the building blocks for every type of practice. Shifting your focus more towards these concepts will enhance the effectiveness of your training.

THE BIG IDEAS

- Shifting your focus to the proper feedback during practice sessions gives golfers more accurate information on making adjustments. This is more productive than haphazardly working on swing aesthetics.
- Focusing on impact fundamentals gives you plenty of valuable information. Face contact, ground contact, clubface angle, swing path, and delivered loft are all helpful.
- After each shot, go through a quick checklist to evaluate how the ball traveled relative to your intended target. Can you identify the piece of feedback that played the biggest role?

CHAPTER 32
DRIVER PRACTICE

IN THE PAST, we referred to shorter clubs as "scoring clubs" (and many still do). But as I learned more about advanced statistics and shed my preconceived notions about scoring, I now believe that the driver is perhaps the singular most critical scoring club for many golfers. Golf becomes easier if you can learn to embrace your driver, hit it farther, and keep it in play. Conversely, you can inflict quite a bit of damage on your scores with errant tee shots. The good news is every golfer has an opportunity to do this relative to their experience and skill level.

I've been fortunate enough to play with many great players. I can't think of one of them that wasn't efficient with their driver. And they all used it as much as possible. But like many of you, I used to fear my driver and looked for any excuse to avoid using it off the tee. I didn't realize it at the time, but I was losing a scoring battle for two reasons:

1. Keeping it in the bag on holes where it was the correct strategic decision made me lose strokes because I would face longer approach shots.
2. When I did use it, I wasn't fully committed and made a lot of scared swings.

But there is hope! Through the years, via many practice methods I'll share, my driver has gone from my most feared club to my most beloved. That doesn't mean I have complete control over where the ball is going, and there are many days when I struggle. But I am committed to using it whenever I can and living with the results.

This isn't an easy task, but putting in the right driver practice can yield massive jumps in scoring potential, whether a beginner or an advanced player.

This chapter will share everything I know about becoming more efficient with the driver through smarter practice methods and understanding ball flight basics.

THE RECIPE FOR DISTANCE

Hitting the ball farther with your driver is fun and will lower your scores. And the best part is that no matter what your starting point is, there is usually an opportunity for gains through strike efficiency, swing speed upgrades, or a mixture of both.

But what creates maximum driver distance? It's predominantly a mixture of three factors - ball speed, launch angle, and spin rate.

A general rule of thumb that will give most of you more distance is increasing ball speed, lowering spin rate, and launching it higher. Those are the conditions that the modern golf ball needs to achieve to travel its farthest distance.

I'll quickly explore each factor and how it plays its role. I'll try to keep it as simple as possible! But I believe understanding this information is crucial to learning to unlock more distance with your driver.

Ball Speed

Golf ball speed is how fast the ball is traveling right after impact. Essentially, ball speed combines your swing speed and impact location on the driver's face. For example, if you swing your driver 100 mph, the maximum ball speed you can achieve is 150 mph based on the governing bodies' equipment rules. That would indicate a smash factor (ball speed divided by swing speed) of 1.5, and you have transferred the maximum energy from the driver to the golf ball.

Most golfers struggle to hit their driver's sweet spot (center of gravity) on every swing. So when you move strike location towards the heel or toe of the driver or vertically, your ball speed will decline.

Of all three distance factors, ball speed is the most important for distance. Increased ball speed can "overpower" less than optimal spin rate and launch angle. Generically speaking, you can increase your distance up to 2 yards for every one mph of ball speed.

That is why impact location is vital for ball speed and overall distance. Many golfers can increase their distance without any changes in club-head speed by learning to strike the center of their driver more often.

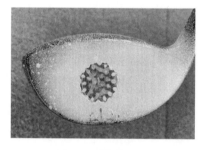

145 MPH Ball Speed
251 Yards

156 MPH Ball Speed
282 Yards

A small difference in strike location can make a big difference in ball speed and overall distance! In this example, moving from lower on the face to the center adds over 30 yards.

Swing speed does play its role as well. All things being equal, an increase in swing speed will also create more ball speed. But this can get tricky. Some golfers will add more swing speed by trying harder, and their swing fundamentals will decline. You might find yourself in a situation where your clubhead speed increases, but ball speed decreases because your impact location suffers so much.

In a perfect world, adding swing speed the correct way will preserve your swing fundamentals and strike efficiency, thus increasing your ball speed. I'll explore in another chapter how I think you can increase your swing speed efficiently.

Overall, ball speed is the top priority to increase your driver distance. Strike quality and upgrades in swing speed are critical.

Spin Rate

Spin rate also plays a significant role in driver distance. If you can find an optimal spin rate, your ball will soar through the air like a rocket. Golfers get into trouble when their spin rates go too low or too high. Extremes penalize golfers.

If the ball doesn't have enough spin, it can look like a duck falling out of the sky. It needs enough spin for it to climb into the air. Conversely, if there is too much spin, the ball can rise too much and rob you of distance. There is a happy medium for your swing like anything else in golf.

As a rule of thumb, most golfers need to find a way to reduce their spin rates to increase distance. But there are outliers like myself that sometimes can spin the ball too low.

Impact location also plays a prominent role in creating spin. Modern drivers are excellent, and if you can strike the center of the face (or even slightly above), you will get optimal spin numbers. When you move towards the toe, heel, bottom, and top of the face, that's where spin can either increase or decrease too much, robbing you of distance and accuracy.

Launch Angle

Launch angle is the angle the ball takes off relative to the horizon. Like spin, it plays its role in distance on a sliding scale.

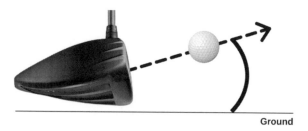

Ground

A visual representation of launch angle

How high or low the ball comes initially off the face of your driver is primarily determined by the delivered loft of the clubface. Research from PING indicates that it is responsible for about 85% of the launch angle. Therefore, playing a driver with the optimal loft plays a significant role in launching the ball at the proper angle.

Additionally, while your driver might have a loft of 10.5 degrees in the center of the face, due to its design, the loft decreases towards the bottom of the face and increases towards the top. So you might deliver as little as 8 degrees if you strike it towards the bottom and as much as 13 degrees at the top.

13 Degrees

10.5 Degrees

8 Degrees

Your driver's delivered loft will change based on where you strike it vertically on the face

But that's not all, folks! There is another influence on launch angle, called the angle of attack. It is defined as the upward or downward movement of the clubhead at the time of maximum compression. If you have a negative angle of attack and the club is moving downward in the impact zone, you will launch it lower. Conversely, hitting up on the ball will increase the launch angle.

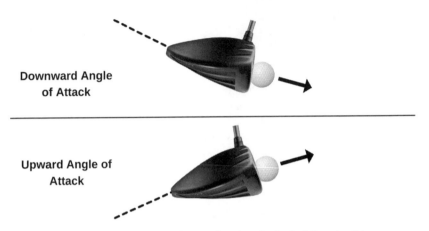

Downward Angle of Attack

Upward Angle of Attack

Angle of attack can significantly alter your launch angle, thereby influencing distance

For most golfers, launching the ball too low is a problem. The ball will not stay in the air long enough to generate any meaningful distance. Typically, the culprit is an extremely negative angle of attack. Learning to increase the angle of attack on its own can generate significant distance upgrades.

This chart from Trackman has become very popular and shows how much distance can be gained at swing speeds under 100 mph by increasing angle of attack. For some golfers, it can add as much as 20 yards.

TRACKMAN — Driver Fitting Chart: CARRY Optimizer

Club Speed (mph)	Attack Angle (deg)	Ball Speed (mph)	Launch Angle (deg)	Spin Rate (rpm)	Carry (yards)	Total (yards)	Dynamic Loft (deg)
	-5	104	14.6	3722	143	166	18.2
75	0	107	16.3	3121	154	178	19.2
	5	108	19.2	2720	164	187	21.8
	-5	113	12.9	3652	160	176	16.2
80	0	115	15.5	3179	171	187	18.3
	5	116	18.0	2648	181	197	20.3
	-5	121	11.9	3669	175	199	15.0
85	0	123	14.5	3164	187	211	17.1
	5	124	17.0	2596	197	223	19.1
	-5	129	11.1	3689	191	215	14.0
90	0	131	13.4	3093	203	228	15.8
	5	132	16.4	2633	214	239	18.5
	-5	137	9.9	3626	207	243	12.6
95	0	138	12.7	3114	219	244	15.0
	5	140	15.7	2595	231	256	17.6

Additionally, this chart from PING shows optimal launch conditions by ball speed and attack angle:

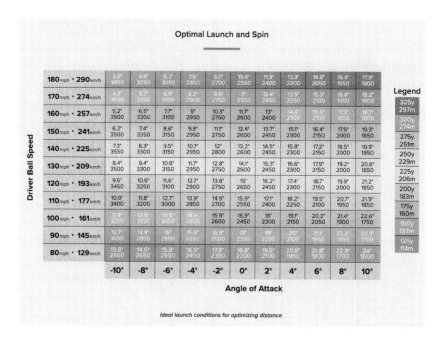

Ideal launch conditions for optimizing distance

How They Work Together

Let's say you were someone who launched the ball lower at around 8.5 degrees with a driver swing speed of 90 mph. Perhaps your driver loft was too low, or you have a negative angle of attack. You would need a combination of more ball speed and spin to maximize distance. Ball speed will be the most crucial factor for you. The more you have, the more you can get away with a lower launch angle.

However, you will need more spin for the ball to climb in the air. If there isn't enough spin, you will experience the duck falling out of the sky.

Some golfers can get away with launching the ball lower with their drivers, but they all have one thing in common. They have a ton of ball speed. Unfortunately, this isn't the case for most players, so launching the ball lower is usually not good for maximum distance off the tee.

The solution to this problem would be a combination of increased ball speed, a higher launch angle, and a lower spin rate. Many golfers fall into this category.

WHY STRIKE SOLVES SO MUCH

The recurring theme of all of my practice advice keeps going back to the same impact fundamental - strike location. Where you strike the ball with every single club in your bag is crucially important to hitting functional golf shots. As you get closer to the center of gravity of the club, all of the factors I discussed (spin rate, launch angle, ball speed) become more optimal.

I believe that impact location with your driver is the number one skill to develop. Modern clubs have come a long way with optimizing strikes around the face, but many problems still occur. You lose distance and accuracy as you get further away from the sweet spot.

Gear Effect

The physics lesson is not over yet. If you've never heard of gear effect, this is a concept I believe every golfer needs to understand. Don't worry; it's a bit easier to comprehend than the theory of relativity.

Gear effect explains why hitting off-center strikes can alter your ball flight with clubs like your driver, fairway woods, and hybrids. It occurs on these clubs because the center of gravity is well behind the face of the club. Gear effect plays a minimal, almost non-existent role with irons and wedges because the center of gravity and clubface are much closer together.

Gear effect becomes a major issue with the driver because the center of gravity is located so far away from the face

Every modern driver is designed with something called bulge and roll. The bulge refers to the horizontal curvature of the face. As you stare down at the driver from above, curvature extends from the heel to the toe.

All drivers have some curvature on the face from heel to the toe, which is known as the bulge

The roll refers to the curvature of the driver's face on a vertical plane. As I showed earlier, the loft of the driver's face changes as you move upward or downward with strike location.

So why is bulge significant? As you strike your driver's face further away from the center of gravity (typically somewhere around the middle) and towards the heel or toe, the driver starts to twist open or closed. If you had a high-speed camera at impact, you would see a driver's face twist open on a toe strike and twist closed on a heel strike. On a center strike, minimal or no twist would occur.

This seems counterintuitive, but here is the most important part. For a right-handed golfer, a toe strike will impart more hook/draw-spin. A heel shot will impart more slice/fade spin.

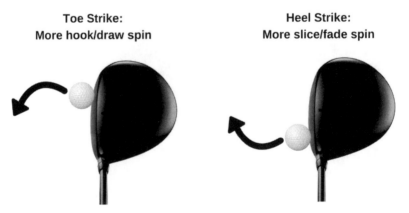

Heel and toe strikes can alter the curvature of your ball flight dramatically due to gear effect

Golf club manufacturers have helped reduce gear effect by increasing Moment Of Inertia in their designs (MOI), which allows the driver to resist twisting on these off-center strikes. But it still does occur.

Horizontal gear effect can work for you and against you. For example, my bias is to miss my driver on the heel, which will impart some slice spin. As someone who draws the ball and sometimes overhooks it, a heel strike can help counteract that. Sometimes it can result in a straight ball flight, a slight fade, or even a slice.

But let's say my strike bias was more towards the toe of the driver - then I'd have a big problem on my hands. I would be adding more draw spin, which would turn my baby draw into more of a hook.

This is why measuring impact location and working toward center strikes is essential. You might hit a slice, or a hook, on the golf course and assume it was because of your swing path. But it could be because you struck the ball too far towards the heel or toe!

Now let's talk about the roll of the driver's face and vertical gear effect. As I mentioned earlier, the driver's face changes loft when you move upward or downward on the face.

As a result, your launch conditions will change. When you strike the ball lower on the face of the driver, three things occur - the ball will launch on a lower angle (due to decreased loft), spin rate increases, and you will lose ball speed. This is not a great combination - you want to avoid hitting the bottom of your driver's face; it's a distance killer!

Conversely, striking it higher on the face is where a little bit of magic can happen. As you progress a little higher on the face, you will start to access a greater loft, and the ball will launch at a higher angle. Additionally, there will actually be topspin imparted on the ball due to gear effect, but the overall effect will be reduced backspin. If you recall, launching it higher and with less spin is one of the key recipes for increased driver distance. So learning to strike your driver a little bit higher on the face (not too high) will add distance for most golfers.

When you combine horizontal and vertical gear effects, you can understand why accessing the center of the clubface, or close to it, is so crucial for distance and accuracy.

Taking all of this into account, working on your impact location during your practice sessions with your driver is one of the most valuable ways to invest your time. You can use the methods I discussed in the previous chapter to generate ideas.

YOU HAVE COMPLETE CONTROL OVER SETUP

One of the biggest reasons golfers struggle to transfer their practice performance over to the golf course is the variability of the game. You are doing most of your practice on a perfectly level surface that isn't even real grass. When you get on the course, you're faced with different lies and uneven terrain, and many players struggle to adjust. I believe this is why adding randomness and experimentation to your practice sessions is valuable.

However, that is not the case with tee shots. You have complete control over everything and don't need to make any adjustments. It's almost the same every time. As such, you can repeat the same setup and know that it's optimal and gives you the best chance of success. But most golfers don't spend the time to figure out how to do that and haphazardly make changes during their rounds.

As a result, I believe driver practice should look a bit different than your wedges or putter. Since those are parts of the game where you'll have to adjust for different distances and more feel is required, I believe random practice can be more beneficial than repetitive (blocked) practice. However, I'd suggest that doing more blocked practice with your driver and repeating the same setup (once you figure out what works best) over and over again can help ingrain positive habits and produce better results on the course. That's why I'll spend some time exploring how experimenting with ball position and tee height is so beneficial.

Tee Height

How high or low you tee the ball with your driver can significantly affect our "big three" launch conditions. For many golfers, tee height will significantly influence their impact tendencies. Additionally, it can alter their angle of attack or whether they are adding or reducing their launch angle.

If I polled 100 golfers and asked them if they took the time to verify how lower, medium, or higher tee height altered their impact location, I'm confident the majority would say no. If you've never experimented yourself, it's time to start testing.

While there are plenty of exceptions, many golfers tee the ball too low with their drivers, and often it can result in them striking the lower half of the driver's face, which you now know is not optimal. But of course, we are all unique snowflakes in this game, and your results could differ.

There is a relatively easy way to test tee height whether you are practicing at home or a driving range. You can purchase different plastic tee heights like the ones shown below. Or a product like Tee Claw allows you to use real tees on a driving range mat.

Start testing various tee heights and keep track of your strike location (you can spray your driver's face with Dr. Scholl's foot spray). For many, you will start to notice some patterns.

In my testing, my strike location tends to follow tee height. If I go too low, then my patterns will veer towards the bottom of the face. If I go too high, I might start accessing the upper portion of the face.

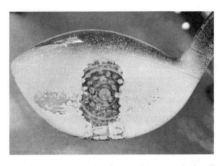

An example of how moving tee height can change vertical strike location

Your results could differ. Overall, you should settle on the tee height that keeps your pattern towards the center or slightly above the center location. You want to do your best to remove tendencies towards the bottom of the face.

Tee height usually will affect angle of attack as well. If I took a group of golfers, measured their angle of attack with low tees, and then compared them to higher tees, most would see a correlation. In other words, the low tees would likely produce a negative angle of attack, and a more elevated tee would either make them less negative or even go to positive territory.

I'll be careful; this does not apply to everyone, but one of the main benefits of teeing the ball higher is that it will get most players hitting up on the ball more, which will make it easier to launch it higher and add distance.

Ball Position

Like tee height, ball position can help give you optimal launch conditions with your driver. There are a lot of variables on how your swing tendencies match up with ball position, so there is no right or wrong answer here. But some guidelines can help.

Hitting tee shots with your driver is not the same as your irons. Some golfers default to placing the ball in the middle of their stance, which is usually a mistake. Typically, this will cause the driver to have a negative angle of attack and launch the ball too low.

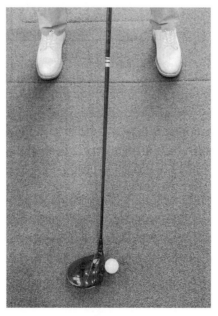

Placing the ball in the middle of your stance is usually not the most optimal position

I would suggest moving the ball forward in your stance for almost all golfers. How far forward is where you'll need to do some experimentation and testing. Ball position can influence your angle of attack, club path, face angle, and for some, impact location.

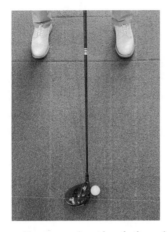 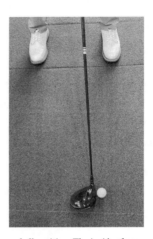

You can experiment how far forward you move your ball position. The inside of your lead foot is about as far forward as you should go.

As you move the ball position around, you'll still want to pay attention to how it changes your impact position (in combination with tee height). Also, you'll want to note the curvature, trajectory, and starting direction of your drives.

For example, moving my ball position closer to the center of my stance will promote more of a draw and lower trajectory. I lose distance and curve the ball too much.

As I move it forward towards my lead foot, it takes curvature off and promotes a higher ball flight. Why does this occur? My swing path is less in-to-out further up in my stance. Additionally, my angle of attack increases further up in my stance. I now have the opportunity to make contact with the ball as the club moves upward rather than downward.

However, if I go too far forward, I find my impact tends to suffer. So generally, I tee the ball a few inches behind the innermost part of my lead foot. This gives me a positive angle of attack, and a slightly in-to-out swing path, with my optimal shots being a baby draw.

My suggestion is to test and refine continually how the combination of tee height and ball position change your ball flight. If you can find the blend that gives you functional impact, not too much ball curvature, and higher launch, now you have the confidence to bring it out on the course and keep repeating that setup.

TRACKING YOUR SHOT DISTRIBUTION

Depending on the driving range you frequent, it might be possible to create a nice visual for yourself to keep track of how well you are controlling your dispersion. As I mentioned in earlier sections of the book, most elite professionals and amateurs have a 60-70 yards driver dispersion. If you can keep most of your drives within that window, you can play well on most courses.

Scott Fawcett, the founder of DECADE, has a neat (and simple) trick. Go on Google Earth or Google Maps, and zoom in on a satellite image of your driving range. Measure about 60-70 yards across, and note where those limits are to your position on the range. When you practice, you can have a visual target and have more accurate feedback on whether you are successfully keeping it within those outer limits. You can also adjust based on how far you hit the ball. It might be more appropriate for someone who drives the ball less than 250 yards to focus on a 40-50 yard window.

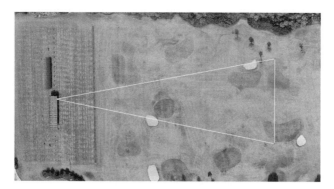

A 65-yard dispersion target at a driving range

HITTING UP ON IT (ANGLE OF ATTACK)

Attack angle can have a massive influence over total distance. As I stated earlier, many golfers have a negative angle of attack, and the club is on a downward arc as it reaches the ball. This reduces the launch angle, which limits your distance potential. It might sound too good to be true, but going from an extremely negative angle of attack to a positive (hitting up on the ball) can add 20-30 yards to your drives without any change in swing speed. Unless you have prodigious speed in your golf swing, I believe most golfers should aspire to have a neutral or positive angle of attack with their drivers.

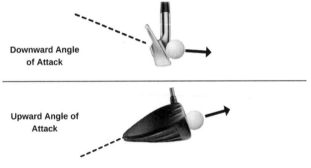

Many golfers struggle transitioning from an iron swing, where a negative angle of attack is more optimal. With driver most golfers should aspire towards a neutral or positive angle of attack

One of the primary reasons a golfer ends up with a very steep driver swing is that they are not making any adjustments from their approach shot clubs. With irons and wedges, we need a negative, or even neutral, angle of attack to hit functional shots. You can't hit up on the ball with an iron and expect good results. But things change when you are on the tee box, and some adjustments are necessary.

Tee height and ball position will both have their role in changing your attack angle with the driver. In general, moving the ball forward and teeing it higher can help move the number higher. For some, that might be enough to optimize their distance more while maintaining a functional ball flight.

But there are a few other ideas you can experiment with to learn to "hit more up" on the ball. As a word of caution, you need to monitor how making these changes will alter your ball flight. If you achieve a higher attack angle, the ball starts on a higher trajectory. But it could also adjust where the ball starts and how it curves. If you remember from our impact laws, those will indicate where the clubface is pointing at impact (face angle) and the path of your club.

So how can you increase your angle of attack? There are a few basic concepts that you can explore in your practice sessions and see how they resonate with your ball flight.

One idea would be to create a physical hurdle you must clear in front of the ball. You can place an empty sleeve of golf balls or even a small row of balls about a foot in front of where your ball is teed. If you are clearing those hurdles, that's an excellent indication that you are hitting more up on the ball.

Another helpful cue is how your shoulders/spine are titled at address and focusing on weight distribution. A common side effect of moving the ball up in the stance is that a golfer will feel like they need to place most of their weight on the lead foot. This can cause your spine and shoulders to tilt forward. As a result, this can cause a downward angle of attack.

When you are practicing, you can try doing the exact opposite. If you look at most great drivers of the golf ball, their shoulders are tilted upwards, and their weight is distributed more behind the golf ball.

Additionally, you'll likely see them more "behind" the ball on the downswing and through impact. Their head and the main weight distribution of their body are still behind the ball. This allows a golfer to impact the ball on a more upward trajectory.

Jon Rahm is a perfect example of an efficient driver. He has been measured at a +5 angle of attack, which allows him to be one of the longest hitters on tour despite having a slower swing speed than some of his peers. Notice at address the ball is teed up closer to his lead foot, and his shoulders are tilted upward. Additionally, at impact he maintains the tilt and keeps his body behind the ball.

I would say this last adjustment is a little more of an advanced concept, and you can experiment in small doses to see how it alters your ball flight and distance. You also want to make sure your body can get in these positions and don't go too extreme; it's possible you could start launching the ball too high!

CONSISTENCY IN BALL FLIGHT

As much as I value consistency in setup, my philosophy is also the same with ball flight, particularly your intended shot shape. Overall, I believe you will find the most success with your driver if you play one shot shape. This is a reoccurring theme throughout the book, especially in the strategy section.

I firmly believe that consistency and simplicity are a winning combination in golf. I want you to practice your driver the same way you would hit it on the course. Instead of adding variables, I want to remove as many as possible. That's why I'm stressing using the same tee height, ball position, and setup. Again, this is one of the few opportunities to perfectly match course conditions in your practice sessions.

On top of that, I want you to make almost the same swing intent each time. I don't care which way it curves; a fade is not better than a draw, and vice versa. If you can remove as much curve as possible off the ball and work towards a straighter ball flight, you will find even more success. Research from PING indicates that a straighter ball travels the farthest.

Pick whatever shot shape comes more naturally, and stick with it. If it's a fade, master that fade. Step up to the tee no matter how the hole is designed and hit that fade repeatedly. With that strategy, you will perform much better than having conflicting swing thoughts and setup positions trying to work the ball in both directions.

LAUNCH MONITOR FEEDBACK

Personal launch monitors have taken off (no pun intended) quite a bit during the last few years. I think they can be very valuable feedback tools, particularly with your driver. I've worked with many of them to evaluate their strengths and weaknesses. I'll briefly go over some of the current technology available when this book was published; you can always visit my website for more up-to-date information.

You can get reasonably accurate readings on your swing speed and ball speeds at the most basic level. If you are working on unlocking the most amount of distance, then working on both will yield the best results.

Overall, you are looking to see how much swing speed you can generate with your driver - this will give you the upper limits of your distance potential. Swing speed training has come a long way, and I'll explore what I feel are best practices in a separate chapter. But at the same time, you want to see how efficient you are with that speed and track your ball speed. Keeping a record of your ball speed will be the number one metric for distance.

A product like the PRGR launch monitor has become the defacto launch monitor for swing speed and ball speed tracking. It allows you to track your swing speed separately without hitting a golf ball doing separate workouts. But when you do hit balls during your practice sessions, you can get very accurate readouts of your swing speed, ball speed, smash factor, and overall distance.

The PRGR launch monitor has become a popular way to track swing speed, ball speed, smash factor, and overall distance

If you want more feedback like launch angle, then products like the Rapsodo MLM and Swing Caddie SC300i are more appropriate. In my testing, I've found that using these products outdoors will give you the best results, while practicing at home with a net will require more space. While their launch angle metrics won't be 100% perfect, I've found them relatively close to enterprise-level products like Trackman.

The Rapsodo MLM and Swing Caddie SC300i are two popular
models that can track your launch angle

As you experiment with factors like tee height, ball position, and adding more angle of attack, you can see how it changes your launch angle. My suggestion would be to look for overall trends; if you started very low, around 6 or 7 degrees of launch, you'll have an excellent benchmark. You can then see if you can increase that number with various adjustments. Think of it like weighing yourself with the same scale. But always, I'd look to your ball flight to verify if you see more positive results.

If you want the best feedback, like spin rate, club path, face angle, and angle of attack, you are looking more towards the most expensive launch monitors. The technology continues to improve, but if you want the complete package, it can range anywhere from $2,000 to $20,000 based on the metrics and accuracy. It might be overkill for many golfers, and they won't know what to do with all of those numbers. Watching your ball fly through the sky and using many of the ball flight laws I've described in the book will help you work backward to these overall trends.

GETTING PROFESSIONAL HELP

If you are struggling with your driver, and none of these concepts seem to help, it might be worth getting help from a professional. Ideally, they would measure your swing on a launch monitor and see how these factors are working together.

Many players get into trouble with their driver when certain parts of their swing get too extreme. You might find that your attack angle is too steep or that your club path is excessively out-to-in (the classic slicer). Either way, the goal should be to neutralize those extremes and return them to functional readings. A teaching pro should give you customized practice drills to help achieve those goals. For many, it's helpful to understand how to fix something when they know their faults and, more importantly, what they should be working toward.

PLAYING THE RIGHT DRIVER

I want to quickly note that playing the correct driver is also crucial to optimizing distance and accuracy.

Driver heads all have different designs that incorporate various trade-offs between the Center of Gravity and Moment of Inertia. Working with a qualified clubfitter to find the right head, set to the correct loft, will play a role in all of the factors I've discussed - most notably ball speed, launch angle, and spin rate.

Additionally, finding a shaft with the right weight, profile, and flex is equally, if not more important, in certain instances.

If you don't get this right, or at least close to right, you will be making it much more difficult for yourself. I have been fortunate enough to learn from one of the best clubfitters in the industry, my dear friend Woody Lashen, the co-owner of Pete's Golf in Mineola, New York. We've performed many experiments throughout the years. I can tell you with confidence that with a few adjustments in driver heads, shaft combinations, and loft settings, you can easily add anywhere from 10-20 yards to a player's drives and narrow their dispersion.

DON'T AVOID YOUR DRIVER!

If your driver is a pain point in your golf game, it's very difficult to expect a scoring breakthrough by avoiding it. Golfers of all levels should devote a significant portion of their practice time, perhaps as much as 20-30% depending on your current performance. Using some of the methods discussed, I believe you can start neutralizing your core issues and seeing positive results on the course.

THE BIG IDEAS

- Your driver is perhaps the most critical singular club for scoring potential. Learning to embrace it and practice effectively can unlock a higher level of golf for just about anyone.
- The goal is to advance the ball as far as possible while avoiding big trouble. It's not fairway or bust; keeping it in play is your primary objective.
- Adding driver distance is mostly about optimizing the trio of ball speed, launch angle, and spin rate.
- Learning to strike the center of the face is perhaps the most important driver skill due to gear effect.
- Optimizing your setup with driver practice is crucial. You have the ability to match conditions exactly to the golf course unlike other parts of the game like wedge play and putting. Focusing on finding the right tee height and ball position can help add distance and improve accuracy.
- Learning to have a neutral, or positive angle of attack is the key to distance for many recreational golfers. Players often have extremely negative attack angles, which limits distance potential.
- You will likely achieve best results by focusing on one ball flight. Don't try to play a fade or a draw to fit certain holes. Get great at one shape!
- Launch monitors are great feedback tools. You can keep track of your swing speed, ball speed, and smash factor. Other models can help indicate your launch angle, which is an important metric to gauge.
- Don't be afraid to ask for help. Getting a lesson or a clubfitting session for the driver can yield tremendous results.
- Driver is the hardest club in your bag to avoid. If you want a

big scoring breakthrough you must figure out a way to neutralize your core issues.

CHAPTER 33
APPROACH SHOT PRACTICE

IF YOU ARE willing to put the work in and shoot your absolute lowest scores, I usually give the same piece of advice - build your game around hitting more greens in regulation and work backward from there.

This statement means a few things. First and foremost, it means keeping the ball in play off the tee and giving yourself an opportunity to hit greens. Additionally, you want to have the proper strategy and select smart targets. But most importantly, you have to be a skilled iron player. And that will require some practice.

Approach play is how golfers primarily score and separate from one another. If things are going well, it is quite boring. You will hit many greens in regulation and even when you miss them, you will have relatively more straightforward wedge shots. So if you are struggling with irons, hybrids, or fairway woods, investing a large portion of your practice time usually will lead to the most significant scoring breakthroughs.

In terms of the different practice methods I've discussed, you can essentially "throw the kitchen sink" at your approach clubs. All of the previous chapters apply - blocked/random practice, tempo, impact training, experimental etc.

Additionally, you will have to pay attention to all feedback forms (though I will prioritize which ones will be most important). Approach play draws on various skills that fall somewhere between driving it well and having distance control with wedges, and your practice habits must change to reflect those truths.

SOLVING THE BIGGEST PROBLEM

Golfers of all levels mostly share the same challenge with approach play. The majority of their shots are missing greens on the short side. Some of that has to do with strategic errors, but a lot of it is influenced by two impact conditions - strike location and ground contact. If you can learn to strike your irons more toward the center of the face and interact with the turf properly, your scores will plummet!

My advice to most of you would be to place a lot of your emphasis on both of those forms of feedback. You can use many of the methods from the previous chapters to experiment with moving strike location around the face. Additionally, make sure you are getting ball first contact and then having your club interact with the turf afterward.

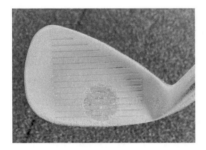 

Place more emphasis on your impact and ground contact using many of the methods I discussed in previous chapters

FACE CONTROL

If you remember from the feedback chapter, where the clubface is pointing at impact (open, square, closed) will primarily influence where the ball starts relative to your target.

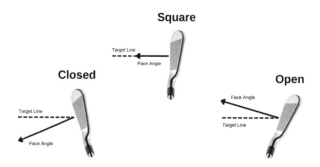

While missing greens to the right or left are usually not as big of a challenge as the shorter side, having face control with your approach clubs is still very important. So you must keep track of whether or not your shots are missing directionally because of clubface that is too open or closed at impact, and make minor adjustments.

I find one of the best practice methods to help establish internal "reference points" with clubface control is intentionally trying to start the ball in different directions. You can take a lower-lofted club like a 6-iron or 7-iron and consciously try to start balls to the right, left, and down the target line. You can begin with partial swings and work your way up to full swings.

Intentionally starting the ball in different directions relative to your target line is a helpful drill to gain more clubface awareness

ALTERNATE BETWEEN METHODS

With approach shot practice, I think it makes sense to transition between the various practice methods I've discussed - block, random, and experimental.

I believe there is plenty of value in repetitive (blocked) with irons. If you are going to hit your 7-iron to the same target 10-15 times, you want to be engaged with the proper feedback. Can you satisfy the following questions:

- How are you striking it?
- Is your ground contact functional?
- Is your ball flight's start direction, curvature, and trajectory allowing you to remain close to your target?
- Are you setting up the ball the same way with ball position and alignment?
- Are you working on specific technical elements of your swing from a lesson you just had?

Each time you are hitting that 7-iron, if you are intentional with your target, noting the proper feedback, and then making adjustments if necessary between shots, I believe you will see results from your practice.

But there is a point where you can overdose, and it will make sense to start picking different targets on each shot. Hit a 150-yard, 120-yard, and then 175-yard shot. Each time you will be forced to select another club, reset to a new target, and test your skills a little more thoroughly.

And finally, you can add a small dose of experimentation to your sessions. What happens when you move the ball position around? Can you try to shape the ball in different directions with varying trajectories? Can you hit your 150-yard club to a 100-yard target? These are not necessarily methods you would employ on the golf course, but they are building your skill as a ball striker.

One idea that can help players is the famous Tiger nine-shot drill. It's a great way to work on every impact fundamental. Your goal is to hit three different heights and curvatures, resulting in nine windows for your ball to go through. For example, on a normal fade shot you would start the ball left of your target and have it curve back to it on a normal trajectory.

High Fade	High Straight	High Draw
Normal Fade	Normal Straight	Normal Draw
Low Fade	Low Straight	Low Draw

The Tiger nine-shot drill is a demanding exercise, but you can simplify it based on your skill level

I will throw in two important caveats. This is an extremely difficult, advanced drill, and you don't need to hit every shot. If you could just learn how to de-loft the club and hit lower shots in just about any direction/curvature, that will be helpful. I find punch shots effective training tools, especially for golfers who struggle with adding too much loft at impact.

The second caveat is that I don't want you bringing all these shots out on the course. This skill-building exercise will help enhance your club-face awareness, manage the relationship between your clubface and club path, loft presentation, and ground contact. If your stock swing is a slight fade with a medium trajectory, let's keep it that way. I am more concerned with helping you get that shot back when it inevitably starts to get out of sync.

WORKING ON YOUR LONGER CLUBS

As we get further from the hole, particularly with approach shot clubs, the scoring level diverges quite a bit. Earlier in the book, I mentioned that a higher-handicap golfer could hold their own in a putting contest from 20 feet with a PGA Tour player because most of the time, both players would two-putt. But if you had a match on who could land the ball closer to the hole from 200 yards, the differences in their games would be pretty stark.

As shots increase in distance, particularly outside of 150 yards, the demands on your impact skills will become greater. Golfers will start to struggle more directionally (left to right) with their misses on top of failing to reach the green. The tolerances in strike location, ground contact, and the clubface/club path relationship become even more critical.

From longer distances, it is not always about getting the ball on the putting surface; it's also about the shot you leave yourself when you miss the green. You would rather have a chip shot just off the putting surface than a 40-yard wedge shot.

I believe it makes sense to devote a significant part of your approach shot practice to longer clubs - don't ignore them! This can be a mixture of longer irons, hybrids, or fairway woods for some. I believe the benefit is two-fold:

1. These are the most significant tests of impact skills. It becomes harder to control your strike, ground contact, start direction, and curvature of shots with longer clubs. Gaining more proficiency will benefit these clubs and all the others in your bag.
2. If you can improve your proximity to the hole from these distances, you will see significant improvements in your scores.

THE BIG IDEAS

- If you want to shoot your absolute lowest scores, you must become proficient with approach shot clubs. Approach play is where golfers separate from one another the most in scoring. You want to build your entire golf game around hitting more greens in regulation.
- All forms of impact feedback become important compared to driver practice or wedge practice. However, you can emphasize some (strike location and ground contact) more than others (swing speed and loft presentation).
- The most significant problem for most golfers is missing greens on the short side. This is primarily due to issues with strike location and ground contact. Many golfers should focus on those two impact conditions with all approach clubs.
- Clubface control is another vital skill to emphasize. Noting which direction your ball starts will help indicate whether the face was too open or closed at impact. Start testing yourself and build internal "reference points" by intentionally starting the ball to the left, right, and down the target line with lower lofted clubs.

- All forms of practice have value with approach clubs, whether it's blocked, random, or experimental. Alternating between them can help challenge your skills. Also, it can help avoid boredom and lack of engagement.
- Do not avoid your lower-lofted clubs! Long irons, hybrids, and fairway woods have an essential role in scoring ability. These clubs present a stout test of impact fundamentals and are excellent training tools.

CHAPTER 34
WEDGE PRACTICE

WEDGE PLAY IS one of the more unique areas of the game compared to approach shots and tee shots. The importance of impact skills starts to change - you are now dealing with more of a finesse shot that does not require a full swing. Distance control and trajectory also become more critical. Conversely, your lateral dispersion (left to right) becomes less of an issue than your full swing shots.

As such, your practice should reflect those differences. To control distance and trajectory, we need to pay more attention to the following impact feedback:

- **Ground Contact:** how your wedges interact with the fairway, rough, and bunkers becomes more critical than approach shots.
- **Impact Location:** distance and trajectory with wedges are heavily influenced by spin rate. Striking the wedge shots closer to the center of the face will help deliver the proper amount of spin to achieve your desired ball flight and stopping power on the greens.
- **Delivered Loft:** with wedges, golfers have more ability to add or decrease loft at impact. Controlling your hand position and shaft lean at impact is crucial.
- **Swing Speed:** wedges are one of the few shots in golf where

you have to vary your swing speed quite a bit. Controlling distance requires matching the proper swing speed to the desired yardage of the shot.

The main challenge of wedge play is matching the feel and technique to specific yardages and lies. It's not the same skill as stepping up to a 7-iron and taking a full swing. Most golfers miss more than 50% of greens in regulation throughout their round. More often than not, that means you will have a wedge shot that will require some precision and feel.

While blocked (repetitive) practice might make more sense in other parts of the game, like your driver, with wedges, I believe it makes sense to divide your time between blocked and randomized practice. You want to hone your technique and distance control, but at the same time, be able to "dial-up" a specific distance at will.

I start every practice session with wedge shots that are less than full swings and urge you to add them to your training if you haven't done so already. This chapter will give you some ideas on practicing your wedges more effectively.

Overall, wedge play is an area of golf that can quickly lower scores for players of all levels. It can help you save more pars, but more importantly, help reduce double bogeys (or worse). Think of wedge play like a security blanket or an insurance policy for your golf game. Additionally, everyone can gain proficiency no matter their skill level or physical capabilities. You'll never hit a 330-yard drive like Rory McIlroy, but you can hit wedge shots like him from time to time.

ESTABLISHING YOUR TECHNIQUE AND DISTANCE CONTROL

When I talk about wedge shots, I'm referring to anything less than a full swing. For example, I hit my 56-degree wedge 100-110 yards with a full swing and my 60-degree wedge about 90-100 yards. However, I use both of those clubs for shots ranging anywhere between 5-85 yards. Those situations require more feel and an alteration in technique (compared to a full swing). Of course, your range of distance and what club you use will look different.

Feel is something that can't necessarily be taught or learned through reading a book like this. You have to earn it through repetition. So whether you are trying to land a wedge shot 35 yards or 80 yards, your body needs to be athletic and "feel" that distance. Through training, your body learns what all of those distances feel like.

On top of that, whether it's a short chip shot around the green or a 3/4 swing with your lob wedge, you need a repeatable technique that you are comfortable with. I don't care what it looks like. What I do care about is, are you comfortable with it? Do you feel confident that you can land the ball on the green most of the time using that technique? If you can satisfy both of those questions, then I would say you're giving yourself the best chance at success.

Sometimes golfers get caught up too much in how things look with wedge play or the ability to play multiple shots. My advice is to excel at one shot rather than being mediocre at four different ones. Your goal is to land the ball on the green most of the time. Getting inside of a 5-foot window all of the time is unrealistic - remember our managing expectations section!

To satisfy both requirements of feel and technique, you will need to put in some work in a blocked format. Since this book is not about the golf swing and specific technical advice, you'll have to find that information elsewhere. I learned the basis for my wedge play through Dave Pelz's *Short Game Bible* and his clock system. More recent books like *Your Short Game Solution* by James Sieckmann or *The Art of the Short Game* by Stan Utley could help you as well. In my opinion, your best chance of getting help with technique would be through taking lessons.

To hone in on various distances and improve your technique, you need to hit shots to the same target continually. I often like to start with a distance between 25 - 50 yards when I practice. When I can lock in the feeling of that distance, I'll move on to another one, like 75 yards. Your goal is for your brain and body to store that information. If you don't practice these distances, you'll be unprepared for them on the course.

In the beginning, it might take more blocked practice to gain skills with various distances and lies. You can get to a place where you need small refreshers and won't necessarily require as much repetition.

TESTING YOURSELF THROUGH RANDOMIZATION

A popular story emerged when Dustin Johnson finally won a major championship in 2016 at the U.S. Open. For years, Johnson knocked on the door at majors mainly due to his tremendous length and accuracy off the tee. However, his weak wedge play prevented him from taking advantage of scoring opportunities.

So how did he fix it? He bought a Trackman launch monitor and started honing in his wedge distances by randomly landing different yardages. The $20,000 investment seemed worth it for the major championship and becoming ranked the #1 golfer in the world!

I don't tell you that story to convince you to buy a Trackman or think you can reach DJ's level of dominance. My point is that no matter how good of a golfer you are, this kind of practice is necessary. For Dustin Johnson, wedge shots were mostly about capitalizing on mammoth drives that left him short approaches on par 4s. For you, it could mean making a few more pars per round and eliminating 2-3 double bogeys when you miss greens.

Once you have put in the work through blocked practice on various wedge distances, you can begin to test yourself. Randomly hitting wedge distances has become one of my favorite practice methods. For those interested in purchasing personal launch monitors, it's my number one recommendation to use them effectively. When my son was three years old, one of our favorite games to play was him calling out random yardages and me trying to land it there with my launch monitor.

You can pick out different targets with each shot if you're at the range. Keep cycling through distances between 20-80 yards.

EXPERIMENTATION

Wedge play is perhaps the best opportunity for a golfer to show off their artistry and individuality. Every shot presents a problem that you can solve in multiple ways. For example, you could have a 30-yard shot with plenty of green between you and the pin. You could hit a low running chip shot with a pitching wedge. Or you could open the face of your lob wedge and land it closer to the hole. Your options between club selection and shot types are vast, and there is no correct answer for all players.

On the course, my preference is for you to keep things simple and rely on a small set of options that you are comfortable with and have proficiency. But that doesn't mean you can't expand your horizons during practice. Wedges are your best opportunity to explore, experiment, and "play" during your off-course preparation.

I suggest taking each of the discussed impact fundamentals that apply more to wedge play and exposing yourself to as many variables as possible. I'll provide some examples to illustrate my point:

- Hit shots from as many lies as possible. See how your wedges react from different lies in the rough, fairway, and bunker. How can you adjust your technique to change trajectory and distance control?
- Try to alter the trajectory of shots. Can you hit a low, medium, and high wedge shot with the same club? Experiment with opening or closing the face and changing ball position. Also, you can add loft or deloft your wedge by focusing on your hand position and shaft lean through the impact zone.

While you won't necessarily do all of these shots on the golf course, going through these exercises will build your overall skill and ability to manipulate your wedges to the desired shot.

TYING IT ALL TOGETHER

Overall, you want to establish your wedge control through repetition and then test yourself through randomization. Additionally, you'll want to add some variation and experiment with variables like different lies and how you manipulate the club's loft at impact.

As a side note, I believe improving these "awkward" wedge yardages will also help your full swing shots. I consider it another foundational form of practice that golfers of all levels should be doing. That's not to say wedge play should take up most of your practice time. For many of you, devoting between 10-30% of your overall time makes sense, depending on your current skill level.

THE BIG IDEAS

- **Different impact conditions become more important when hitting wedge shots that require less than a full swing. Your practice sessions should reflect this change, and you need to alter the type of feedback you pay attention to.**
- **You need to earn your feel and technique for various yardages through more repetitive practice. So when on the course, if you face a 35-yard shot or a 75-yard shot, you can recall what that will feel like.**
- **Testing yourself by cycling through random yardages from shot to shot is equally important. Make sure to introduce a level of randomness to your wedge practice to challenge your distance control.**
- **Experiment with different lies and shot types to help build your overall skill.**

CHAPTER 35
PUTTING PRACTICE

I LIKE to think that putting is a different game inside of golf. For starters, the ball is not flying through the air anymore, so many impact laws change. I also believe it's a part of golf where you can be more instinctual. For example, your depth perception becomes more important. You are sensing how far away you are from the hole, the slope and speed of the greens, and trying to match your putting stroke to all of those factors. While putting doesn't look very athletic, I believe it is a part of the game where your inner athlete can shine more.

So many golfers approach putting with the wrong attitude and expectations. I know I did for a very long time, and I'm still learning. As you read in earlier sections, putting is more demanding than most people think. TV broadcasts lead us to believe that PGA Tour players are making putts from 20 feet all of the time, but they only average about 15%. This is also the part of golf where it is often hardest to separate because of its difficulty. Some 5 and 10 handicaps can putt almost as well as a tour player, whereas their driving and approach play are on different planets.

So what should be your overall putting practice goals? In my opinion, it's pretty straightforward. Improve your chances of making putts inside of ten feet, and reduce your chances of three-putting as you get further away from the hole. Golf is a game of proximity, and putting is perhaps the best example. Once pros start moving outside of 15 feet, their chances of making putts drop precipitously, and their odds of three-putting start to increase. Amateur golfers face even more extreme trends.

According to Shot Scope's database, a 25-handicap will three-putt roughly 25% of the time. As you move down in handicap level, this number reduces quite a bit. A Scratch golfer three-putts only about 8% of the time. For many of you, there is an opportunity to save several strokes on the greens, and a lot of it has to do with how far you are leaving yourself on the second putt.

Three primary skills work together on every putt - face control, speed control, and green reading. You don't have to get all of them right, but if you can improve at each of them, you'll see a reduction of three-putts. Additionally, you'll be able to make some more of those eight-footers for birdie or par that seem to give us an extra pep in our step.

I'm going to focus mainly on face control and speed control with my advice on practicing more effectively. You can improve green reading by working on speed control, almost as a secondary benefit.

DON'T IGNORE PUTTING, BUT DON'T OVERDOSE ON IT EITHER

There needs to be a balance in how much time you spend on each part of your game since it's likely a small, finite amount. Some golfers ignore putting completely, which I believe is a mistake. With some targeted practice, you can achieve some quick wins.

Conversely, you don't want to spend too much time either. If you were spending 50-75% of your time putting, you are likely honing a skill that might only marginally improve your scores, whereas more significant gains could come from more work with your driver or iron play.

I think 10-25% of your practice time is a reasonable amount. And if you want the best information on where you need the most help, use advanced statistics to determine your putting performance, which I explore in a separate chapter.

FACE CONTROL AND SETUP

As I mentioned earlier, impact laws change with your putter. Since we are not worrying about the ball curving through the air, the path of your putting stroke dramatically loses its influence. We are primarily concerned with starting our putts on the intended line, and that is almost entirely controlled by where the putter face is pointing at impact (closed, square, or open). Technically, you could fade or draw a putt with a very extreme club path by adding so much sidespin, but I don't think any putting instructor in the world would recommend that method.

As you get closer to the hole, controlling the putter's face becomes more important, particularly inside of ten feet. From 8 feet, where PGA Tour players make 50% of their putts, your putter needs to be less than 1 degree closed or open for the ball to go in.

There are so many examples of different putting styles that can work. Some players have plenty of arc in their stroke, and they rotate the face quite a bit. Others are the opposite.

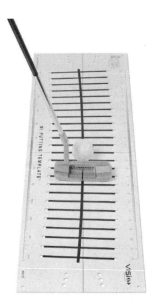

A popular training aid from Visio shows the visual of a slight arc in the putting stroke. The putter face gently rotates open on the backswing, returns to square at impact, and then rotates slightly closed on the follow through.

Either way, good putters can square the face at impact to their intended line. I'm not here to tell you how to putt from a mechanical perspective, but I want you to spend some time exploring how to build the skill of face control.

Luckily, almost all of us have the opportunity to work on this skill at home with a putting mat and possibly some other training aids.

Many of the other practice fundamentals I've discussed can apply. Here are some ideas:

- **Experimentation:** Putting is very personal, and I believe there are more opportunities to experiment with your stroke style, setup, and grip technique.
- **Repetitive & Random Practice:** There will be some value for both approaches, but you don't want to get too stuck with

hitting the same putt over and over again. Changing targets and distances will help you mentally reset and pay more attention to the task.

- **Challenge Yourself:** One of my favorite ways to work on putting at home or the course is through games and challenges. How many putts in a row can you make from a certain distance? How many times can you cycle through various lengths and targets without missing? Working with physical cues like gates can help as well.

Feedback also becomes more straightforward. If you are working on distances from 3-10 feet on the same surface indoors, you are almost wholly removing green-reading and speed control. Pay attention to your directional misses, look for patterns, and make minor adjustments. For example, is your tendency to miss one side of the hole more than the other?

I believe your overall goal is to establish your own personal "feel" and setup that will give you the best chance of making a completely straight putt from 5-8 feet. How far you stand away from the ball, your hand position, posture, and where your eyes are located over the ball all make a difference. Then you will have to combine that feel and setup on the golf course with your speed control and green reading skills.

Through years of practice and experimenting, I've settled on my own feel to combat one of my main tendencies, which was closing the putter's face at impact. I use a pencil grip style, which helps remove the influence of my right hand. With the help of a putting mirror, I make sure I have a consistent setup with my eyes over the ball and shoulders square to my target (my shoulders tend to get closed). Also, my goal is to have a slight arc on my stroke (I'll use a visual aid for that as well) as I come back and through to the ball. Additionally, my putter (made by SeeMore) has a unique system that helps give me the same ball position, hand position, and alignment on every putt.

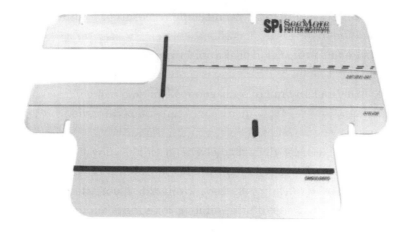

The putting mirror I use to practice from SeeMore. It has visual cues for shoulder alignment, eye position, aiming, and the arc of the putting stroke. Tools like these can be helpful to verify you are in the same posture and setup as you address the ball.

Hopefully, that gave you a few ideas. My overall philosophy is doing the right kind of practice to help remove variables in your setup so your skill can perform. Several training aids can help, such as mirrors, gates for your stroke (or as targets), and visual aids that represent the arc of the putting stroke.

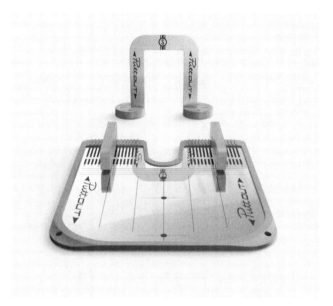

Some golfers respond well to physical barriers for their putting stroke and having the visual cue of a gate to verify they are hitting their start lines (designed by PuttOUT Golf)

Putting mats like this model from Perfect Practice can help hone your face control at home with the extra challenge of a smaller hole.

SPEED CONTROL

If you want to become a better putter, speed control is the most important skill to improve. You can have impeccable face control and read greens accurately, but your putting performance will suffer if you can't control your speed. Think of speed as the glue that holds everything together.

Whether during practice sessions or a round, I believe most golfers place way too much emphasis on their lines. That's not to say that getting the proper read and starting the ball on the intended line is unimportant. But I believe if you shift your focus more towards speed, you will see better results.

Unfortunately, speed isn't something that I can describe to you. I could talk about controlling the tempo of your stroke, the length of your backswing, or striking the putter closer to the center of the face. These factors will affect your speed control, but those are all variables that can change from one player to the next.

Like many of the other skills I discuss, speed control is more innate and unseen. You are using your senses to evaluate how far from the hole you are, the speed of the greens, and the undulations of the putting service. Then you will take all of that information and try to match it with your putting stroke. This area of golf, in particular, will call more upon your athletic ability, no different than trying to hit a tennis ball to a specific part of the court or throwing a football to hit your receiver in stride down the field. It's instinctual. And as many of you who play other sports know, you don't build those skills through studying mechanics; it's more through practice and play.

Speed control requires more feel and adjusting technique (another way to describe skill). It's hard for any golfer to expect to develop speed control if they cannot play or practice it much. Whether you're playing the same course, or different ones all the time, green speeds change daily. You have to adjust and recalibrate constantly.

When I think back on how I've built the skills with me today, I always return to my experience as a junior golfer. When I first learned the game at my local town course, my friends and I would spend hours on the practice green. We would compete against each other on how close we could keep the ball to the hole from various positions around the green. The pressure was real. Our upstairs had a long, carpeted hallway in my parents' house. I used to randomly pick targets and keep the ball as close as possible. I didn't know it at the time, but this was a highly effective practice at developing speed control. As adults, we tend to move away from a playful approach and more toward repetitive routines that focus more on technique.

That's why practice drills and performance games can be very effective at improving speed control.

Overall, I believe it makes much more sense to lean on random practice for speed control. If you have access to a putting green and can practice from various distances, I would not recommend repeatedly hitting putts from the same distance. You won't be learning too much because it will no longer be as challenging after a few putts. Conversely, you will be more engaged and challenged if you hit putts from 15, 35, 25, and 10 feet randomly.

PRODUCTIVE PUTTING PRACTICE

If possible, I would suggest dividing your putting practice between two methods for the most part:

1. **Putts inside ten feet**: work on setup and mechanics such as face control and stroke arc. You can alternate between repetitive and random practice methods.
2. **Speed control**: move further away from the hole and challenge yourself from various distances. Shift your focus away from mechanics and engage your instincts. Try to solve a new problem each time.

In a perfect world, most golfers would benefit by doing more speed control work, but that usually requires having access to a putting facility. At the minimum, everyone can do setup and mechanical practice at home with a putting mat. How you spend your time will depend on those circumstances and your current skill level.

THE BIG IDEAS

- Try to think of putting as a different game inside of golf. The demands change, and you can rely a little more on your instincts.
- Statistics show that putting is where golfers typically separate themselves the least from one another in terms of scoring ability. A recreational golfer could never match the play of a pro golfer off the tee or with approach shots, but they can get closer to them with their putter.
- Your practice should seek to improve on two primary goals - increasing make rates of putts inside ten feet and reducing three-putts from further distances.
- Don't overdose on practice or ignore it either. Spending 10-25% of your overall time can yield scoring results. However, there will be diminishing scoring returns at a certain point compared to other parts of your golf game like iron play or driver performance.
- While practicing shorter distances, you are working more on mechanical skills and setup. Can you create a setup and stroke that helps you start the ball on your intended line?
- You are primarily working on speed control over longer distances, arguably the most critical skill. Rely more on your instincts and challenge yourself with random distances.
- Divide your practice between putts inside ten feet (mechanical work) and longer distances (speed control). Most golfers would benefit more from speed control in an ideal scenario, but it will depend on your current skill level.

CHAPTER 36
USING STATISTICS TO GUIDE YOUR PRACTICE SESSIONS

GOLFERS CAN GET CAUGHT up in a cycle of spending time at the practice facility with no plan and working on the wrong parts of their game. I'd like to give you some ideas on spending your time more productively with the guidance of statistics.

EFFICIENCY WITH LIMITED TIME

With limited time, recreational golfers need to be efficient and work smart when they have the opportunity to practice. Since no one explains the hows and whys of what that looks like, many mistakes are pretty common.

For starters, there is usually no overall plan. I would show up to the driving range for years and haphazardly hit balls. I know I was not alone. The other range stalls were filled with other clueless hackers.

Another big mistake is that golfers spend time on parts of the game that will yield little or no results. There are a few reasons why this occurs:

- We'll continue to hone a mostly developed skill by gravitating towards what comes easily, and further gains are likely minimal.

- Spending time on shots that we don't encounter all that much on the course.
- General misconceptions about which parts of golf will most impact scoring. For example, investing 50% of your practice time on five-foot putts will not improve your handicap dramatically.

Meanwhile, other more important elements are ignored. Your time is a precious resource that needs to be invested wisely. You want to look for opportunities that can achieve significant returns.

HOW STATISTICS CAN HELP

I spoke a lot about statistics in the strategy and managing expectations section, extolling how strokes gained analysis clarifies performance. Understanding how scoring occurs in golf and then using your statistics as a guide can help you spend more productive time at the range.

To be clear, I'm not talking about traditional statistics. Tracking how many fairways you hit each round or total putts is not enough information. At best, they can give you a few clues on where you need to spend your time. However, for many, they can be misleading.

A myriad of apps and shot-tracking systems are available now to make this process more streamlined for those who are more analytical and willing to put a little more effort into their games.

Whatever system you use, the advantage will be receiving a clear, top-level explanation of your golf game's relative strengths and weaknesses. For example, if you are a 15-handicap, many apps will compare your performance to other handicap benchmarks.

An example of comparing performance versus different handicap benchmarks using strokes gained. Negative values indicate areas that need improvement, and positive values indicate areas of relative strength.

You will see where you are gaining and losing strokes on tee shots, approach shots, wedge play, and putting.

Usually, seeing top-level strokes gained data is an eye-opener. It could reveal that areas of the game where you are spending most of your practice time are already a strength, and there isn't much "juice left to squeeze." Conversely, there could be easier opportunities where targeted practice yields quick wins.

Strokes gained statistics are a great starting point, but you will have to do a little more detective work. I'll provide some examples of how that can look in each part of the game.

DRIVING

Your performance off the tee is a combination of how far you can hit the ball while keeping it in play and avoiding big trouble.

We primarily relied on fairways hit as a measuring stick in the past. But that number can be misleading. You could average 75%, which would mean you are a great performer off the tee on the surface. However, let's say you were only averaging 200 yards with your tee shots; you could be losing strokes off the tee versus a player who hit it farther but only averaged 55% of their fairways.

Taking a stat like fairways hit in conjunction with strokes gained performance is a better starting point. Additionally, with most systems, you can dive deeper into your shot distributions and see a visual representation of your tendencies off the tee.

If you found yourself losing strokes off the tee versus a handicap level you are looking to achieve, I would suggest finding the answers to the following questions:

- Is this a distance issue? If you find yourself comparable in avoiding big trouble (penalties, trees, fairway bunkers) and fairway accuracy, then adding distance is likely the only way to gain strokes. Perhaps it's because you are not using your driver enough or need to learn how to hit your driver farther.
- Are big mistakes costing you strokes? Are you finding yourself in recovery situations and penalty areas?
- Is your dispersion reasonable? Most shot-tracking systems will show you a visual representation of your tee-shot distribution. It is possible that you aren't hitting enough fairways to keep up.

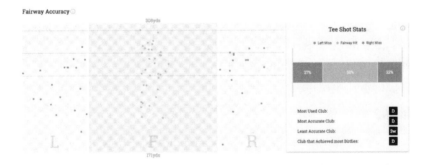

An example of how you can see visual representations of your tee shot performance from Shot Scope

Alternatively, if you are not using a stat-tracking system, you could use my definition of a successful drive as a better measuring stick. You could track the following three scenarios in each round:

- Fairways hit
- Successful tee shots: you advanced the ball close to your average distance, have a clear path to the green, and a reasonable lie (think light rough).
- "Oops Swings" - whenever your ball ends up in a recovery situation, penalty area, or out of bounds.

If you increase the amount of successful tee shots, and decrease the "oops swings" then you know you are on the right path.

APPROACH SHOTS

Typically, approach play is the most critical part of golf in how golfers separate themselves from one another in scoring. I still believe that Greens In Regulation (GIR) is a fundamental statistic, and golfers should build their game (through practice and strategy) around hitting more greens. GIR has the highest correlation with scoring and handicap level than any other stat.

However, approach play primarily comes down to proximity to the hole, which GIR cannot measure. Additionally, when you are missing greens, where you end up plays a significant factor in scoring potential. For example, if you miss a green in a bunker and are short-sided, that shot will lose more strokes than where you had a short chip and plenty of green to work with.

If you want the most precision, using a combination of GIR, strokes gained, and analyzing where your approach shots end up will give you a very clear picture of what you need to work on.

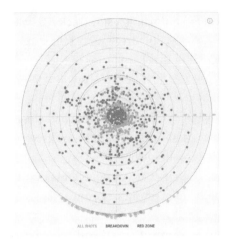

ALL SHOTS   BREAKDOWN   RED ZONE

You can see visual representations of where your approach shots land relative to the target. Seeing these patterns in aggregate, or sorting by various distances is very helpful (Shot Scope dashboard)

Here are some questions that I find are helpful to answer:

- Examine your misses from a distance perspective (short and long). The majority of golfers miss in front of the green rather than behind. Some of these are strategic mistakes. Other times it can be an inability to strike clubs on the center of the face. Impact training is a great way to work on these issues.
- Analyze your lateral misses. Do you see a pattern towards left or righthand bias? Are you short-siding yourself relative to pins quite often? Again, these could be strategic mistakes. But usually, it's controlling where the clubface is pointing at impact and managing the club's path through the impact zone.
- Is ground contact an issue? Controlling the low point of the golf club is very important in approach play. Think back to shots where you are missing the green, and try to evaluate if you are getting the ball first and then turf contact.

An example of approach play analysis from Arccos

WEDGE PLAY

Some apps define wedge play as inside 100 yards, while others use inside 50 yards as their benchmark. Either way, proximity to the hole is the measuring stick to determine whether you are outperforming or underperforming from these distances.

Distance control becomes more critical as you get closer to the hole, and lateral (left to right) dispersion is usually not as big of an issue. I find strokes gained particularly helpful with wedge play because they reveal certain distances where you are having problems. For example, you might find out that you are a great wedge player from 60-100 yards but struggle as you get closer to the greens.

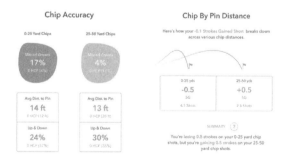

This golfer is showing a slight weakness on wedge shots closer to the green (Arccos dashboard)

If you find yourself deficient in one or several distance categories, I find that wedge play is where golfers can quickly pick some low-hanging fruit. So many golfers don't practice their wedges at all, and if you refer to the chapter on wedge practice, I think you'll get some great ideas.

PUTTING

Putts per round is another traditional statistic that can be very misleading. I could provide plenty of scenarios where someone with 30 putts over 18 holes could outperform or underperform golfers at the same skill level. It's just not enough information. Strokes gained is far more prescriptive in explaining your putting performance and what distances you need the most work.

You will need to do more work to track your strokes gained by putting statistics effectively. Some automatic GPS shot-tracking systems will identify when you made contact with the ball, and you can tag where the pin was on each hole. Sometimes, GPS is not precise enough (yet) to tell whether you had a 6-foot putt or an 11-foot putt.

Those who take detailed statistics of their putting walk off the distance of each putt and note them on their scorecard after each hole. How far you are from the hole on each putt will allow strokes gained to assign a value to each stroke. While it might be a little more tedious, it will give you much more valuable information on where you need to practice more.

Like wedge play, you will receive your strokes gained performance based on proximity to the hole. You also usually can see your make rates by distance, three putting, and how many putts miss short or long of the hole.

Putting by Putt Length

Here's how your -2.6 Strokes Gained Putting breaks
down across various putt distances.

0-10	10-25	25-50	50+ ft
-1.8	**-0.7**	**-0.2**	**+0.1**
SG	SG	SG	SG
21.5 Shots	7.3 Shots	3.5 Shots	1.2 Shots

SUMMARY (?)

You're losing 1.8 strokes on your 0-10 foot putts,
but you're gaining 0.1 strokes on your 50+ foot
putts.

*Putting inside of 10 feet is the biggest weakness in this player's
performance (Arccos dashboard)*

The three primary putting skills are speed control, face control, and green reading ability.

If you were losing strokes from the 0-10 feet range, I would suggest that face control (your ability to start the ball on your intended line) is likely your biggest issue. Those are the distances where you have an excellent chance of making putts, and as you miss more and more of them, your strokes gained will dive deeper into negative territory.

Speed control becomes more paramount as you get further away from the hole.

As you get outside of 10 feet, and your chances of making putts decrease dramatically, putting becomes a game of proximity. If you are losing strokes from further distances, it's because you are leaving yourself outside a reasonable range from the hole, not because you didn't make the putt. Speed control becomes more crucial, and your ability to reasonably determine the break of the putt. Working on those skills will likely save you strokes and eliminate the common culprit - three-putting.

Overall, going through a detailed analysis of your statistics is one of the most efficient ways to plan your practice sessions. There will be plenty of opportunities for many to create quick wins in parts of the game you are deficient. But you need to know where to look!

THE BIG IDEAS

- With limited time, golfers need to be efficient with their practice methods.
- Using advanced statistics can help identify deficiencies in your game. Spending some time on your weaknesses rather than your strengths can lead to quick wins.
- Many stat tracking apps can do advanced strokes gained calculation, giving golfers tour-level analysis of their games. Taking a deeper dive into each part of your game can unlock important clues to guide your practice sessions.

CHAPTER 37
SWING CHANGES & TECHNICAL WORK

THERE IS MORE information than ever on the golf swing. Where it used to be several magazines and books giving out swing tips, there are now thousands of outlets on the internet that golfers can access. I am quite sure many of you regularly watch videos on Instagram, YouTube, and other platforms about various swing philosophies. While a lot of the advice is high quality (and plenty of it is poor), it can create a problematic cycle. Golfers show up to the range every week, perpetually trying new swing techniques. Initially, they might see positive results. But for most, eventually, they get frustrated, and they're on to the next idea several weeks later.

This cycle wastes a lot of precious practice time. Rather than working on specific swing moves they saw on a video, I strongly feel most players would benefit from working on many skill-based ideas I've discussed. But I am not against swing changes or working on your technique. I've gone through several of them myself, and they have all led me to a higher level of golf.

Armed with the correct information and feedback methods, you can spend a portion of your practice time working on specific technical elements of your golf swing. I will explore some ideas to help guide you through this process and what I believe will give you the best chance of success. More importantly, I'll be honest about how long it might take to make a swing change and what you'll have to commit to doing.

WHAT IS RELEVANT?

At this point, we know more about the golf swing than we ever have. Many myths have been debunked, and plenty of golfers are getting better faster because of this increased knowledge. But that doesn't always mean more is better.

There are so many great instructors sharing their knowledge. Much of it is available for free and easy to consume. But golfers fall into a common trap. They believe that learning more and more about the golf swing from as many voices as possible will make them better. If anything, it usually makes them worse.

The biggest problem I see is relevancy. Every golfer has multiple puzzle pieces in their swing. The goal is to make them all fit together to hit functional golf shots by satisfying various impact fundamentals. When you start taking random pieces, like changing your takeaway or your wrist angles at the top of your swing, and inserting them into your swing puzzle, often they don't fit.

For example, a few years ago, the concept of shallowing the shaft in the downswing became very popular. Many videos on social media and YouTube were extolling its benefits and showing how various pro golfers and elite amateurs were executing the move. If done correctly, it can be a very beneficial tool to control the relationship between the club path and face angle in the impact zone. Conversely, for a player with swing tendencies that don't require that specific move, introducing it could make them hit the ball all over the course and lose control.

Golfers have to be very careful when introducing various movements and positions they've seen online into their swing. If these changes are not relevant to their particular swing and what their body can do, they will do more harm than good.

CONTINUITY

Your mind needs to be quiet and in a reactive state to play your best golf. As you'll read about in the forthcoming mental game section, you want to step up to the ball as committed as possible and not have your mind worrying about multiple swing thoughts. Another big problem I always see revolves around continuity.

I'm confident that if I sent a video of your golf swing to ten highly-trained swing professionals, they would all come to different conclusions on what you needed to do to improve from a technical standpoint. They would all find different ways to communicate what needed to change and perhaps some drills you could pursue in practice.

Let's say you chose one of those teachers to work with and decided to commit to their plan fully. With their guidance, there's a better chance you will see meaningful improvements in your game if you stick with the program.

What do you think would happen if you listened to all ten of them at once? You would probably start getting confused by all of the ideas. Are you focusing on just your takeaway? What about getting the clubface less closed at the top of your swing? Is your trail shoulder rotating enough in the backswing? Having all of these thoughts is no way to play your best golf.

This is the scenario that so many golfers create for themselves. By listening to so many voices, they have collected a library of conflicting swing thoughts in their head. And when it comes to executing their swing on the golf course, it's placing them into a confused, conscious swing state rather than a subconscious one.

That's why cruising the internet for swing tips usually doesn't work. You have two significant odds stacked against you:

1. The information is often not relevant to your golf swing.
2. Because it's so easy to consume, you lack continuity.

RISK/REWARD

Any time you start tinkering with your swing, you have to ask yourself what you stand to gain and what you stand to lose. There is plenty to lose for the more skilled golfer with many years of experience and consistent swing patterns. Conversely, there could be more upside in their performance for beginners to intermediate players by going through a swing overhaul.

Balancing the risk and reward is one of golf's enduring challenges. There are countless examples of top professionals who ruined their careers because they were on an endless quest to perfect their technique. Also, just about every driving range is filled with recreational players on a similar goose chase.

SO WHAT SHOULD YOU DO?

Unless you have a very advanced understanding of your golf swing, I suggest most golfers get off the endless swing education train. This might not be an issue for some, but if you're nodding your head to what I'm saying in this chapter, I think you should cool it.

Essentially, golfers have two choices to make. Are you going to go at it alone or get some help?

Currently, it is estimated that around 10% of golfers take swing lessons. It makes sense to me why that number is so low. Lessons can be expensive, and golfers don't have endless budgets. I wish that number were higher, though. I think that if golfers took the $500 they spent on a new driver, found a good instructor, and stuck with their program, they would see much better results in their game than the new driver would provide.

If you are going to work on technical changes in your swing to get better, you'll have the best opportunity to improve if you get customized advice from an expert.

But if you're not in a position to get lessons or can't find an instructor that you are comfortable with, I'd suggest moving away from playing amateur swing doctor. In my opinion, introducing many of the practice fundamentals that focus on building impact skills will help you reach a higher level of golf. In a perfect world, I'd suggest getting help from a swing professional at some point and working on impact skills at the same time - one doesn't necessarily have to come at the expense of the other.

FINDING AN INSTRUCTOR

If you are interested in getting help on your swing, who you work with is important. Like any profession, swing coaches have different philosophies and skill levels. I don't have a foolproof method for you to find the perfect coach, and your geographic location might limit your options, but I will give you some advice.

Perhaps the best place to start is through word of mouth with other golfers you know. Also, finding a coach online is pretty easy these days, and you can check around various private and public courses. If you can find several you're interested in working with, I think it's best to have a conversation with each of them to learn more about their teaching philosophy and how they work with their students.

I believe it's vital to work with someone you feel comfortable with, and their communication style suits you well. You can usually start with an introductory lesson. Some questions you can ask are the following:

- How do they work with technology? While I am a proponent of launch monitors and other diagnostic tools, you want to ensure that an instructor does not overload you with complicated, extraneous information.
- Learn more about their philosophy on the golf swing. I prefer golfers to work with instructors who aren't forcing them into one model golf swing. Can they take your existing swing tendencies and make meaningful adjustments to address your specific ball flight issues?
- What kind of practice plan can you expect? You'll have a much higher chance of success if the instructor can give you various

drills and challenges to make your practice more meaningful and effective.

- Do they offer playing lessons? There are so many things an instructor can't see in your game on the practice tee. If possible, going out on the course with them for a playing lesson is often quite valuable.
- Will they help you with other parts of your game? Most coaching defaults to just the golf swing, which is unfortunate. But if you can find an instructor willing to take a more holistic approach to your game, that is a bonus. Having conversations about your recent rounds, reviewing stats, and all of the other elements of the game that I am focusing on throughout this book will be very helpful. We all need support!

I don't want to give you the impression that they should answer all of these questions perfectly, but these are good starting points. As a secondary option, online lessons are becoming more and more popular. Many coaches who have become popular on social media offer packages to review your swing videos and give you customized advice. While I prefer in-person lessons, this is another excellent option if you are looking for help.

YOUR COMMITMENT

Instruction is a two-way street. A lot of golfers make the mistake of assuming that by just showing up for lessons, they will automatically improve. If you invest your time and money, you have to make sure you are fully committed or you will not get a return on either.

Getting a lesson is just a starting point. You have to be prepared to practice between sessions to see a change. Any adjustment to your swing changes your motor patterns - that requires time. So if you don't have available time for practice sessions outside of the lessons themselves, it might not be worth pursuing. It might make more sense to space out your appointments over weeks, or even months, to make sure you can do the work in between and measure your progress.

While not necessary, I think it's a good idea to commit to a series of lessons. Getting two or three sessions is usually not enough. That doesn't mean you have to work with an instructor forever, but as you see progress, it might make sense to either space your sessions further apart or just have check-ins from time to time to make sure you are still on the right track.

GO SLOW, BE INTENTIONAL, AND EXAGGERATE

Making any kind of change to your swing can be daunting. Your existing tendencies are often so ingrained that even the most minor adjustments can feel extreme. On top of that, you have to be prepared that your performance on the course can change and be frustrating. For some golfers, making changes towards the end of their season or even in the offseason can be beneficial because it can remove the pressure to play well. So it's helpful to go into the process with realistic expectations.

The first step is often the most challenging. Expecting to make full-speed swings with these new swing changes and seeing better ball flight sets you up for disappointment. A common piece of advice that works quite well is moving slowly and exaggerating the new pattern.

On top of that, when you are first making the changes, try not to worry about ball flight feedback. You can spend some time in a mirror at home with or without a golf club, and as you slowly rehearse the swing movement you are looking to create, you can see what is happening. People often refer to this as "feel vs. real" in the golf swing. You want to visually verify what is occurring and how that feels in your body.

SLOWLY CLIMBING THE LADDER AND ADDING LAYERS

After you are starting to feel comfortable with changing the movements in your body and verifying how they look and feel, it's time to start adding a few more layers. You can start adding the feedback of ball flight at the practice range. I'll caution you not to be too hard on yourself, as you'll likely experience some setbacks. But you will want to see some evidence that the swing changes are making meaningful improvements to your ball flight (thereby satisfying impact conditions).

Hopefully, you can move to the golf course as you get more proficient and comfortable at the range. This is where things can get tricky. Your old patterns will likely return when you add the context of being out on the course. So don't get too discouraged. I recommend not even keeping score the first few times out and viewing them as practice sessions in a different environment.

Naturally, there will be setbacks and frustrations on the golf course. You'll have to return to the range environment where the pressure is off to reinforce the new movements. But over time, the goal is for these new changes to feel natural and improve your ball flight.

HOW LONG SHOULD IT TAKE?

Before you commit to making a swing change, you should also under-stand some reasonable guidelines on how long it should take.

Like everything else in golf, it depends. If you are making more minor changes, like going from a weak grip to a strong grip, it might only take several weeks to feel comfortable and see better results. But if you were doing a more extensive overhaul, then several months might be a more accurate expectation.

Another factor is how much time you have to practice and your dedi-cation level. Are you willing to spend some time at home making those swing rehearsals in the mirror? Can you go to the range several times a week? Can you play enough rounds to apply more pressure? While everyone is different, it will require repetitions in practice and play to make these new changes stick.

Overall, if you can satisfy most of these requirements, it should take around 2-3 months to make a successful swing change. Some might see progress in a shorter period. However, if it's taking longer, I would question if you are doing enough work, or in a worst-case scenario, it might not be the correct swing change for you.

THOUGHTS ON VIDEO

Taking a video of your golf swing while making swing changes can be beneficial. But I would be careful about how you use it. At best, it can provide valuable feedback and verify what you are feeling in your swing. At worst, you can abuse it - golfers can get a little too obsessed with swing positions, leading them down a dangerous rabbit hole.

If you are not working with an instructor, I would advise against taking videos of your swing. Most golfers have no idea what to look for. Often, they'll start making changes to make their swings look nicer. But every action has a reaction. You might not like that your shaft comes a little past parallel at the top of your swing, and try to shorten it. But that change could have a disastrous effect on your downswing and prevent you from getting into a functional impact position. For most, haphazardly making changes will be more trouble than it's worth.

Also, videos can be very misleading. Changing camera positions in each session can dramatically alter how your swing looks. You can make the same swing look pretty different by adjusting the height and position of a camera.

For the best chance of success, I would suggest asking for help from your instructor. Have them show you how to set up the camera for a down-the-line or face-on position. Most importantly, you should clearly understand the faults you are trying to correct and some essential checkpoints you are looking to satisfy.

Last but certainly not least, don't think you have to record every swing you make. Use it to check in and verify what you are feeling. Remember, the most crucial feedback is how the golf ball is flying through the air, not all of the physical checkpoints in your swing.

SHOULD YOU DO IT?

Technical swing changes is a topic I'm very passionate about, and it's one of the reasons I started Practical Golf. I have seen many golfers struggle who are in an endless pursuit of swing changes because the industry has led them to believe that is the secret to better play. Most golfers are just changing lanes in a traffic jam and getting nowhere.

But if you can get help and put meaningful work on technique changes relevant to your swing, it can bring you to a much higher level of golf.

THE BIG IDEAS

- There is so much information on the golf swing, which creates a double-edged sword for golfers. While plenty of helpful information is easily accessible, consuming too much becomes counterproductive.
- The biggest challenge is relevancy. You might find a great piece of information, but if the swing advice is not relevant to your tendencies, it can likely cause more harm than good.
- Continuity can be equally important - you don't want ten coaches' voices in your head; your best chance of success is picking one.
- Golfers must balance the risk and reward of a swing change. What do you stand to gain, and what do you stand to lose?
- Your best chance of success is getting customized advice from a qualified swing professional. Be prepared to commit to the process, which can take several months.
- If you are going at it alone, it's much harder to diagnose and employ the correct technical changes. Devote more time to skill-based drills that focus on impact fundamentals.
- Be careful with taking video of your swing! How you set up the camera can make your swing look different. Also, if you are not working with a coach, you may not know what to look for, and the whole process can cause more harm than good.

CHAPTER 38
ADDING SWING SPEED
THE RIGHT WAY

CERTAIN GOLFERS ARE GIFTED when it comes to swing speed. Whether it's their genetics or skills they have built playing other sports, we have all been around players who can effortlessly generate tons of speed. But for the rest of us, increasing our swing speed is a more learned process. All things being equal, more swing speed is a scoring advantage. You'll hit your tee shots farther, have higher lofted clubs into greens, and be able to hit more effective shots from the rough.

Unfortunately, as we all age and become more sedentary in our daily lives, we start to lose speed. Golf starts to become more difficult because our proximity to the hole increases. But there are ways to reverse this trend. There have been many advancements in understanding what creates speed and training more effectively throughout the last decade.

While it is not 100% necessary, I encourage many golfers to start training for swing speed. It's one of the areas of practice where I have changed my mind quite a bit after learning from some of the top experts in the industry and going through various regimens myself. The reasons are twofold:

1. **Speed is a skill you can take to the course every day.** It

directly translates to more distance, which will lower your scores over the long run. We used to think of it as something you either had or didn't have, and it was set in stone. I now believe swing speed should be considered a skill no different from putting or wedge play, which means it's an area of the game you can improve upon.

2. **Many responsible methods to increase swing speed will also improve your overall health.** I am a huge advocate of exercise and its benefits. I can tell you without exaggeration that if you're not currently exercising, but you add some of these methods, you will improve your quality of life and overall health. A mountain of evidence suggests regular exercise is the key to longevity and preventing conditions like heart disease, certain cancers, and diabetes.

So if you're interested in hitting it farther, lowering your scores, and improving your health - I believe this chapter can help!

LET'S CLEAR UP BOMB AND GOUGE

There is no question that professional golf has changed. Tiger Woods caught everyone off guard with his prodigious speed and power, and two decades later, we are seeing the effects. Additionally, now that we understand what creates speed and its benefits, you see almost every elite golfer coming out of college with tremendous speed. The cat is out of the bag.

Many people say professional golf is just a game of "bomb and gouge," which means hitting your drives as far as possible without regard to where it lands. I believe that's a misnomer - the longer hitters on tour have incredible accuracy and well-rounded ball striking skills. Either way, what's happening in the professional world has not transferred over to the recreational game.

Various studies have confirmed that regular golfers have not experienced any massive jumps in swing speed or overall distance. The results are similar, whether it's the Distance Insight Report from the

USGA and R&A or data from shot-tracking companies like Shot Scope and Arccos. The average male golfer is driving the ball about 225 yards, which has held steady for a long time.

The evidence is quite clear - regular golfers need even more help with speed and distance than the pros do. One of the great takeaways from Mark Broadie's book *Every Shot Counts* is that recreational golfers stand more to gain from a scoring perspective by adding 20 yards of distance than a pro golfer does.

Another unmistakable trend is that handicap level directly correlates with distance. Better golfers tend to hit it farther. Adding swing speed (responsibly) is one of the great investments you can make in lowering your handicap.

The good news is that you don't need to undertake any kind of intensive training regimen. If you are doing the proper work, you can spend as little as 45-60 minutes a week and see tangible results. More importantly, it's pretty fun and rewarding to see your progress. Who doesn't like showing up to the course and hitting their drives past their buddies?

INCREASING SPEED THE RIGHT WAY

Any change you make in your golf game comes with an inherent risk. There are examples of pro golfers who have chased speed, which has damaged their technique and belief in their golf swing. While there are no guarantees, I believe the methods I'll suggest have a much higher chance of adding speed and improving some of your impact fundamentals. I should also note that you should consult with your doctor to ensure your body can handle specific exercises.

Either way, you can't expect just to swing harder and see better results. Swinging harder might increase your speed, but impact conditions suffer when golfers don't take the appropriate steps. Most notably, a player will struggle to access the center of the clubface and lose distance through lack of ball speed.

The winning recipe trains your body to move faster without feeling like you are trying harder on the course or swinging any differently. You are just changing what "normal" feels like. Think of it as removing the governor from a golf cart. You'll press the pedal just the same, but the cart moves faster.

Based on my testing and research, I believe there are two main methods that everyday golfers can pursue to add speed - speed training and golf fitness training. It's hard for me to say which one is better, though I think you have the best chance of success if you do a mixture of both. Typically, I use my offseason months to train more for speed and go into "maintenance mode" during my full golf season.

Speed Training

Several products have been released throughout the past few years that focus specifically on adding swing speed. SuperSpeed Golf is the most popular and uses a series of weighted sticks to help golfers train through a concept called Overspeed Training. This is a successful method in other sports such as track and field. In a sense, you are tricking your brain and muscles into believing you can swing the club faster.

SuperSpeed Golf uses a series of weighted sticks to help increase your speed

I have added speed through this kind of training, and it's been a very effective training method for all levels of golfers. The workouts take between 15 - 30 minutes, and you should be prepared to do them 2-3 times a week to see results over months.

Additionally, you'll want to secure a swing speed radar like the PRGR Launch Monitor to monitor your progress along the way. It's crucial to have feedback on how fast you are moving after each swing and track your progress.

Golf Fitness Training

There are a lot of misconceptions about how to train your body for golf and, more specifically, how to create more speed. The term "golf-specific exercises" gets referred to quite a bit and generally is misunderstood. If you are training for golf, you aren't always doing exercises that mimic the golf swing. Instead, you are doing targeted workouts that directly benefit the physical movements that golf requires.

Running 20+ miles a week might improve your overall cardiovascular fitness, but there will not be much transfer over to your golf game. How often do you run on the golf course or require stamina for intense physical exertion? Tiger Woods publicly stated that he regrets running so much earlier in his career and attributes it to many injuries, particularly his knee problems.

For years, the golf world shunned activities like lifting weights for fear of ruining a player's swing or injury. Thanks to organizations like the Titleist Performance Institute (TPI), we have a much clearer understanding of how to train efficiently for improved performance on the course and injury prevention. Almost every professional golfer now trains their bodies just as hard as their swing.

Luckily for you, this information and workout regimens are not reserved for pros who have large budgets for personal training. You can add a fitness regimen with limited equipment at home or your local gym. They are not complicated, you will improve your overall fitness, and best of all, you'll add speed and have more control over your golf swing.

I have to credit one golf fitness professional for a lot of my understanding, Mike Carroll from Fit For Golf. His programs focus on the three fundamentals widely accepted as the cornerstones of improved golf fitness - strength, mobility, and power.

I'll quickly summarize their importance:

- **Mobility:** Your spine, hips, shoulders, and other parts of your body are all required to twist and turn during the golf swing. Since so many golfers lose mobility from lack of exercise and aging, reversing this process through targeted exercises can help improve your swing and prevent injury.
- **Strength:** Your overall strength is perhaps the most critical factor for increased swing speed. Think of it as the overall horsepower of your engine or ability to produce force. The stronger you can get, the higher your potential. Unfortunately, strength training has earned a bad reputation. Its benefits are profound, especially as we age, and it's never too late to start. Bread and butter strength training exercises for your lower and upper body will increase your golf performance, prevent injury, and improve your overall quality of life.
- **Power:** Some people refer to power as explosiveness, and it plays a big role in swing speed. Doing exercises that require jumping or medicine ball throws directly transfers to swing speed and is another critical component of golf fitness.

I am a strong advocate of workout programs like these because the benefits can be profound on and off the golf course. And if you are using your time wisely, it won't take more than 2-3 workouts a week of about 20-30 minutes to see actual results.

For further information, I would recommend checking out the Titleist Performance Institute website - www.mytpi.com. They have plenty of educational resources, and you can find a TPI Certified trainer in your area.

I also highly recommend the Fit For Golf app. For a small monthly fee, you can get access to plenty of programs that can be performed at home or in a gym. I've used it myself, and it's fantastic. The programs are easy to follow and used by touring professionals and recreational golfers. You can learn more at www.fitforgolf.blog

THE BIG IDEAS

- Swing speed is a fundamental golf skill. You can improve upon it no differently than your putting or wedge play.
- Adding speed and distance is a scoring advantage. While there are exceptions, there is a direct correlation between handicap level and swing speed.
- We have a much clearer understanding of what creates speed and how to train for it. Whether it's a fitness regimen or working with a product like SuperSpeed Golf, golfers of any level or age can see tangible results.
- While not necessary for all golfers, working on your swing speed can be a fun endeavor to benefit your golf game and overall health!

CHAPTER 39
WORKING WITH TRAINING AIDS

MANY GOLFERS HAVE SUCCESSFULLY USED certain training aids to make their practice sessions more productive and improve their ball striking or putting. But at the same time, tons of these products collect dust in basements and garages worldwide. Most golfers know the excitement of receiving a new product that promises big results, only to be disappointed shortly afterward. Whether it's poor product design, lack of commitment or both, training aids can be tricky.

Through the years, I've tested a lot of training aids to see if they were something I can recommend to Practical Golf readers. Eager inventors usually tout the magical benefits of their device and how it can help golfers of all levels. Unfortunately, I have found that most of these products fail at two key parameters:

1. **They are not engaging:** The best training aids I have found are easy to set up. They also walk a fine line between being moderately challenging and not boring the end user. Many products I have seen cannot satisfy those requirements.
2. **They are not relevant to your swing:** The golf swing has endless matchups that create functional ball flights. Many training aids promote a specific move or position, which might sometimes provide more harm than benefit.

In addition to my testing, I've asked many teaching professionals whom I respect about their thoughts on training aids. Usually, their answers are a mixed bag. Some teachers have products they like and will use them in certain situations if they believe they can help their students with a specific swing issue. To me, that is a responsible use of a training aid. On the other hand, when I ask many swing coaches if there are any products they think can help golfers, they struggle to answer.

The industry makes billions of dollars every year selling products to golfers with the promise that they'll get better. I have come across some wonderful companies that actually want to help. But I've also been behind many closed doors where the discussion is usually about how much money someone made. So when it comes to this topic, I can be a little cynical because the last thing I want is for people to spend their money on something that has little or no chance of helping their golf game.

There is a short list of products that I like, and you'll notice some mention of them throughout the book. While my opinion is not the end-all-be-all, I prefer simplicity and utility. Perhaps the best training aid isn't even made by a golf company, and it costs less than $20 - it's a foot odor spray!

IS IT RELEVANT?

You have to do your best to decide if a product is relevant to your swing (hopefully with the help of a teacher) and commit to using it. For example, I worked with the DST Compressor training aid years ago. It has a curved shaft that helps promote shaft lean at impact and controlling the clubface direction. At first, it was incredibly frustrating to use. I hit massive pulls, shanks and watched the golf ball do all kinds of crazy things in the air. At that point, it would have been relatively easy to give up. The design made it almost impossible to cheat. But after a while, I started to hone in on the impact position it was promoting, and it was a bit magical for me. I believe it's helped me become a much better iron player.

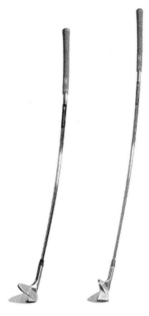

A product like the DST Compressor could work wonders for certain
players, but for others, it might not be relevant

But before you go rushing out to purchase this product, the opposite could have been true for a golfer with a slower swing speed. If that player used an aid like that, it potentially could give them excessive shaft lean and delofted the club at impact too much. As a result, they would lose distance on their iron shots because they did not generate enough ball speed to allow the ball to climb into the air.

I have also tested full-swing trainers, forcing me into positions that don't make sense with my swing matchups. I've used my judgment to quickly abandon them because I did not believe they would help me. So you can see that these products can present a bit of a double-edged sword.

My advice is to be careful and don't believe the hype. If you're watching an infomercial on the Golf Channel, the odds are that product will not transform your golf game like they say it will. That's not to say all training aids are bad, but you shouldn't collect them like swing tips - more is not better.

THE BIG IDEAS

- Training aids usually overpromise and underdeliver - be careful of marketing hype!
- Some products promote techniques in the golf swing that might not be relevant to your game. However, if you can find the right match and put the work in, they can be valuable additions to your practice sessions.
- Some of the best training aids are basic - foot odor spray for impact location, and alignment rods are prime examples.

PART FOUR
THE MENTAL GAME

CHAPTER 40
A COMMITMENT TO FUN

AFTER READING the managing expectations section of this book, you are now on a better path to understanding reasonable outcomes when you play. In this chapter, I'd like to discuss a concept that many golfers gloss over. Consider this your introduction to the mental game.

Sports psychologists rely on performance-enhancing techniques to get professional golfers into peak states. The pressure of playing golf is substantial. To play their best, they need a massive "mental game toolkit" to access. Professional golf is a serious endeavor, and results are everything.

Luckily, that's not the case for you! Golf is a recreational sport. And in case you forgot, let me share the definition of recreational with you:

Relating to or denoting activity done for enjoyment when one is not working.

Many golfers forget that we should be playing this game for fun and enjoyment. I know I did for a long time. It is easy to let your results dictate your enjoyment level. But when you play for your score, you are setting yourself up for disappointment and frustration. How is that fun?

Perhaps my number one piece of advice is committing that you approach golf as a playful activity no matter what. This might sound silly, but I consider this a prerequisite for anyone who wants to increase their performance.

Paradoxically, making this decision will likely lead to better results for most of you. I know what it's like to go through 18 holes, having my satisfaction level ebb and flow with the outcome of each shot. Great things will happen when you can remove the shackles of scoring expectations. Overall, you must do your best not to let your score dictate whether or not you had fun!

Each of you will have your unique path in this game. The most challenging part is figuring out how to balance improving with making sure that the process is enjoyable. Most of this book shares methods to lower your scores efficiently. But my main hope is that everyone can have their cake and eat it too. I want you to get better and have more fun simultaneously. I believe it's possible for everyone.

This section will explore mental techniques that you can employ regardless of your skill or experience. I will talk about pre-shot routines, mindfulness, grit, acceptance, consistency, and gratitude. You can choose which concepts you would like to introduce in your golf game. I don't want you to think it's an all-or-nothing proposition. However, I want you to keep thinking about everything through the lens of playfulness and fun. Try to consider how you will strike your balance between improving and fun because it looks different for each player.

THE BIG IDEAS

- **You are not playing golf for a living - remember, it is a recreational activity!**
- **Committing yourself to enjoy your days on the golf course is necessary for progress.**
- **View golf as a playful activity and think about how you will**

balance your improvement process with your enjoyment of
the game.

CHAPTER 41
NOBODY CARES HOW YOU PLAY

A PERVASIVE FEAR amongst golfers is worrying about what others think about your game. I've heard this from many readers of Practical Golf throughout the years, and I know exactly how everyone feels.

A couple of years ago, I got to play with a renowned figure in the golf industry. He was someone I admired and learned a lot from. I was nervous as we were about to tee off, even more so than some of the biggest tournaments I've played. I wanted to live up to the level of play that I assumed he expected.

After a somewhat shaky start (from both of us), I was honest about my feelings. The interesting thing was that he revealed that he felt very uncomfortable as well. I was worried about playing in front of one of the great minds in golf, and he was worried about playing with a plus handicap. It was an interesting moment and revealed an inherent truth about the game. We all struggle with our confidence and vanity, no matter our experience and skill level.

THE TRUTH IS NOBODY CARES

I have communicated with thousands of golfers worldwide since I started my website. I feel like my inbox is a virtual confessional booth. Players come to me with their fears, anxieties, and worries.

Every golfer, on some level, cares about how they look to their playing partners. It's only natural because we are only one swing away from making fools of ourselves. Golf has a way of making us all vulnerable.

But at the same time, all of us are consumed with our games. This section of the book is dedicated to helping you deal with the thoughts that will run through your head during a round of golf. You will notice all of them will be about you and not your playing partners! That's why golf is a game of mental solitude.

The truth is that nobody cares all that much about your game because they are too busy worrying about their own. And on top of that, everyone knows how embarrassing it is to top their opening tee shot or have a day where nothing seems to go right. We are all united by our folly.

So if you are carrying the burden of worrying about what others think of you, try to breathe a sigh of relief. Generally, we're all rooting for each other to play well.

For the most part, golfers care more about disruptive playing partners. The golf course is a shared experience. Your playing partners might have no clue what score is for the day, but they will notice if you lose your temper and hold the group up.

Overall, the burden of our expectations makes this game challenging enough. Try not to add another mental weight of worrying about what others think of you. Because I can assure you, they are primarily concerned with themselves.

THE BIG IDEAS

- **Every golfer has insecurities and worries about what their** playing partners will think of their game.

- Try to remember that most players are so consumed with their own game that they will not notice what's happening in yours.
- We all know what it feels like to play terribly and embarrass ourselves. But we are all rooting for each other!

CHAPTER 42
STAYING IN THE MOMENT

As you know, we have so much time to think during a round. Each shot only takes seconds, but we have hours to let our minds wander. This extra time presents one of the game's great challenges - the ability to stay present.

Often, golf is a battle between the past and the future. We tend to ruminate on shots that have occurred and worry about the remaining ones. Conversely, champions of the game talk about "taking one shot at a time, and staying focused in the moment." Through much trial and error, all great golfers figure out that remaining in the present is one of the keys to success. Most players know this theoretically but struggle to employ any strategy to improve their ability to focus on the task at hand.

There is a technique that can help all of you. Luckily, many of you are likely using it at some level in your golf game without even knowing it. I'm talking about mindfulness. I'll explain what it is and how it can help, but first, I want to make sure we're all on the same page.

WHAT THE STRUGGLE LOOKS LIKE

My golf game was crippled by fear and an inability to stay focused for many years.

Before I even hit my first shot, I started to worry about how I would play that day. I might start thinking about challenging holes on the course or what swing flaws were plaguing my game at the time.

Once I got out on the course, the fear would build. I'd look at trees, bunkers, hazards and fixate on them. As the round unfolded, frustration would mount if I hit a few poor shots and couldn't put them behind me. On top of that, I'd start to worry about how they would affect my score for the day, and pressure would build on how well I'd have to play for the rest of the day to reach my target score.

I was obsessed with results. They dominated my mind and made it almost impossible to enjoy myself and be engaged properly on each shot.

I'm confident that every golfer reading this book knows how I feel. Through the years, I've received countless questions from players struggling to free their minds from the past and future during rounds.

"I always seem to blow it when I have a good round going. How can I stop being so scared when a great score is within reach down the stretch?"

"My first tee nerves are overwhelming; what can I do to alleviate them?"

"Whenever I get paired up with new people, I struggle to play well because I am so worried about what they think. How do I get past this?"

The questions are different, but they all have the exact root cause. Golfers get so worried about performance and results that it can make the experience of playing unpleasant and prevent them from improving.

To be clear, I don't have a magic wand to eliminate all of your fears and properly focus your mind on every single shot. I've gotten better at this over time, but there are still plenty of days where the past and present can weigh me down. However, there is ample opportunity to improve and see meaningful results.

WHAT IS MINDFULNESS?

Whenever people hear the terms mindfulness or meditation, they often think of someone sitting on a floor in a dark room doing breathing exercises. While this is often a way to train your mind in these practices, there are plenty of techniques you can employ on the golf course.

Here is a commonly used definition of mindfulness:

> *Mindfulness means maintaining a moment-by-moment awareness of our thoughts, feelings, bodily sensations, and the surrounding environment through a gentle, nurturing lens.*
>
> *Mindfulness also involves acceptance, meaning that we pay attention to our thoughts and feelings without judging them—without believing, for instance, that there's a "right" or "wrong" way to think or feel in a given moment. When we practice mindfulness, our thoughts tune into what we're sensing in the present moment rather than rehashing the past or imagining the future.*

Sam Harris, a thought leader in this field, describes it as the following, "Mindfulness allows you to experience your life in the present without ruminating about what just happened, what should have happened, what almost happened."

When I first started to explore mindfulness, it made perfect sense to me why it's a common mental technique used in golf.

LEARNING HOW TO MEDITATE

Before Phil Mickelson won the 2021 PGA Championship, he openly admitted to having problems focusing on the golf course. He turned to mindfulness and meditation to help regain the mental acuity he once had earlier in his career.

While I watched Phil coming down the stretch on Sunday afternoon, I could see him going through miniature meditations before each shot. His victory was one of the most exciting (and improbable) majors, and while we'll never know for sure, his commitment to mental training could have been the deciding factor that week.

While you don't need to have the same intensity and dedication as Phil, you too can learn how to employ meditation and the practice of mindfulness on the golf course.

There are plenty of apps and websites that can help train your mind. I recommend the Waking Up app from Sam Harris. I used it for several months, and the guided meditations that took 5-10 minutes per day taught me valuable lessons. Calm and Headspace are also popular options.

Some might scoff at the idea as being a little too "out there," but I'd encourage you to try it if you are struggling with fear, anxiety, anger, or any of the other emotions that golf seems to conjure out of us.

WHAT IT CAN LOOK LIKE

If you're skeptical, allow me to provide some tangible examples of how I've used these techniques to calm myself down in extreme pressure, and more importantly, have more fun while playing.

- A repeatable and specific pre-shot routine is a perfect way to stay engaged in each moment before each shot.
- Consciously slowing down the pace of your steps when you are nervous (almost every golfer speeds up).
- Focusing on your breath. Feeling the sensation of breathing slowly through your nostrils and exhaling through your mouth.
- Humming songs between shots, or even as you prepare for a shot.
- Engaging with your surroundings on the course. Looking at the wind moving leaves on a tree, the sound of birds chirping, or the beauty of the landscape.

- Simply enjoy the company of your friends and playing partners.

Every golfer can have their unique way of staying present on the golf course. Sometimes we forget what a gift this game is and how special the experience is.

Mindfulness can be a powerful tool to help mitigate many of our mental woes, and it's pretty simple to employ with a bit of practice. I encourage you to go through a few guided meditations and start thinking about ways you can introduce these techniques while you play.

As always, this is not an all-or-nothing proposition. Whether you are a beginner golfer or seeking to compete in elite competitions, there are ways to make this fit with your current game.

THE BIG IDEAS

- **Golf can be a battle between worrying about past shots and ones that haven't occurred yet.**
- **The ability to stay grounded in the present is one of the game's great challenges.**
- **Mindfulness is a technique that can help by learning how to bring awareness to your surroundings and feelings without judgment.**
- **Learning how to meditate on and off the golf course can help players deal with negative emotions and bring more enjoyment to their playing experience.**

CHAPTER 43
WHAT CAN YOU CONTROL?

ONE OF GOLF'S grand illusions is giving you the impression that you have more control over the game than you think you do. This is one of life's most significant challenges, so it's no surprise that we all share this struggle on and off the golf course. The age-old advice, "focus on what you can control and accept what you cannot," proves even more true in becoming a better golfer.

The overall goal is quite simple. First, I want to help you distinguish between what's within your power and what's not. Then I'd like you to shift your focus to working on the former while accepting the latter. The last thing I want you to do is to waste mental energy worrying about something on the golf course that will be beyond your influence!

THE BIG THREE

There are three main categories that I believe golfers can exert control over:

- Preparation
- Routine
- Reactions

You don't have unlimited mental energy. Think of it as an overall budget. If you can learn to spend that budget in the areas you can control and stop wasting on what you cannot, great things will happen in your golf game.

Preparation

There is quite a bit you can do off the course to improve your performance on the course. Proper preparation can make your decision-making process much more manageable, allow your skill to shine, and get your game in a more "autopilot" state.

Here are a few examples that make sense for everyone:

- Practicing effectively
- Studying a golf course and developing a strategic plan
- Getting your body ready (pre-round warm-up or exercise)

You can break down each of those elements further into various categories, but I consider those to be the pillars of preparation that you can have plenty of control over. If you ignore them completely, don't expect improved performance in your game.

Your Routine

Many golfers ask me what they can do to deal with nerves and pressure. Whether it's a tournament, a match with your buddies, or your typical Sunday round, my advice doesn't change that much. I tell most people to commit to going through a routine before every shot, no matter what happens. Simple advice, but difficult to stick with.

I believe all pre-shot routines should have the following elements:

- **Analysis**: Evaluate your position on the course and think about an optimal target and club selection.
- **Preparation**: Establishing your thoughts for the shot.
- **Execution**: Initiating your swing with total commitment.

If you can develop this kind of routine and commit to going through it on every shot, no matter how bad or good things are, you'll create one of the best habits a golfer can have.

Your Reaction

Most golfers don't think about having a post-shot routine, but how you react to each shot is sometimes just as important as preparing for it. You can exert a great deal of control over this process. That's not to say you can't get upset or pump your fist in celebration; those are natural instant reactions.

A good post-shot routine should accomplish the following – internalize your good shots and objectify your bad shots. Most golfers don't give themselves enough credit for good shots or even realize when they've hit one. Conversely, they take it very personally when the bad ones occur, and the negative feelings seem to drag on throughout the round.

While this is incredibly difficult, and you'll never be perfect at it, you have to do your best to separate yourself emotionally when big mistakes occur. Take a step back and think about if you could have done anything differently.

Perhaps you chose the wrong club and misjudged the wind. Or you picked too aggressive of a target when aiming at the green. Many times, it's just a regular occurrence with your technique. This process shouldn't take too long once the shot is over.

My favorite time to do a more in-depth analysis is after the round, while the information is still fresh in my mind.

WHAT YOU CAN'T CONTROL

Now let's examine concepts that are beyond the scope of your control.

The Variability of Your Technique and Skill

How often have you gotten frustrated when you can't take your ball striking from the practice tee to the course? Or have you been wholly demoralized when you have one of your best ball-striking days, and less than 24 hours later, your swing feels like a mess? You're not alone because this happens to every golfer on the planet.

Variability is perhaps one of the most complex parts of golf to accept. You cannot control how your golf swing will perform daily, and it can be maddening.

This is a relative concept, as many things in golf are. All players have what I would call a baseline skill level. Some days they'll perform on the lower end of that potential; other days, they can reach the upper limits. On the whole, most rounds will fall somewhere in between. The hardest part for any golfer is understanding what that variability looks like and accepting that it will happen.

Through practice and playing more, it's possible to increase your base skill level. In other words, your bad days aren't as bad, and your good days are a little better. Additionally, you can make interventions and adjustments on days when you struggle with your swing. But no matter what, you will experience randomness.

The Universe

As you know, golf is played outdoors on various terrains with a small white ball. Your skill and the quality of your swing determine how the ball will initially come off the clubface. After that, you are subject to the rules of the universe.

Weather and the laws of physics seem to torture our souls constantly. The truth is it's not personal. But it feels that way sometimes.

You can select an optimal target to execute the shot exactly how you want, and things still might not work out because of a gust of wind or the way the ball bounces off a small hill.

The great philosopher Forrest Gump sums it up nicely in this quote, "sh*t happens."

People often tell you to control the process, and the results will follow. And essentially, that's what I'm saying as well. However, along the way, many of those results won't be what you want them to be because golf is played in the elements and on uneven ground. Almost all other sports are played on a consistent field (think basketball, hockey, football, baseball, etc.), and it's one of the reasons golfers who play other sports seem to struggle with managing their expectations appropriately. That is part of golf's beauty and challenge.

Overall, golf has so much randomness that you will have to give up a significant amount of control.

STRIKING THE BALANCE

While there are plenty of other concepts to explore regarding what you can control and what you cannot, I consider these "The Big Five."

I'm not telling you to go out there and become perfectly zen with all this advice. I'm still figuring it all out myself!

I hope one or several of these concepts opened your eyes up to something you assumed was true about the game but wasn't. A small inkling of a renewed perspective can have a massive, positive influence on your relationship with the game.

No golfer can strike a perfect balance of control. But you can get better. Remember, it's just a game!

THE BIG IDEAS

- **Learning to take ownership of what you can control in golf and letting go of what you cannot is monumentally difficult, but worth pursuing.**
- **You can take control over your preparation, routine, and reactions.**
- **You cannot control the inherent variability of the game. Every day your swing and performance will change.**
- **You also cannot control the universe. Golf is played on uneven terrain and in the elements. This creates randomness that you have to accept!**

CHAPTER 44
GROWING YOUR GRIT

As MUCH AS I want you to have fun and enjoy your golf game, I have to be honest. There are plenty of moments that will test your patience and emotional stability - that's one of the main challenges of this game. Hopefully, you don't see this as counterintuitive or contradictory, but I'm going to change gears here a bit. If you want to become a better golfer, you will need to learn to dig in when things aren't going your way and change your habits. That's why grit is a valuable asset in your "mental toolbox."

I'll try to be careful as I explore this concept. Whenever I mention words like grit, resiliency, or grinding it out, inevitably, I get the response, "well, that doesn't sound like much fun!" But it's all a matter of perspective and commitment level.

If you are reading this book to become the absolute best golfer and want to lower your handicap, this chapter will be vital, especially if you lack grit. You will need to make changes, and humans do not like change.

However, golf might not be as serious as an endeavor for you. Or you might not even have many opportunities to play. I'll let you make the ultimate decision, but grit might not be relevant or necessary for some. That's the beauty of golf - there is no right or wrong in your approach.

EXPLORING GRIT

When somebody hears the word grit, it can elicit multiple reactions. Often, people envision a negative state. I will not suggest you white-knuckle it through your round of golf. Grit is now primarily associated with positive psychology.

A psychologist who wrote a wonderful book entitled *Grit: The Power of Passion and Perseverance*, Angela Duckworth, defines grit as "persever-ance and passion for long-term goals."

In her research, Duckworth found that grit is a more significant predictor of success than talent. In my journey through golf, I have found that to be the case as well. I've seen so many players with outstanding abilities who can't seem to excel or enjoy golf. Conversely, those who genuinely want to improve and love the process find ways to problem-solve to reach their goals and outperform. More impor-tantly, the satisfaction they derive from that process is gratifying. Personally, I like to hang my hat on grit.

Golf is a very peculiar but addicting game compared to other leisurely pursuits. Let's face it; our tribe is a little crazy to chase a small white ball around a large field. It's hard to explain precisely why golf can be so addicting. A lot of it has to do with how challenging the game is and how good it feels to have those moments where we think we figured it out. But with those incredible highs comes a lot of lows. And I believe those lows are why many players quit the game or find themselves in perpetual limbo.

Unfortunately, we can't have it both ways. You can't become the golfer at the top of your mountain (which is different for each player) without climbing through some mud at the bottom.

Angela Duckworth's words are better than mine:

> One way to think about grit is to consider what grit isn't.

> Grit isn't talent. Grit isn't luck. Grit isn't how intensely, for the moment, you want something.

Instead, grit is about having what some researchers call an "ultimate concern"—a goal you care about so much that it organizes and gives meaning to almost everything you do. And grit is holding steadfast to that goal. Even when you fall down. Even when you screw up. Even when progress toward that goal is halting or slow.

Talent and luck matter to success. But talent and luck are no guarantee of grit. And in the very long run, I think grit may matter at least as much, if not more.

Many golfers can identify with some of these words. And, of course, I want your pursuit of better golf to be primarily fun and playful. But because this game can be so challenging and mentally exhausting at times, adding a bit of grit is almost necessary for most.

WHAT GRIT CAN LOOK LIKE OFF THE COURSE

There are so many examples of how you can add grit to your golf game.

While I'm no master of grit, my experience has shown me its value over the years. Some parts of the game came easier to me at times than others. But eventually, I hit a lot of frustrating walls.

I was utterly terrified of intermediate wedge shots for years and would do anything to avoid leaving myself 30-80 yards from the hole. Eventually, I realized this was impossible to do, and to get better, I had to conquer the problem head-on. So I poured over Dave Pelz's *Short Game Bible*. I highlighted, took notes, and made a genuine effort to absorb the information.

Then I spent hours of meaningful practice to settle on a wedge technique that I could feel comfortable with. Slowly, I became more and more comfortable with these shots while I played. But there were still plenty of times where I chunked a shot, or worse, the dreaded shank! But because I was so determined to solve the problem, I felt confident I could overcome these adverse outcomes.

In a way, I was shifting my mindset and identity. While I still have to work on these shots to maintain my skill, I believe I am an excellent intermediate wedge player. One of my favorite authors, James Clear, describes these as identity-based habits.

When you're looking to solve a problem in your golf game, having grit and the proper habits is usually a winning combination. I recommend the book *Atomic Habits* to just about everyone who follows Practical Golf.

James Clear writes:

> *The key to building lasting habits is focusing on creating a new identity first. Your current behaviors are simply a reflection of your current identity. What you do now is a mirror image of the type of person you believe that you are (either consciously or subconsciously).*
>
> *To change your behavior for good, you need to start believing new things about yourself. You need to build identity-based habits.*
>
> *Imagine how we typically set goals. We might start by saying, "I want to lose weight" or "I want to get stronger." If you're lucky, someone might say, "That's great, but you should be more specific."*
>
> *So then you say, "I want to lose 20 pounds" or "I want to squat 300 pounds."*
>
> *These goals are centered around outcomes, not identity.*

Golfers fall into the same trap. Saying that you're a 20 handicap and want to become a ten handicap is not enough information. You will have to take a much deeper dive into your game to figure out what is holding you back and what habits you need to change to get there. I've given you some ideas earlier in the book on doing this more efficiently and analytically. Grit is the fuel that will keep you going as you face inevitable setbacks in creating this new identity.

I've had to go through this same process with my driver and putting. In my quest to become a better tournament player, it became apparent by watching other golfers and benchmarking my performance that these were also problems that needed to be solved. The predicament was that I kept telling myself, "I'm a great iron player, but I just struggle off the tee and on the greens."

It wasn't easy, but now I genuinely believe that I am good at both. But I had to change my processes and habits along the way. As I kept slowly chipping away and celebrating my tiny accomplishments, I was also proving my new identity. I did not want to be the dissatisfied golfer who looked at the course with fear anymore.

USING GRIT ON THE COURSE

I have had my share of mental battles on the golf course, and I know how many of you will struggle. For years, I would approach golf as a make-or-break proposition. I would go out to play with a devastating combination - lack of preparation and unrealistic expectations. My score was the only litmus test of success, and when I felt it was out of reach, I would give up on the day. I had almost zero grit.

I found myself in a binary state - I was either trying way too hard or entirely checked out.

Along the way, I witnessed many of the same behaviors in others. What is most interesting is that having grit elsewhere in life does not necessarily mean it will translate to your golf game. I've played with successful business people, professional athletes, and plenty of other high achievers who undoubtedly have serious grit. But it was nowhere to be found once they teed it up. After a few bad swings, they would lose their composure and continue in a negative mindset for the rest of the day.

There are many reasons why "golf grit" is harder to develop. It's much easier for some to give up when you become embarrassed and your ego is damaged. I know that was the case for me.

So what is grit on the golf course? For me, it's a straightforward definition. It's a commitment to yourself that you will not give up and stay mentally engaged no matter what happens. And this is another moment where you have to choose your adventure. For some, this level of commitment might not make sense or isn't fun. And I have to stress that it's not an all-or-nothing proposition; there is no perfection with grit.

Every round of golf is an opportunity to learn, grow, build new habits, and work on your grit. I used to play a terrible game with myself where I would either turn on or turn off for the day. Let's say I had a bad opening stretch of holes; I would tell myself, "OK, you're done for the day." And then six holes later, I might have a few good shots and then say, "wait, you're back! This is a real round." This mental inconsistency is not productive.

With these earlier chapters in the mental game section, I'm ultimately building a process you can commit to on every shot. I will get into specifics on what I believe are productive elements of pre-shot and post-shot routines. Overall, grit is the commitment to going through these routines on as many shots as possible.

I hope you can start building more consistent and positive habits on the golf course. In concept, this all sounds very simple. But to this day, despite what I consider a very high grit level, there are still rounds where I have to struggle to stay engaged. And I believe on those days, it's where you have your best chance to grow your grit and solidify these habits. This is no different than someone trying to establish a fitness routine - the moments you feel tired and lazy are the actual test.

THE BIG IDEAS

- Grit is a necessary component in your "mental toolbox" - it is defined as perseverance and passion for long-term goals.
- Have a positive mindset and solve problems through analysis and change your habits.
- Altering your identity and being specific about what habits you will change is crucial.
- Growing your on-course grit and staying engaged in rounds no matter your results is how many golfers break through to the next level.

CHAPTER 45
THE HARDEST BALANCING ACT

THROUGHOUT THE LAST 25 YEARS, I'm confident that I have either made or witnessed every mistake imaginable in golf – especially in the mental game. And I now know that it is critical to strike a balance and avoid extremes when it comes to your attitude and engagement level. While this might sound generic and simple, I can guarantee that getting this right (or improving) will be part of your keys to getting better at this game. We can all use help in this department.

Almost every golfer plays their best when they can exist in the space between caring too much or not at all. This is very hard to do.

In other words, you can't live and die at the result of every shot. But at the same time, you need to be engaged enough to control your emotions and approach each shot analytically.

Finding the happy medium between caring too much and not enough might look different for all of you. We each bring our unique personalities to the game. However, I know that tipping in either direction too heavily does not work out in the long run.

I find that two words - consistency and acceptance, can help you all find your balance.

LIVING AND DYING ON EACH SHOT

18 holes (or even 9) is a long time. Each round of golf usually has different acts. They can even be as dramatic as some of your favorite movies. There is heartbreak, hubris, triumph, and even redemption.

For a long time, one of my most significant flaws as a golfer was that I reacted too dramatically based on the result of each shot.

An errant drive might send me into a panic – all of a sudden, I'm walking faster and worrying about what my next mistake might be. Conversely, an early birdie might have had me "peacocking" a bit too much and wondering how well I would score that day.

You cannot become a better golfer if you are constantly in this state.

PLAYING "I DON'T CARE GOLF"

On the other end of the spectrum, there is a desire to check out when things get tough mentally.

Unfortunately, golf doesn't work this way. There are ample opportunities to bail out or say to yourself, "I don't care what happens." Often, I find golfers do this as a defense mechanism. We're scared to find out how badly we might score if we keep trying after a rough patch. Sometimes it feels like we are staring into the abyss (yes, this game can make us feel that way).

This extreme doesn't work either. If you are going back and forth between caring and not caring, there is no opportunity to grow as a player. Of course, we care how we play!

APPROACHING THE GAME WITH MORE CONSISTENCY

For several years, I got to play with a golfer named Tom, who embodied the word consistency. He was one of those players who made the game look way too easy. Watching him play was actually quite boring and an important lesson for me. Tom seemed to hit almost every fairway and green. When he (rarely) got into trouble, he got out of it quickly and didn't panic. His demeanor and performance were as consistent as it comes.

Tom's skill was the result of decades of hard work. After almost every round, he was on the range, working on whatever part of his game he felt was deficient. There was a wear mark the size of a dime on his driver in the perfect impact spot - a reminder that he worked very hard at the right things to make the game look easy.

I tried my best to learn every time I played with Tom. He was one of the best tournament players in our area for a long time. He wasn't forthright with many of his secrets, but I could see his game was well-rehearsed and thought out after playing many rounds with him.

One of the few nuggets of wisdom he did impart on me sticks out to this day. He told me that he tries to do everything exactly the same when he plays in tournaments. While that might sound generic, Tom said that even the rhythm he walks and picks up his tee after a shot is identical.

At the time, that level of consistency seemed a little overboard to me. Who would do such a thing? But throughout the last decade, as I've gone through my competitive journey, I've realized that little details like that are essential. I find myself clinging to consistency at the tiniest levels - even how I take my tees, ball markers, and divot repair tool out of my bag before I tee off.

Consistency is a relative concept, just like everything else I discuss. You can choose your level of commitment.

Golf can be an uncomfortable game - variance and chaos can reign supreme. Being as consistent as you can with your emotions, routine, practice, and just about anything else in this game helps mitigate the variability.

ACCEPTANCE

Acceptance is another word that goes hand in hand with consistency and is a cornerstone of a solid mental player. There is so much in golf that you have to accept rather than reject.

Several years ago, I played with an avid golfer who was also an accomplished psychiatrist. Like anyone else, he was searching for secrets of the game. He told me that most of the standard psychological advice he saw for golfers was a bit of a letdown and asked if I had anything better to offer.

I confessed that I wasn't sure that I did, but I did talk about how much I struggled over the years with accepting all of the feelings and outcomes golf presents us with. Then I hit a tee shot into a penalty area on a Par 5. The moment felt interesting, and I tried to explain how I used to deal with that moment versus how I currently try to deal with it.

Most likely, the old me would have scolded myself and lost my temper. Perhaps that disappointment would have carried over to the next shot, and I would have made a mental error that cost me more strokes.

The newer me (still not perfect, but trying to get better) did a quick post-shot analysis. I determined it wasn't a bad swing. I struck the ball well, and it probably traveled about 20-25 yards right of my target due to a slightly open clubface at impact, which was a perfectly reasonable dispersion. I realized my error was strategic. I had not done my homework on this hole and realized that the penalty area (a small creek) on the righthand side was in play, and I should have taken less club. Either way, I had to close the chapter on that shot and make a good decision on the next one.

It was an interesting choice because I had to drop the ball behind a tree. I was 220 yards from the hole and still had an opportunity to reach the green and make par, or even birdie. But I did have to hit a reasonably large fade to avoid the tree. Since that is not my natural shot shape, that would introduce a dreaded double-cross into another penalty area up the left side of the hole.

So I chose the more intelligent, high-percentage shot and hit a low punch to wedge distance. I got it on the green and two-putted for bogey. As our conversation continued, I explained how that was a perfect circumstance where I would have rejected the outcome of the tee shot in the past. My frustration likely would have chosen the more aggressive, low percentage shot when presented with a recovery situation. Overall, while not a glorious scenario, I felt it illustrated how acceptance saves strokes in the long run.

I could write a whole other book on all of the things that you have to accept about golf rather than fight against.

You must accept that you will feel complete control over your golf swing and then be completely clueless another day. Heck, that can even happen in the span of six holes!

You must accept that you will have moments where you feel nervous, anxious, or embarrassed.

You must accept that a great round could be derailed by one errant swing or an unfortunate bounce.

You must accept that you will still make mistakes no matter how disciplined or skilled you become.

FINDING YOUR BALANCE

Striking a balance between being too engaged or not engaged enough while playing can be complex. This is a concept you'll have to reflect upon and how it relates to your demeanor on the course.

Not everyone's balance will look the same, but I think adding more consistency and acceptance to your overall approach will likely help.

THE BIG IDEAS

- **Having strong reactions, positive or negative, to each shot creates a "mental rollercoaster" that makes it hard to enjoy golf and improve.**

- Working on your mental consistency can be just as important as your swing. Golfers need to learn to balance between caring too much or not enough.
- Learning to accept all outcomes, particularly the negative ones, is a sign of a solid mental game.

CHAPTER 46
WHAT SHOULD YOU THINK ABOUT WHILE YOU SWING?

WHEN MOST GOLFERS are introduced to the game, it's all about their swing. We are programmed to consciously think about what our bodies are doing at all times. Keep your head still, get your hands in a certain position in your backswing, don't forget to rotate! No matter what level of player, the dominant form of instructional content focuses on the body's movement.

We collectively assume (and are taught) that we should be thinking about these things before, during, and after we hit a shot. Often, this results in playing "golf swing" and not golf. Make no mistake; those are two entirely different concepts.

But what if there were more productive thoughts that had nothing to do with the golf swing? While we can't completely control our minds on the golf course, I strongly encourage you to experiment with shifting your focus away from the swing and the various movements your body makes. Many skilled players figure this out on their own terms, but that doesn't mean they should keep the knowledge.

I stumbled upon many of these concepts throughout the years through trial and error. Also, talking with better players has given me more feedback on how golfers shift their focus depending on their skill level and the kinds of shots they are playing. Additionally, my podcast co-host, Adam Young, helped refine my thinking on this topic.

THE BIG THREE

Generally speaking, there are three different focuses of attention as it pertains to golf (or just about any other sport):

- **Internal Focus:** Concentrating on the movement itself, your actual golf swing. For example, what your arms or wrists are doing throughout the swing.
- **External Focus:** Thinking outside your body. This could be concentrating on striking a particular part of the clubface, brushing a blade of grass in front of the ball, or envisioning a specific trajectory or shot shape.
- **Neutral Focus:** Unrelated to the movement or process of the shot. A simple example is focusing on breathing. Another could be humming a song.

These can be broken down further, especially external focuses, but it's best to think of them in these three buckets for simplicity.

Most sports default to preaching an internal focus - it's all about what your body is doing. But over the years, a growing body of research in motor learning is pointing out that it might be detrimental to the growth of certain players, and moving towards more external (task-related) thoughts can speed up skill development.

Internal Focus - The Default

You have likely seen this image before on social media.

While it's become satirical, there's a lot of truth to it.

For the most part, golfers play the game thinking about all of the internal movements of the golf swing. While internal thoughts can be productive and suit certain players better, they can limit many golfers from reaching their potential.

For example, if you were playing catch with a friend – would you think about what your arm and wrist need to do to throw the ball properly to the target? Probably not. If you did think about those things, you would likely struggle to complete the task and miss your mark.

We generally do not obsess over form and mechanics in other sports as much as golf. So then why should golf be any different?

I believe that if some golfers start to move away from internal swing thoughts, especially on the golf course, and start to shift their attention elsewhere, they will free their bodies up to execute athletically. Most players can hit the kinds of shots they want to; sometimes, they have to get out of their own way!

One of the greatest examples I can think of comes from Dave Stockton's book, *Unconscious Putting*. He likens putting to someone driving a car on a highway. When driving, you don't think about where your hands are on the wheel or how hard you have to press the gas pedal. However, if you suddenly see a police car in your rear-review mirror, your body will likely tense up, and you will start thinking about what your hands, arms, and legs are doing. Instead of driving the car, you are guiding the car.

Stockton believes that most golfers putt like they have a cop car in their rear-view mirror. I'll take his example even further; I think most golfers swing that way too.

While no rule of thumb fits all golfers, I believe practice sessions are the time to concentrate more on internal swing thoughts. Also, lower-skilled players who are still learning the game and making swing changes can still benefit from internal thoughts on and off the course. Nonetheless, I believe the overall goal should be to put more conscious swing work off the course, so you can unconsciously perform on the course.

This is why an external focus on the golf course can be so helpful to many golfers. It can get you out of "swing jail," where you are constantly thinking about what your body is doing and moving more towards creating the result you want. And if you are a golfer who benefits from internal thoughts, your brain can't possibly tolerate five of them while you prepare and execute a shot. One or two would be more appropriate.

The Power of External Thoughts

Many golfers can have breakthroughs in their games when they shift their focus outside of their body and more on a task. I've seen the power in my own game.

While there are many forms of external focuses, many of the examples I gave in the practice section of the book are external:

- If you're striking it too close to the heel of the club, consciously try to hit the toe.

- Are you struggling with a nasty slice? Try to hit the biggest hook imaginable.
- Do you hit your iron shots "fat?" Try striking the ground several inches in front of the ball during practice.

If you notice, none of these tell you to externally rotate your shoulder more or ask you to get your hands higher in your backswing. That's because I genuinely believe if you self-organize around a task like trying to strike the toe of your clubface, your body will start making the required movements without consciously thinking about them. In my opinion, this is where you want to get to with your game, especially on the golf course.

When I'm playing my best golf, I'm not worried about what my arms, legs, and hands are doing during my swing. I focus on striking the turf with my irons in front of the ball. Or perhaps I'm envisioning playing a fade with my driver as a way to counteract an excessive hook that I'm fighting that day.

It's not to say golfers can't succeed with internal swing thoughts on the course. There are plenty of examples of that working. Internal thoughts have their time and place – perhaps when making a swing change or on the range. However, if I had to place a bet, more golfers are struggling because of the wrong internal thoughts than being helped by them.

I'd rather players unlock their inner athlete by trying to shift their attention away from the swing (as hard as that is to do).

Neutral Swing Thoughts

There is a third category of focus that doesn't even involve golf. These are neutral thoughts such as humming the rhythm of a song or focusing on deep breathing in times of stress.

Many athletes refer to these thoughts as being "in the zone." I've had a lot of success in tournaments humming songs to myself (sometimes songs my kids listen to). Or, when I'm feeling a lot of pressure, I will consciously slow my body down and focus on slowing my breath in an almost meditative state.

Neutral thoughts aren't for all golfers. On the whole, they're probably better suited towards more skilled players. Thinking about something entirely different from golf can help certain players get out of their way and allow their bodies to do what it knows how to do. Either way, they can be as impactful as an external focus for a beginner or intermediate player.

EXPERIMENT ON YOUR OWN

Now that you (hopefully) know there are different things you can think about other than the movement of your body, it's time to experiment. Since our brains work differently, it's best to test what kinds of thoughts can help you get better results. An excellent place to start is always on the practice tee, and then you can slowly bring it on the course.

On the whole, many of you will see incremental success going from internal to external thoughts. And for more experienced players, a neutral focus can help just as much.

The focus of attention is another tool during your pre-shot routine. When you can start to hone in on what kind of thoughts are most productive for different styles of shots on the course, you can incorporate them into your routine.

For example, I find that neutral thoughts are most productive for me while putting. I'm often humming a song to myself as I make my read and go through my routine. Conversely, I have a more external focus with my iron and wedge shots, such as where I am trying to strike the turf (in front of the ball). I'm also in a primarily external focus with my driver, but more so on shot shape. While it might sound counterintuitive, I'm thinking about the opposite shot shape than my fault, which generally helps me hit a straighter ball flight with less curvature.

So when we get to the pre-shot routine chapter, keep these concepts in mind. It can help during your preparation and execution phase.

THE BIG IDEAS

- Most golfers assume they should focus on their bodies before and during the swing. It doesn't have to be this way!
- There are three primary ways to consciously focus - internal (movement of body parts), external (the task itself), and neutral (unrelated to the movement).
- Internal thoughts are better during practice sessions, swing changes, and for players still learning the game. But having too many of them, especially on the golf course, can prevent you from performing your best.
- Shifting to an external focus, or focusing on the task itself, can benefit golfers tremendously. It frees your body to self-organize athletically.
- A neutral focus, such as focusing on your breathing, can be calming and effective for higher-skilled players.
- Experimenting with these concepts can be effective during your practice sessions and pre-shot routines.

CHAPTER 47
BUILDING A SUCCESSFUL PRE-SHOT ROUTINE

MUCH OF THE advice I give golfers about the mental game is tied together in the pre-shot routine. Everything you do before you hit each shot can influence its outcome. Overall, a consistent routine can help clear your mind, deal with nerves, access your skill, and make smarter decisions.

However, I see many golfers go through routines that aren't productive. Many players will do things before a shot just to do them. Golfers often copy what they see on TV or perhaps a playing partner of theirs that is a better golfer. In this chapter, I'll try to break down each part, advise how I think you can create a successful process specific to you, and take ownership of it.

When a golfer comes to me with questions on how they can deal with varying mental issues that arise on the course, my answer is usually the same:

> **Commit to going through your routine before each shot, pick a smart target, execute, and accept the result. Then move on to the next shot and do it all over again.**

That sounds incredibly simple, and it will be much harder to do while you're playing, but I believe in that statement. Golf is a series of independent events. Your routine is a way to reflect that truth. Additionally, it's a way to bring more consistency to your game.

GETTING INTO A REACTIVE STATE

Before I took up golf, I played every sport imaginable. Like many of you, I quickly noticed the difference between golf and everything else.

In most sports, you are reacting to an opponent. There isn't much time to think before execution.

Whether a pitcher throws you a fastball, you are about to shoot a basketball, or you are chasing down a tennis ball - these decisions happen in a split second. Many times you are not initiating the action. You are responding to it. There isn't much time for thoughts about technique; it just happens.

Conversely, in golf, there is almost too much time to think. Before each shot, there is ample opportunity to fill your mind with thoughts about the golf swing and plenty of other things that can distract you from accessing your inner athlete.

I genuinely believe that most golfers have potential to hit better shots on the course if they can get themselves into a more reactive state over the golf ball. It's not easy, but a routine can more often help you access this zone.

A good routine should be like hitting an autopilot button before and during each shot. It is so familiar that you can do it without consciously thinking about it.

Several years ago, I played in a golf tournament with several ex-athletes. It was a real treat for me since I watched them compete in their respective sports on TV. Luckily for me, they were all happy to answer my endless questions.

The one I was interested in speaking to the most was one of the best kickers in the NFL when he played. Unsurprisingly, he was a great golfer too. Anyone that watches football knows that the kicker is one of the most pressure-packed positions in all sports. They only get called to the field several times a game, and the result of the entire game often hangs on whether they make or miss a field goal. Both he and I agreed that there were some parallels to golf. I thought I could glean some mental knowledge from him since his entire professional career dealt with extreme pressure.

When I asked how he dealt with the pressure of kicking in front of tens of thousands of fans and even in a Super Bowl, his answer surprised me. He said he was obsessed with routine. In practice, they would kick field goals repeatedly with the same timing down to the millisecond. He would follow the team down the sideline kicking into a net with the same exact routine during games.

Eventually, when he was called upon to kick the field goal, he could perform because he felt like he was just executing the routine that was so familiar to him. It allowed him to block out thoughts that might affect his performance.

His talent, work ethic, and other factors made him a great kicker. But it was interesting to hear at the highest level of sports that such small details that seemed so simple were one of the cornerstones of his career.

Of course, I don't want all of you to think that you need this type of focus and commitment. But a good pre-shot routine that you can repeat unconsciously can help you deal with golf's pressures and get you into a more reactive, unconscious state.

WHAT A ROUTINE CAN AND CAN'T DO

Before we get into the elements of a productive routine, I want to manage your expectations.

Like anything in golf, there are no guarantees. You can analyze your shot, pick a smart target, go through a mentally precise routine, and still have an undesirable outcome.

Additionally, pre-shot routines can not overcome a lack of skill. They are not some kind of magic wand that will have you hitting incredible shots suddenly. You'll still need to put in some sort of work to enhance your ball-striking skills.

One of the most common complaints I hear from readers of my site is that they can hit all of these incredible shots on the practice range, but when it comes time to execute on the course, that golfer is nowhere to be found. And I know exactly how they feel.

I believe routines can help golfers access those great shots more often by getting them into the "reactive state." This is a way to allow you to access more of your potential by getting into a more unconscious state rather than consciously worrying about all of the things that could go wrong with your swing.

IT DOESN'T NEED TO BE LONG, AND IT SHOULD BE CONSISTENT

Another thing I'd like to clarify (I promise we'll get to the nuts and bolts soon) is how much time it should take. In recent years, I've noticed in tournaments that many players take longer and longer to go through routines before they hit shots, especially on the putting green. Many players take their cues from watching professional golfers on TV.

I firmly believe that a successful pre-shot routine should not take that long. There's some evidence that suggests that faster is better.

Several years ago, Dr. Matt Bridge conducted a study at European Tour events that measured how long pro golfers were spending before each shot and compared their performance. Over 22,000 shots were measured in five tournaments. The conclusions supported that less time over the ball increased performance, especially with putting. Here are some of the key findings:

- On putts inside of five feet, less time doubled the likelihood of the putt being holed.

- Shorter time leads to a 90% increase in the probability of strokes gained with putting.
- Overall, spending less time over the ball could earn a tour player more than $200,000 per season.

For most recreational golfers, the more time you spend before the shot is an opportunity for indecisiveness to creep in. It's improbable your confidence is going to increase as more time elapses. Also, you want to respect other players' time, so spending 90 - 120 seconds before each shot will not please the other golfers in your group.

So when you are trying to formulate your pre-shot routine, don't do something for the sake of doing it. Make sure it has a specific purpose.

Another essential element to consider is consistency. If you were to watch clips of Tiger Woods or Annika Sorenstam in their prime, you could take a stopwatch to their pre-shot routines, and they would be almost the same each time. It wouldn't matter if it were the opening shot of the tournament or the 72nd hole with a major championship on the line.

Consistency was another critical factor in Dr. Bridge's European Tour study. He found that players who were more consistent over the golf ball were 50% more likely to make cuts than less consistent players.

Of course, it will take some time and work to develop a concise, meaningful, and consistent pre-shot routine. It won't happen overnight. Routine is a part of your game that needs some work, just like your swing.

THE COMPONENTS OF A PRE-SHOT ROUTINE

After a massive build-up, I'm pleased to present you with the components of a successful routine. This is your opportunity to exert complete control in a game where many things are out of your control.

I'll go into more detail, but here are the three main elements:

- **Analysis:** examine the conditions you're facing on each shot -

the lie, distance, wind direction, elevation change, the area surrounding your target, etc.

- **Rehearsal and Preparation:** standing behind your ball and establishing your thoughts for the shot. This part can be personal and include practice swings, visualization, target focus, and alignment.
- **Execution:** Crossing the "imaginary line" and initiating your swing with complete commitment.

Analysis Phase

The first step is going through your analysis of the shot. There are a few ways to do this. A lot of this phase will incorporate many of the principles from the strategy part of the book.

Overall, you are trying to figure out what club you're going to use, your target, and your shot type. I want to stress the importance of this phase - this is where a lot of players throw away shots on the course because they're not going through any kind of analysis or consistently make poor decisions.

A lot of analysis can occur before you get to the golf course or even before you get to your ball. For example, in my chapter on studying golf courses, I gave a few suggestions on how you could plan out your tee shots using satellite imagery. Additionally, you can do some preparation before you arrive at your ball (which is one reason I love walking the course, it allows me more time to do this).

I'll reiterate some of the strategic concepts briefly, but here is what you'll need to consider.

- **Lie:** where the ball rests will most influence your decision-making. For example, if you had a bad lie in the rough or were facing a lip in a fairway bunker, you should be making an entirely different decision than if your ball was in the fairway.
- **Distance:** you'll need to decide how far you want to hit the shot. This should consider a few different factors - elevation changes, wind direction, the areas surrounding your target (is

there trouble?). A distance measuring device or phone app can make this more efficient and accurate.

- **Target and Shot:** once you have determined how far you want to hit the shot, it's time to pick a very specific target and the shot type. As discussed in the course management section, this will consider your typical shot patterns and what is surrounding your landing zone.

I often view the analysis phase of a pre-shot routine similar to Texas Hold 'Em for poker players. Each shot is a new and different situation that needs to be sized up. No different than a poker player who has to calculate odds quickly as each card series is dealt out.

As you become more familiar with proper strategy, you can make decisions quickly and more decisively before each shot. This is why I tried to offer you a simple framework for course management - you don't want to spend a long time in the analysis phase.

One of the most challenging parts of the analysis process is acknowledging all of the trouble on the course. You'll want to use this information to pick a more intelligent target. However, once you decide on your target, you'll have to focus on it exclusively. This balancing act is one of the hardest things in golf and requires a lot of experience and commitment.

Ideally, you'll step up to your ball, take a quick look at your lie, check your distances, and evaluate some other factors in seconds to arrive at your target, club selection, and shot type. As I mentioned earlier, much preparation can occur as you approach your ball or even before you reach the golf course.

Overall, the goal is to be as committed to your decision as possible. Once you move on to the next step of the routine, no new analysis should be done. Think of it like mentally closing a colossal bank vault! Pulling your club out of the bag should represent the end of the analysis phase.

Rehearsal and Preparation

Now that you've picked your club selection and target, it's time to move on to the rehearsal and preparation segment of the pre-shot routine. Preparation can be very personal; there is no right way to do this. However, you want to be specific with your intentions. Don't do something like a swing rehearsal unless it has a particular purpose.

I'll deconstruct this phase with what I do before each shot to give you an example.

- I stand several feet behind my ball, mainly focused on my target and visualizing my shot.
- I take two swing rehearsals. Generally, I'm thinking about my stock "swing feel," which is not too mechanical. If I'm trying to make an on-course correction, such as altering my swing path or feeling how open or closed my clubface is at impact, I will incorporate that into the swing rehearsal.
- I return my focus to my target. I have a unique alignment method, where I position my clubhead pointing at my target and leave it there as I get set over the golf ball.

This phase is an opportunity to gather your focus for the shot. Again, this can be very personal, and you can use the swing thoughts part of this book to get some ideas.

Some golfers might stand behind their ball, mentally rehearse their swing thoughts, and then take several practice swings to solidify them. Others might just look at their target, commit to it, and step up to the ball without any swing rehearsals (or thoughts).

If you look at professional golfers, you'll see that they each have different methods. But you will notice consistency, which you should strive for when you go through your rehearsal. I derive a lot of comfort going through the same process before each shot, and it helps get me into the "autopilot" mode where I try to turn off my conscious thoughts.

If I had to simplify a framework for golfers, it would look like this:

- Stand behind your ball with a visual focus of the target and shot you are trying to play.
- Physically rehearse a swing with your specific focus for the shot (optional).
- Return your focus to the target and have a method to align yourself.

Pulling The Trigger (Execution)

When you're finished with your analysis and pre-shot rehearsal, it's time to step into the shot and execute. This phase is where a lot of things can go wrong for golfers.

It's helpful to think of crossing an imaginary line. Behind the line, you've considered all of the elements necessary to pick a smart target, club selection, and shot type. You've also gone through a mental and physical rehearsal. Once you cross the line, it's time to execute. Ideally, there should be no new information. You're not changing targets or thinking of new swing thoughts - it's time to pull the trigger and hit the shot!

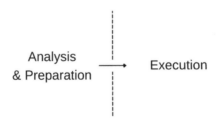

The execution phase is where most players struggle. You'll see golfers spending enormous time over the ball, almost frozen in time. Usually, their minds are filled with tons of swing thoughts or fear about what could happen. They are trying to control the shot rather than letting it happen. It's highly counterintuitive, but everyone who plays falls victim to thinking they can have complete control. You have to do your best to let go and give up control over what could happen.

To give yourself the best chance of having success, you should be as decisive and fast as possible. It should not take more than a few seconds over the ball (perhaps after a few waggles to settle yourself) to start your swing.

Additionally, you don't need a laundry list of swing thoughts. No checklists are necessary. I would prefer the opposite. Based on your skill level and experience, I'd suggest going back to the swing thoughts chapter to explore how internal, external, or neutral thoughts can help as you stand over the ball. Either way, they should be as simple as possible.

For example, I focus on a small area of grass in front of the golf ball as a mental cue for ground contact with approach shots. When I'm on the putting green, I take one last look at my line and usually say to myself mentally, "good speed" so I can focus on matching the speed of the putt to my mind's view of the target (no different than throwing a baseball or football).

The whole point of practice is to consciously work on your golf swing and build your skill and technique. Those are the times to engage in the golf swing mechanics when you're off the course. However, when it's time to pull the trigger, you must try to perform the swing unconsciously.

In other words, I want you to step into the shot and just hit it! You have to do your best not to let your brain get in the way. Every golfer is different, but for most of you, I'd argue that spending less time over the golf ball and learning how to initiate your swing will lead to better results. We even saw this was the case with professional golfers in the study I mentioned earlier.

Having a mental or physical trigger for some golfers can help initiate the swing and prevent the dreaded "frozen over the ball" scenario. You'll notice golfers with very subtle triggers, like slightly leaning the shaft of the club forward before they swing. Others might have a countdown in their head saying, "three, two, one, go." When I'm on the putting green, I make a small move to square my shoulders to the target before moving the putter, which helps correct an alignment flaw.

While it is not necessary, it might help some of you to introduce a trigger into your execution phase to signal to your brain and body that it's time to initiate your swing. Eventually, it could become so comforting that you won't even think about it anymore.

PRACTICING YOUR ROUTINE

Hopefully, I've given you some good ideas on building your pre-shot routine or altering your existing routine to make it more effective. If you are interested in making a change, it will take some work and time.

Earlier in the chapter, I mentioned my conversation with the NFL kicker, who told me one of the keys to his success on the field was making his routine the same during practice. Golf is very similar.

If you want to give yourself the best chance of improving, start going through your pre-shot routine during your practice sessions. I believe the benefit is twofold:

- It will help you stay more engaged in your practice sessions and avoid "zombie range sessions."
- You will start to build comfort and experience with your routine, which will improve its effectiveness on the golf course.

This skill needs to be developed, no different from accessing the club-face's center. Treat it as such!

THE BIG IDEAS

- **Having a consistent, meaningful pre-shot routine can help alleviate many of golf's mental challenges.**
- **One of the overall goals is to get a golfer into a reactive, subconscious state before each shot rather than being bogged down by various swing thoughts.**
- **A productive pre-shot routine does not need to be long. There is plenty of evidence to prove that taking less time will**

yield better results. Each element should have a specific purpose.

- There are three main elements to a pre-shot routine: analysis, rehearsal/preparation, and execution.
- The analysis phase considers your lie, distance, and other factors to pick your target and shot type. A lot of this draws upon your course management skills.
- In the rehearsal and preparation phase, you shift your focus more to your target and shot type.
- Imagine crossing an imaginary line into the execution zone when you are done with your analysis and rehearsal. You should be fully committed to your decision, and no new information is processed.
- The execution phase should be short - perhaps a few waggles of the club, and then you pull the trigger! Having a singular focus, like brushing a blade of grass in front of the ball or some kind of trigger to initiate the swing, is very helpful.
- Practice sessions are also a time to work on your pre-shot routine. Build your process, and make it your own.

CHAPTER 48
BUILDING A POST-SHOT ROUTINE

NOW THAT WE'VE covered the pre-shot routine, what should you do after you hit the shot? A post-shot routine can be equally important and sometimes more influential in your development as a golfer. Unfortunately, this part of the mental game is usually overlooked.

One of my greatest struggles was how I reacted to each shot. A combination of unrealistic expectations, poor emotional control, and impatience made each round a bit of a roller coaster. I had no kind of system or mental framework to form a post-shot routine.

For years, I never gave much thought to the process or even gave it a name. Surprisingly, reading a book about wedge play clarified the concept and reinforced a few things I was starting to figure out as my mental performance improved.

In James Sieckmann's book, *Your Short Game Solution*, he discusses the notion of a post-shot routine. Despite it being a great read on how golfers can take a more modern approach to wedge play, this section is one of the most valuable.

After plenty of reflection and learning from other mental coaches I respect, here is my current definition of a productive post-shot routine:

Internalize, take ownership, and celebrate your great shots. Be proud of them! Conversely, view your poor results through a non-emotional, objective, and analytical lens.

Similar to the pre-shot process, I will deconstruct each element. This will be a new way to think about each shot on the course for many of you. You'll also have to put some work into this, and with experience, this process should not take very long on the course.

CAN YOU IDENTIFY A GOOD OR GREAT SHOT?

It seems like a minor miracle when you dig into the physics of what it takes to hit a golf ball remotely close to your target. But most of us gloss over these small victories while we play and only seem to react and notice the negative results.

Most golfers don't even know what a good or great shot is for their skill level. Consequently, there are a lot of missed opportunities to internalize and celebrate these small wins.

For example, many of you probably wouldn't pat yourself on the back for the following:

- Hitting a wedge on the green, 15 feet away from the hole from 100 yards.
- Making bogey after hitting your tee shot in the trees.
- Sinking an 8-foot putt.
- Hitting a drive close to your average distance, in the rough, with a clear, unobstructed path to the green.

If you recall some of the stats I gave in the managing expectations section, you now know that many of those results are equivalent to or better than PGA Tour performance, and you should be happy!

Overall, the first step in establishing a successful post-shot routine is to familiarize yourself with what kinds of outcomes on the course can be deemed positive for your skill and experience level.

CELEBRATING YOUR WINS

A big part of improving your mental game is to build a library of positive memories in your brain. These are extremely helpful, especially when things aren't going so well. However, you can't create this library without filing these positive memories when they occur.

So when you stripe a drive, drain a 20 footer, or hit an excellent approach shot, take a second to internalize the shot. You don't need to go crazy with a Tiger fist pump, but perhaps a small fist pump or telling yourself "great shot" could be in order. The more and more you do this, you'll build a very valuable habit.

In addition to enjoying yourself more, this self-love can build confidence in your game. You can even incorporate these small memories into the preparation phase of your pre-shot routine. Sometimes, when I'm struggling with a specific part of my game or feeling pressure in a tournament, I'll try to bring back memories of my great shots as I visualize my target standing behind the ball. These are small reminders to yourself of what you are capable of.

Understanding positive results relative to your skill level and then taking the time after these great shots to internalize them is half of the equation. The other half is a little more challenging but equally important.

THE MOST COMMON TRAP

Unfortunately, golf provides us with many undesirable outcomes. No matter how good you get at this game, there are a lot of moments where you will have to deal with adversity.

After a negative outcome, the most common tendency is for golfers to let their emotions take over. We scold ourselves, our body language suffers, and tempers can flare up. Admittedly, I've had my fair share of anger and disgust.

These reactions are often unwarranted because golfers don't understand what good results are for their ability level. But there are plenty of times when you'll hit a tee shot out of bounds, get stuck in a bunker, or draw a dreadful lie in the rough.

So, what can we do to keep our round going rather than allow our emotions to take over in these moments?

OBJECTIVE ANALYSIS

As hard as it may be, the best solution to any bad shot is to remove your emotions from the situation and go through a quick, objective analysis. When you're done with your round, you can dive deeper into each situation, which I'll cover in the next chapter.

A good question to ask yourself is, "could I have done anything differently?" You want to do a little detective work based on the intent of your shot and the result.

Sometimes, you can trace the lousy shot back to a strategic mistake such as the following:

- A target that was too aggressive.
- Not taking into account the wind or change in elevation.
- Choosing the wrong club or shot type.

Or perhaps the mistake was more mental. Was there something you could have done differently in your pre-shout routine? Were you not mentally committed to the shot?

Last but not least, I like to examine my ball flight and work backward to impact fundamentals. Was the issue rooted in ground contact, face strike, club path, or face angle? Is there a pattern developing that needs an in-round adjustment?

Many of these variables are intertwined, and sometimes there is no answer other than, "it's just the inherent variability of golf."

Either way, transitioning from reacting with emotion to objective analysis is one of any golfer's most potent tools. It can completely change your mindset, enjoyment level, and performance.

A FEW CAVEATS

This chapter is another opportunity to present my usual disclaimer. How you react to shots is essential, but I don't want you to think that this is easy or you have to be perfect.

It's impossible to control your emotions completely. If you hit a tee shot out of bounds and release a little pressure from the balloon (so to speak), that's completely understandable.

As usual, I'm always striving for incremental improvements. Let's say you were having emotional reactions to 80% of your bad shots. If you got it down to 40-50%, that's real progress, and I think you'll see reductions in your scores and increases in your fun level.

LETTING GO AND MOVING ON

To be clear, post-shot routines (like pre-shot) should not take that long once you become accustomed to doing them. There is ample opportunity after your round is over to dive deeper, but the internalization of good shots or analysis of poor ones should only take seconds. Once that is complete, the most critical part is letting go and moving on.

I'll quote James Sieckmann:

> The last step of a quality post-shot routine, and perhaps the most important, is 'letting go'. Once you've mentally corrected a bad shot, be done with it. Don't take the negative experience of the last shot to the next one. Don't take it to the next hole. And for sure, don't take it home. Negativity stifles the learning process and makes peak performance impossible. It's like carrying around a ton of bricks; it tires the body and burdens the mind. Is that what golf is supposed to be like? No! Golf is a journey that should be filled with joy! Regardless of what happens, each round has the potential to be a great one.

In other words, when the shot is over, it is OVER. There is nothing you can do to change the result, and you do your best to go through your pre-shot and post-shot routine with as little mental baggage as possible.

THE BIG IDEAS

- A quick post-shot routine should internalize your successes and take ownership of them. Conversely, looking at your poor results from an objective, analytical perspective is equally important.
- Take time to identify your good or great shots. Celebrate and remember them!
- When mistakes occur - ask yourself if you could have done anything differently.
- Once this process is complete, it is time to move on to the next shot. Close the door on the last one because it is OVER.

CHAPTER 49
POST-ROUND MENTAL ANALYSIS

IN EARLIER PORTIONS of the book, I discussed how many clues to a better version of your golf game are hiding in your rounds. Going through a post-round review (as best you can) can give you ideas on adjusting your practice routines and strategic decisions. I also find it helpful to review your mental state during the round.

This doesn't have to be complicated or take much time, but it is beneficial.

To give you some ideas, here are some questions you can ask yourself:

- How was your overall experience? Were you in a positive frame of mind most of the round? Did you struggle with your reactions to shots? Most importantly, did you have fun?
- Were you able to be consistent with your routines?
- Did you take the time to consider the proper target/club selection? Factoring in the wind, elevation change, areas surrounding your target?
- Did you struggle with commitment to certain shots?
- Were you able to remain present, or did you worry about shots that had already occurred or future holes?

- How was your grit? Did you check out for the day early because things didn't go well?

If you've noticed, I've centered these questions around the topics of each chapter in the mental section. At the minimum, exploring where your mind went and making some internal notes for next time is a way to get things moving in the right direction.

THE MENTAL SCORECARD

If you love keeping data and measuring your progress, a more disciplined approach might be helpful.

In recent years, it's become more common for players to keep track of their mental performance, just like their scores or stats. In Dr. Michael Lardon's book *Mastering Golf's Mental Game,* he refers to a mental scorecard concept.

Dr. Lardon's mental scorecard allows players to score themselves on each phase of the pre-shot routine - analysis, preparation, and execution. By breaking down each shot on every hole and grading yourself, you'll arrive at a percentage score out of 100 for the round.

Let's say you were on a par 5, and you made a bogey. You now have six shots to evaluate whether or not you successfully went through all three phases of the pre-shot routine. If you did it on four shots, your mental score would be 4/6. After tallying each hole, you arrive at a percentage at the end of your round. A top tour player would routinely score in the high 90s. However, according to Dr. Lardon's research, a great recreational player would be closer to the high 60s or low 70s, so perfection is unnecessary.

For golfers who are more committed to improving their mental performance, I think it's a wonderful idea.

I also think you can adjust and simplify this concept to whatever you find are some of your biggest mental challenges. There is no right way to do it, in my opinion. Overall, like anything else in golf, if you can start to track your mental performance, it can help motivate you and make your work more efficient.

DON'T LET YOUR ROUND DISAPPEAR

A post-round review is a valuable habit. It's an opportunity to internalize everything positive about your round. Even if you didn't play all that well, just taking a moment to be grateful that you got to play in the first place is an important reminder for many of us!

Additionally, you can start to analyze your mental performance. Quantifying your mental performance can be helpful for certain golfers to keep track of their progress.

THE BIG IDEAS

- **When your round is finished, don't let the information disappear! Doing a quick analysis of your decision-making and emotional state while playing is helpful.**
- **For golfers who love deeper analysis, keeping a mental scorecard can quantify the effectiveness of your routine and commitment on each shot.**

WHAT'S NEXT?

THANK you so much for taking the time to read this book. As a reminder, I want you to be selective about what you do next with the information I provided. Golf is not an all-or-nothing proposition. You can take a few of these concepts at a time and apply them to your game where you see fit. I hope you refer back to *The Four Foundations* for years to come. Please remain patient, strive for incremental progress, and have fun!

If you want to continue your education, I would encourage you to take The Four Foundations of Golf Video Masterclass.

To credit you for your book purchase, you can use coupon code **READER** at checkout to receive a $25 discount. Please visit the following URL to learn more:

https://fourfoundationsofgolf.com/masterclass

The video course provides the information from the book in a more visual, conversational format. Additionally, there are more examples and bonus materials from other coaches. This is a great way to reinforce the key concepts you have learned.

To receive updates on new blog posts from my website, podcast episodes, and special offers on products, you can subscribe to my newsletter by visiting the following link:

https://practical-golf.com/newsletter/

Did this book help you in some way? If so, I would love to hear about it. If you can leave an honest review on Amazon it will be helpful to other readers.

Also, if you prefer audio format, you can check out the podcast I co-host with Adam Young, The Sweet Spot. We have a growing library of episodes that can help with every part of your game.

If you would like to chat with me directly, you can always find me on Twitter - @practicalgolf, or contact me through my website.

ABOUT THE AUTHOR

Jon Sherman is the owner of Practical Golf, a website dedicated to being an honest resource for the everyday golfer looking to enjoy the game more and improve. He lives on Long Island with his wife, son, and daughter. Jon is a member and club champion at St. George's Golf & CC in East Setauket, NY. He also is an aspiring competitive mid-amateur golfer - playing and learning along the way just like everyone else.

 twitter.com/practicalgolf